Praise for *A Darker Sh*

"*A Darker Shade of Blue* is the riveting account of Superintendent Keith Merith's thirty-one-year journey as a Black municipal police officer. He has chronicled experiences that will take you through a full spectrum of emotions from anger to triumph. The author is only the fifth Black police officer in Canada to write a book about their experiences, though the year of this book's release marks 140 years of police service by Black Canadians (Peter Butler III, Ontario, 1883). While much has improved, the author illuminates the significant work ahead to achieve true fairness and equity in our great country." — DAVID MITCHELL, founding president of the Association of Black Law Enforcers

"An illuminating and insightful exploration of the intricate intersections of race and law enforcement. With impeccable research and a deeply personal narrative, Merith brings to light the nuances of being Black in the blue uniform. This is a must-read for anyone seeking to understand the complexities of modern policing and the transformative potential of inclusion. A landmark work." — DR. AKWASI OWUSU-BEMPAH, professor and author of *Waiting to Inhale: Cannabis Legalization and the Fight for Racial Justice*

"In the 2000 movie *Shaft*, John Shaft, a former detective from the NYPD, said he was 'too Black for the Blue, and too Blue for the brothers.' Superintendent Keith Merith's book serves as a powerful reminder that this burden and struggle are very real for Black Canadian police officers. The narratives and experiences in this book have reignited my commitment to doing the right thing. I wholeheartedly urge you to read this book and rekindle your own dedication to promoting equity, fairness, and justice." — DR. FRANK TROVATO, founder of TNT Justice Consultants

"A must-read for those interested in policing and the subtle and not-so-subtle effects of racism. Superintendent Merith leaves us with sensible suggestions for improvement and an appreciation of his love of service." — KENT ROACH, C.M., author of *Canadian Policing: Why and How It Must Change*

A POLICE OFFICER'S MEMOIR

A DARKER SHADE OF BLUE

KEITH MERITH

This book is also available as a Global Certified Accessible™ (GCA) ebook. ECW Press's ebooks are screen reader friendly and are built to meet the needs of those who are unable to read standard print due to blindness, low vision, dyslexia, or a physical disability.

Get the ebook free!*
*proof of purchase required

Purchase the print edition and receive the ebook free. For details, go to ecwpress.com/ebook.

Published by ECW Press
665 Gerrard Street East
Toronto, Ontario, Canada M4M 1Y2
416-694-3348 / info@ecwpress.com

Cover design: Jessica Albert
Cover image: Amy Brathwaite Photography / amybrathwaite.com

To the best of his abilities, the author has related experiences, places, people, and organizations from his memories of them. In order to protect the privacy of others, he has, in some instances, changed the names of certain people and details of events and places.

LIBRARY AND ARCHIVES CANADA CATALOGUING IN PUBLICATION

Title: A darker shade of blue : a police officer's memoir / Keith Merith.

Names: Merith, Keith, author.

Identifiers: Canadiana (print) 20230561713 | Canadiana (ebook) 20230561772

ISBN 978-1-77041-679-6 (softcover)
ISBN 978-1-77852-306-9 (ePub)
ISBN 978-1-77852-307-6 (PDF)

Subjects: LCSH: Merith, Keith. | LCSH: Police, Black—Canada—Biography. | LCSH: Police—Canada—Biography. | LCSH: Police misconduct—Canada—Prevention. | LCSH: Racial profiling in law enforcement—Canada. | LCSH: Police—Recruiting—Canada. | LCGFT: Autobiographies.

Classification: LCC HV7911.M47 A3 2024 | DDC 363.2092—dc23

This book is funded in part by the Government of Canada. *Ce livre est financé en partie par le gouvernement du Canada.* We acknowledge the support of the Canada Council for the Arts. *Nous remercions le Conseil des arts du Canada de son soutien.* We acknowledge the funding support of the Ontario Arts Council (OAC), an agency of the Government of Ontario. We also acknowledge the support of the Government of Ontario through the Ontario Book Publishing Tax Credit, and through Ontario Creates.

PRINTED AND BOUND IN CANADA

PRINTING: MARQUIS 5 4 3 2 1

MIX
Paper from responsible sources
FSC® C103567

To my wife and life partner, Cheryl,
and to two incredible women I'm privileged to call my daughters,
Jasmine and Brianna

With a special dedication to my current grandchildren, Nova and Dash
Your light shines brightly.
The future belongs to you both.

TABLE OF CONTENTS

PROLOGUE

I'm fifteen years old, living in a small village. It's summer in the late eighteenth century and nothing could be better, so I think. I am blessed with both my mother and father, who have loved and cared for me all these many years of my life. My brother, who is twelve, and my sisters, nineteen and seven, are my world as I know it. My love for them knows no bounds. On this clear, hot summer day, like many others, I gather several jugs and head to the creek to replenish our water supply. As I near the clearing, I am violently knocked semi-conscious by a thick, heavy, broad net that falls from a great height, where it had obviously been suspended. My first thought is that it is a trap set for animals; I have the wherewithal to get out from under it. The weight is surprising but not insurmountable. I get to my knees, but then the dull cold grey steel of a rifle butt slams into my temple — immediately I am enveloped in darkness as random shooting stars invade the abyss. Now I am unconscious.

As the light returns to my eyes, I see shadows of men, hear voices of men. In my groggy state I am able to discern that I am on a cart, and we are moving. My head feels split in two; the pain is that immense. As my head clears slowly, I now realize that I am trembling and caked in dry blood. Both my arms and legs are bound by rope and latched to people on either side of me. I remain this way for several hours, not quite understanding what is happening. When we reach the coast, that's when I know. I have never seen them before but have certainly heard some of the stories. We are heading to the ships that belong to the white devil.

And those devils are everywhere. Strange in appearance, strange in their language, strange in the tools they possess and stranger still in the brutality and callousness of how they treat most of the people with me. You see, there are literally hundreds of us, who I now consider kinsmen, kidnapped native victims being led from other similar carts or walking, bound as I am, and being dragged towards the skiffs that will bring us to the mother ship. Now the group of men that I'm bound to grow increasingly terrified, screaming in abject fear. I join them, understanding that this is part of the slave trade and those are slave ships.

As we are removed from the cart, the resisters are further beaten in the most brutal fashion. Teeth smashed out of mouths via rifle butts. Arms broken by heavy wooden truncheons applied liberally and without mercy. My shoulder blade is cracked by a swing that misses the man behind and catches me instead. As they drag me along the sand, the screeching is unbearable. Guttural calls for help fall on deaf ears. I am eventually loaded onto the mother ship and bound by heavy wrought-iron shackles around my ankles, wrist, and neck. Shuffling, I am led into the bowels of the ship. The darkness is ever so slightly broken by the whiffs of light provided by oil lamps that hang on distant posts. We are made to lie side by side, body to body. The intent is to fit as many of us into this godforsaken vessel as possible. From this point forward, I am now considered cargo.

The journey takes three and a half months. Many of us will not survive. As bad as the conditions were on our departure, they are absolutely nothing compared to the voyage across the Atlantic. The days are extremely long and sufferingly hot. My movements consist of sitting up or lying down. The chains have opened up raw festering wounds where they rub against our skin. I am caked in my own feces and urine, as I have been given no receptacle in which to relieve myself. The stench is unbearable. The vomit and infected wounds compete with the defecation and urine, vying for a championship spot as the all-time nauseating repugnant smell. The captors are inhumane in their lack of sympathy, empathy, or care. They are utter sadists. There is glee at the suffocation. They bathe in the subjugation. They relish in the torment of the black-skinned ungodly sinners, who are now in the right hands for a Christian God to finally give them an opportunity for redemption; under God and his overseers, the "white man." One meal a day consists of a dried piece of either yam or bread (not both) and water. The nights are frigid, giving my body some slight reprieve from the pain of wounds, infections, cramps, and dysentery. The cold renders some pain and inflicts its own judgement by way of an unholy discomfort attached to the early onset of hypothermia. For 106 days I suffer in that dark, stinking, claustrophobic tomb, where moaning, crying, sniffling, coughing, choking, screams of agony, gasping for air, and sounds of whimpering fear are ever-present and haunt me. And finally, the silence of those souls who are destined not to finish the journey. The dead are unceremoniously removed and summarily tossed into the ocean to form sustenance for those inhabitants lurking beneath the surface.

Oh, how I long for, beg for, plead for, cry for death. If only I could see, for even a few moments, my family again. They don't know where I am, what has happened to me, or if I am alive. I wonder and fear for their safety. My state of depression forms the core of who I am. The cargo hold is dark, it stinks, it's slamming me from one side to the other, it pulls and tugs on my chains, it's robbing me of every vestige of freedom and goodness that I thought I possessed. It's the belly of an eighteenth-century transatlantic slave ship.

My final destination is the island of Jamaica. All of us disembark and are stripped naked. Buckets of water and lime are dumped on us. I am to clean myself as best I can. I am commanded to cover my body with oil. This, of course, is to highlight the best parts of me, so I am more marketable. My captors make me walk a quarter of a mile in chains to the central market. It is a bustling place, noisy with more white people in one place than I have ever seen in my life . . . though that's not saying much, as this whole experience is my first encounter with the white devil. Soon thereafter, I am poked, prodded, pinched, spread, bent over, rubbed, grabbed by the lip to expose my teeth, then auctioned off. My slave master is a rich white man who owns a three-hundred-acre plantation. He is vicious, with a large contingent of overseers. He does not hesitate to lash the skin off my back for any misdemeanour observed, pointed out, or just plain made up. There is no point in denying the accusations, for that only enrages him further. The beatings are severe and are always preceded by a verbal onslaught that begins with, "Nigger, who the fuck do you think you are?"

No matter what I endure, my spirit will not be tamed. I resist him and them with every fibre of my being, longing to be free. He and they resist me and mine for believing that we have a right to exist outside of tyranny and subservience.

∞

As a young man, in the early '70s, I along with many others, watched Alex Haley's *Roots* on television. This was an earth-shattering series depicting the plight of human beings who had been kidnapped from continental Africa and enslaved, mostly in the southern United States. This series moved our Black community into a consciousness fraught with a tremendous dislike for white people. It penetrated my soul, causing me real pain for many years.

I believe the story I have just told came to me from ingesting every part of that series, and over the years it's haunted my dreams, become a waking vision, and inhabited me as if it truly happened, as if I'm seeing a past life. It's fully formed in my head and feels like it actually happened . . . I can't shake it. But it also gives me the strength to keep moving forward, to hope that things will get better.

INTRODUCTION

In 2017, I retired from the York Regional Police Service at the rank of superintendent after thirty-one years of service. For the most part, they were wonderful years, though operating effectively at the senior officer's level demanded all of me most of the time. I grew weary of the exceedingly long hours combined with the constant internal nagging of wanting to spend more time at home with my family. After so many years of service with one organization, I felt it was time for me to move on and discover another side of life that I knew would be extremely rewarding if I put the effort into creating it. I must say, I have not been disappointed.

During my tenure with the York Regional Police, I considered myself very fortunate to have been able to take advantage of placements in many of the various units, departments, and bureaus that were part of the service. I managed to transfer to a new position every three to five years in order to have a well-rounded and satisfying career. To that end, I have held command positions in a variety of portfolios, which included Bureau Commander of Information Management, Court Services, officer-in-charge of Investigative Services, Organized Crime Bureau, Duty Inspectors Office, and Professional Development. I have also worked in Intelligence, Criminal Investigations, Training and Education, Drugs and Vice, Uniform Patrol, and completed a three-year secondment with the

Provincial Weapons Enforcement Unit. Having worked in so many areas is somewhat outside the norm, but I was fortunate to have been able to capitalize on opportunities that presented themselves to me.

Retirement has given me the chance to chart my own course as I experience what I affectionately call "part two." For several years, I did exactly that: travelling the world, enjoying the white sands and warm waters of the Caribbean, taking in the Aztec culture of Mexico, absorbing the ancient ruins of Greece, sampling the various seafood dishes of the Azores in Portugal, visiting Buckingham Palace in England, walking the Avenue des Champs-Élysées in France, and venturing deep into the savanna while on safari in South Africa. I remember waking up one morning around 4 a.m. a year or so ago with a compulsion to write about my exposure to systemic racism, with a focus on my policing career. I didn't quite comprehend at the time why this desire was upon me. But the more I wrote, the more I realized that I truly had a story to tell that was experiential and contemporary to what has happened, is happening, and will continue to happen in the world of police interaction with the citizens they are sworn to serve and protect.

This book is my perspective on policing, based on my personal experiences. It's about my journey as a Black man manoeuvring through three decades of policing, taking the reader with me on some of the intimacies and intricacies of certain calls for service, leadership within a police organization, and lessons learned along the way. I speak to this noble profession that entrusted me with the power and authority to keep the peace, maintain order, and put myself in harm's way, if necessary. I tell tales of the many funny, fascinating, and terrifying situations that could never happen in any other profession. I have seen the best of policing and the officers who truly love and cherish the job that they are sworn to do. The majority are very special people.

The book will discuss why race matters, both internally within a police organization and externally, and touches on the importance of social justice reform. It is about Black and brown and Indigenous people of colour and why they matter. When folks express frustration about systems, whether in the realm of justice, housing, finance, or social services, what do they really mean and how does it affect them? I knew that I was able to speak to many of these issues as I had experienced them first-hand. Deep down, I felt that several of the recent killings of Black individuals by police officers, primarily in the United States — including but not limited to Philando Castile, Breonna Taylor, Tamir Rice, and George Floyd — was having a negative residual effect on me. Add to this the absolute madness that is once again surfacing across nations with the rise of white supremacy, bigotry, and hatred, which includes police officers.

The issue of police brutality, which has largely targeted Black lives, has lit a fire in me and driven the direction of this book. For thirty-one years, I was part of a system, organization, culture, and specific operations that have targeted Black and brown people. The negative aspects of this targeting were never my personal intention; however, if you are part of the system, then you are part of the whole. Having policed for as long as I have, I know that we in the policing community, the justice system, and other law enforcement institutions can and should do better.

The book provides a glimpse into my life, my career, my experiences, and my passionate drive for systemic changes and social justice reform. It provides the reader with the opportunity to walk in my shoes, to see through the lens of a Black man, charged with a duty to serve, to gain an understanding and appreciation of what some officers of colour face and deal with inside their institutions of work. The book speaks to what I believe is the right way to lead and build stronger teams.

I want the reader to know and respect the fact that growing up Black in North America and pursuing a career in law enforcement is not and has not been easy for many. Despite this reality, countless do succeed, but most often there was a price to pay that was not levied on our white counterparts. There were times my legitimacy came with the uniform. There were times without the uniform that I was put in the category of "less than." I suffered along with my family.

In the late '90s I owned a boat that was moored at a marina just north of the town of Newmarket. One lovely day, a friend of mine visited with his wife and his two young boys, aged ten and twelve. My two daughters, around the same ages as the boys, and my wife were there as well. The day being so nice and warm, we decided to use the pool on the grounds, which we are entitled to do as part of my slip rental contract. The kids jumped and splashed around the pool along with several other children, having a blast while the parents lounged. Within ten minutes, I was approached by a security guard and the grounds manager requesting identification and wanting to know who I knew at the marina to gain access to the pool. You see, someone or some group at the pool hadn't liked what they were seeing. My friend was tall and Black. His wife was Korean. Their two boys were biracial. Both my wife and I are Black and my two little girls are Black. The marina, at that time, had all white members. We were anomalies that needed to be addressed. The manager took a stern stance with me until she finally recognized who I was. I had dealt with her about my renewal contract the year prior and I had been in my police uniform at the time. She respected the hell out of me then. I want the reader to be able to see and recognize this disparity, and hopefully be inspired to do their part to contribute to the betterment of all.

I have taken the time to delve into some American politics, which I believe have, and will continue to have, a direct impact on Canadian politics and policies and will have plenty of residual effects on Canadian policing. My critical analysis should not be taken as anti-police in any way, shape, or form; rather, it is a personal perspective that comes from having real-world policing experience and relatable incidents.

There is no great call to action other than treating all people decently and appealing to our sense of humanity. I do, however, speak to some of the systems that over time have unfairly placed me and others like me at a disadvantage. Current movements of exposing, addressing, and reforming these injustices must formulate a day-to-day passion, which includes a corrective, persistent action from the majority of us until the time comes when this will no longer be necessary. My hope is that this book will inspire some to do the right thing, at the right time, for the right reason.

Back in the early '80s, in order to be qualified and sworn in as a police officer in the province of Ontario, every potential officer was required to pass a thirteen-week program at the Ontario Police College. This training consisted of a variety of courses deemed necessary in order for us to be capable of managing the immense power, authority, and responsibilities that would be vested in us. An essential component of that training consisted of the application of use of force. This is where the term "stop resisting" had a profound impact on me.

In the world of policing, officers use the term "stop resisting" to justify and supplement their use of force. This command is used by police to clearly articulate, with as few words as possible, that a non-compliant person must stop their combative behaviour and allow the officers to place them under control. It is also a form of communication to witnesses that the use of observed force applied by officers is a direct result of the subject's aggressive behaviour. There is another reason why that term is used: it lays the foundation in court proceedings that force was necessary and applied with justification, as the party had been told to comply and did not. This is taught to police officers all over North America and beyond. Listen for it the next time you view police physical interaction with the public.

Here is the rub: officers are prone to use this term to support their aggressive behaviour along with augmenting charges such as resisting arrest or assaulting police. Now, some folks will no doubt purposely resist, assault, and even intend to kill officers — that is a fact. This book deals primarily with circumstances when police operate outside their authority and mandate, negatively impacting the citizens that they are sworn to serve and protect; at that point, citizens will resist. The police want compliance and the people want justice.

"Stop resisting" has a dual meaning. Police and the network of governmental social systems are called out for sometimes focusing on resisting the people rather than having their better interest at heart. If the opposite were true, then it is conceivable that the people would cease resisting what is perceived to be injustice.

Throughout the book, I have extrapolated the term "stop resisting" and applied it to the many individuals and systems that work by design to put people of colour in a position of having no choice but to resist at every occasion and at every level. The systems feel that we should not resist, and as a result they apply even more pressure by telling us to stop resisting as they mandate compliance. The objective truth is that the more compliance is demanded, the more resistance is required by the aggrieved. As the system and their arbitrators resist us, we the aggrieved resist them. This book is infused with the juxtaposition. Keep that in mind as you read through my many thoughts and experiences.

Throughout my career, I ran into that resistance time and time again, over and over. And it never stopped. There were times when I decided to acquiesce, but that was never the right thing to do and was always met with more oppositional resistance. My pushback was, for the most part, situational and often strategic — it had to be. The times when I acted like a raging bull in a china shop caused quite a bit of havoc. Although, in some cases, that shock factor was absolutely necessary.

While writing the book, to my surprise, some unresolved experiences surfaced that made me realize they still bother me. The fact that it pains me to recount these stories years later tells me that they are unreconciled at my core. I believe the feelings infused in the stories recounted in my book are impactful not only to me but also to the reader. There are many stories that I'm telling for the first time to folks outside of family members. I realized the importance of the various situations I have personally experienced, as they put context to current affairs and race relations that play out every day. There are wounds and scars that are left in the wake of bigotry, discrimination, unfair work practices, human rights violations, and other such acts of prejudice and hate. Even proudly wearing the uniform of a Canadian police officer, rising to the level of a senior commander, was not enough of an insulation to prevent the battering and bruising. The darker shade of blue. Writing this book has deepened my view that life is not fair, it is not balanced, and it certainly favours some more than others.

Three decades of service might seem mundane to some, but I assure you it was not. My investment was in the people I encountered, which presented unique opportunities to leave a lasting impression. The act of caring often resulted in unpredictable endings, but each day presented its own challenges along with its own chances for success. Caring was not exclusive to the citizens I was sworn to serve and protect; it included partners, superiors, subordinates, friends, associates, and family, each deserving of the quality time and the respect due to them. Navigating the external and internal operations required the expenditure of a great deal of time and energy, which often was exhausting. The infusion of mutual respect, professionalism, and care were non-negotiable. However, there is a profound cost for this type of service.

The cost for me was that of leaving a part of myself behind after each encounter. Caring took a tremendous amount of energy to sustain over those many years. It did, however, elicit a value that was not tangible in any physical way but oh so rewarding to the soul. I would describe it this way: the piece of me that landed on someone else made a difference. "Was the impact big, small, or almost insignificant?" This was the one consistent question I asked myself. The answer is certainly within the heart and mind of the receiver. Caring is the ability to be empathetic when required. To be honest and true when need be. To be there in times of need or to just be there. To be responsive to our natural instincts to do no harm. To acquiesce to our accepted and innate instincts of giving. It's about doing the right thing, at the right time, for the right reason. This to me is our earthly connection.

During my thirty-one years as a police officer, I came to realize that the greatest piece of equipment I possessed, that I never left the station without, was a smile. I gave it liberally and generously, and the results were astounding. Often there was no interaction with the community other than a fleeting smile. There were times when the impact was immediate and noticeable with a reciprocal smile. Other times my smile was met with very little reaction, but I'm sure there were positive residual effects that I will never know about. My belief is that we are all connected and the way to test this theory is through the universal language of a smile: try it and judge for yourself.

· PART ONE ·

FROM CHILDHOOD
TO POLICE COLLEGE

COMING OF AGE IN A
WORLD OF WHITENESS

I was born in Wolverhampton, England, of Jamaican parentage. England during the '50s and '60s was unforgiving where race was concerned. During this time, there was a mass exodus from colonized Caribbean countries to England, as the people were considered British subjects and did not require a visa to enter the country. There was work and opportunity to provide for one's family; thus many people took the chance. My parents, Ina and Leonard, were born on the island of Jamaica and would have been considered middle-class in status and income. But both of them knew there were better opportunities abroad, so they chose England and made their move. They made two critical decisions that charted the course of my extended family's future. In 1953, my dad arrived in the UK by way of an ocean liner that took three weeks to dock in the port of Southampton. My mother followed two years later, taking that three-week journey across the Atlantic, leaving my two older siblings, Hazel and Dennis, behind. Both Dennis and Hazel had been born in Jamaica. In addition to me, my elder sister Monica, my younger sister Shirley, and my younger brother Carl were born in England.

The house that we lived in had some unique characteristics, starting with no central heating. Instead, it had two fireplaces that warmed the house via coal, which was purchased and stored outside. We had a coin-fed hydro meter inside the house. We consistently experienced lights-out due to the meter expiring and would stumble around in the dark with a handful of coins to feed it. There was no bathroom in the house, nor hot water. We had a galvanized portable tub that we filled with hot water heated from the kettle and cold water from the tap in order to take a bath. The single toilet was housed in a separate structure attached to the house, but there was no access to it from the inside. We had to go outside to use the toilet. As kids, we would use a chamber pot at night. The house was always damp and infested with mice. But we called it home.

I remember as a young boy how difficult it was being in school and looking quite different from most other children. I remember how hard it was for me to relate due to my cultural upbringing at home being dissimilar to that of many of my classmates. There was constant teasing, which is typical among kids, but in my case the teasing was based on looking different, something that I had no control over and had no idea how to deal with.

I recall being around six when my father had a street fight outside our home due to a stranger calling my brother and me "Black Sambo." At the time, we lived in linked housing that was street-facing with no front yard — the front door opened up to the sidewalk. We were playing handball against the brick of our home when this man took issue with two little dark kids having a bit of fun. With a thick cockney accent, he threatened to slap the tar off us Sambos, using several pejoratives better left unwritten. I immediately called for my dad, and he confronted the man. The fight, as I remember, didn't last very long and was clearly one-sided. My father was in his prime. He had the righteous cause of defending his children and was vicious in his attack, delivering several thundering strikes to the stranger's face that dropped the man instantly to the ground. It did not end there. My father seemed to up his fury, pinning the culprit by the throat and delivering half a dozen more blows while yelling that he would kill him if he ever came near us children again. I clearly remember the sounds of the punches connecting and the sight of the blood-soaked sidewalk. Even at our tender age, my father's reaction in defence of his children being threatened by this white stranger etched in my mind that I should never have to put up with that kind of bullshit. I needed to be ready to fight anyone at any time to honour my self-worth. I am convinced that this incident lit the fuse of my no-nonsense approach to racism and standing up for the underling.

My uncle on my mother's side had immigrated from Jamaica to England then Canada some years prior, and convinced my parents that opportunities were considerably better in Canada. This prompted my dad to leave England in search of the promised land. In 1964, he arrived in Canada with the intention of exploring the possibilities of relocating his family. In 1968, we packed up and moved to this new land. Because we had not seen my father for four years, the reunion was euphoric.

On my tenth birthday, Canada became my new home. We lived in the downtown core of Toronto for about a year, then moved into government-subsidized housing in a tough area of the city known as Rexdale. After only days at my new school, Greenholme Junior Middle School, I found myself in a full-fledged fist fight defending my little brother from racial taunting and bullying. This trend continued from junior school to middle school. By high school, I had developed somewhat of a reputation as being able to scrap and certainly willing to stand up and defend myself.

Rexdale was classed as high-risk and was heavily policed. We had two distinct hot spots: Orpington Crescent and Jamestown Crescent. These areas were ethnically diverse. Many Black and white families lived here in this poor part of town, surrounded by gang activity that equated to crime and violence. Interestingly enough, I knew many of the Black and white gang members but was never involved directly with them when it came to gang activity. One year there was a full-on battle in the Jamestown core between the Black gangs and the white gangs. I remember being in the middle of the storm quite by accident while visiting a friend. Hearing the commotion on the street, I went outside and, just like in the movies, folks were fighting, wielding golf clubs, baseball bats, nunchakus, bicycle chains, and all manner of crazy weapons. I knew most of the combatants and moved through the streets without confrontation of any degree of hostility by either side. It was a mess! The craziness petered out in the next couple of days, and life resumed as usual.

Growing up, I never knew we were considered poor. I really lacked nothing noteworthy. Yes, we were in subsidized housing in a rough area, but both my parents worked, we had a car, and were never without a decent meal. Our clothes were as close to being in fashion as our discount stores, Honest Ed's and Kmart, could provide. My high school days were great in the sense that I really fit in. In those days, there was a resurgence of Blackness, with disco, funk, and soul music topping the charts. Afros and Jheri curls — the wet-hair look for men and women — were in vogue. The *Shaft* and pimping image were popping, and Black men were popular with the women. Weekends consisted of one party after another. We would put on our best, hippest outfits to spend a Saturday night at the discotheque. Although a terrible student, I was still very popular at school due to my athletic ability. In ninth grade, my first year of high school, I made the varsity football team and won top male fitness champion. The school was surprisingly diverse and strangely cohesive. As young maturing adolescents, we were more interested in what we had in common than our subtle differences. The common theme was dating, music, dance, fashion trends, and sports. Our cliques were inclusive to all races and cultures. We saw very little in the way of racism and discrimination.

In the summer of 1974, a friend told me that if I wanted a part-time job, the Canadian Armed Forces were hiring to augment their militia program. Although fifteen at the time, I submitted my application as a sixteen-year-old, and with the assistance of a friend of a friend, my application was accepted. Yes, I joined the army: 2nd Field Combat Engineers out of Fort York Armoury, Toronto. I attended the armoury one or two evenings during the week and most weekends for full days. I spent my summers at Base Borden or Petawawa doing Class B service, which was considered full time for those working months. Those were fabulous days. Being combat engineers, we trained to be soldiers and engineers. We learned how to march, parade, and drill. We learned to use the FN C1 rifle, Browning 45-calibre pistol, submachine gun, and FN C2 automatic rifle. We learned how to lob grenades, and ran bayonet drills too. As engineers, we learned compass navigation, large-scale water purification, and how to construct a Bailey bridge (a pre-formed steel bridge for foot traffic or vehicles). We also learned to operate large equipment and drive troop carriers. There was a component where we set demolitions, explosive booby traps, and anti-personnel and anti-tank mines. For all of this and more we were paid around $160 every two weeks, which would amount to $900 in today's dollars. What else could a young man want? The downside was that it came with a great deal of racism and discrimination. 2nd Field Engineers was a unique group among troops, as we had a large contingent of Black personnel. This was simply because of geography and word of mouth. We were based in the big city, where the numbers of diverse people were significant, and once word got out that brothers were present in greater numbers than in other troops, our numbers grew disproportionately relative to the others.

As militia women and men, we would periodically train with the full-time soldiers known as "Regulars" or just "Regs." These units were made up primarily of white men who didn't take kindly to the invasion of their base by "darkies," as they referred to us. This being the case, we were cautious to the point of moving around the base in groups. It was not uncommon for single Black members of our group to be assaulted. It was particularly treacherous for us when we attended the bars on base in the evenings. We were severely outnumbered, and those boys were always itching for a fight — alcohol-induced, of course. One evening, five of us sat around the bar having a pint when a large contingent of Regs surrounded us. One member took one of our newly ordered beers from the counter and drank it, a sure signal that we were not welcome and needed to leave. We did so under protest but were extremely glad that we made it out alive.

The military is an entity unto itself, very different from civilian life. The bases operate as mini independent towns with their own governmental structure, rules, and regulations. Our group loved and hated the base with equal passion. We were training, learning, testing our mettle, and growing each day we spent on base. However, we were different;

we knew it and they knew it. We got into many bad situations when confronted with the racial shit that we were subjected to, and there was very little in the way of support to address or redress this nonsense.

For example, my fellow trooper Daniel Simpson and I had spent the better part of the day driving senior officers to and from their appointments on base. It had been a long, exhausting day. We were finally relieved of duty and headed to the mess tent to have dinner. Daniel and I joined the long line outside the tent. When we were about a dozen soldiers away from reaching the doors, a lieutenant led a large platoon up to us and told us his men were joining the line in front of us. Daniel and I had been in line for approximately thirty-five minutes by then. We were the only two Black men in the line. A white lieutenant walks up to us and orders that his men (all white, I might add) will be entering the line in front of us? We were furious and took a stand. We both refused to step aside and got into a verbal confrontation with this senior officer. They arrested and paraded us in front of the regimental sergeant major (RSM). He told us in no uncertain terms that we were heading to Edmonton (the base where military prisoners are held) on a court martial for insubordination and a litany of other charges. He had no interest in our points of view and had already condemned us to internment. We were sent back to our housing unit to await deposition. There was little doubt that we had already been tried and convicted.

Daniel and I had the presence of mind to write a letter addressed to the base commander outlining the situation and that we were prepared to go to the press and the Human Rights Commission with a racial complaint against the Canadian Armed Forces. That same evening, we were summoned back into the RSM's office for what I was sure would be our detention orders. On our arrival, the lieutenant was in the room. We immediately presented the letters to the RSM. I remember the look on his face when he read the contents. He looked somewhat stunned and confused. This certainly was completely unexpected and nothing he had anticipated. We were ordered to stay in place and the RSM, along with the lieutenant, left the room. When he returned, his demeanour had changed to an apologetic tone, claiming there had been a misunderstanding and that he was prepared to dismiss the entire situation. "And oh, by the way, there is no need to take this any further," he said. As I recall this story, looking back, I can only assume the reason we did not pursue the claim was the fact we felt we were no longer in trouble and had escaped jail. I do remember wanting this whole experience to be over.

So let me tell you about one of the more serious situations that four of us faced one summer evening on base. It started with one of the Regs, who was a cook for the base's non-commissioned officers' mess. I don't remember why or what it was about, but he and I got into a verbal confrontation. The result was that we squared off to fight and I punched him in the face. A whole bunch of folks jumped in and sorted us out. Later that afternoon, four of us left the base and drove seventy-four kilometres away to a sleepy town called Renfrew, which just happened to have the only discotheque near the base. In the wee hours of the morning, we arrived back on base at the front gatehouse and were advised that military police (MPs) were looking for us and we needed to report to them immediately, which we did. They advised us that we had been accused of raping a civilian female on base earlier that afternoon. We did *what*? Who did we rape? It turned out to be the wife of the cook whose ass I'd whooped earlier. Both he and his wife had made a report to the MPs that she had been raped by four Black guys and they named us. We explained as calmly as we could manage that we hadn't even been on base at the time of the supposed sexual assault incident. Based on our testimony and other contributing factors, the MPs deemed that we were not suspects. We never heard another word about the incident, even though we complained like hell to anyone who would listen to us. To this day, I still have conversations with two of the guys that were accused with me. We laugh about it now, but believe me, at the time it shook us to our cores.

After graduating high school, I enrolled in the Law and Security Administration program at Humber College. My mind was set on becoming a police officer. A career in policing had always interested me from childhood. What better way to show your maturity into manhood than being a guardian of society by way of law enforcement? Although

I always felt this way, there was one defining incident that solidified my commitment to making it happen.

At the age of sixteen, after a couple of attempts, I finally passed my driver's licence test. My girlfriend at the time had a car, and one day we decided to drive down to the Canadian National Exhibition (CNE). I was driving, and I remember it was a lovely warm day with light traffic on the road all the way. So far, so good. We entered the parking lot and slowly moved down several aisles, looking for a space. As we proceeded down one row, we found ourselves head-to-head with a police cruiser heading in the opposite direction. We made eye contact, and immediately the roof rack light bar lit up and the officer motioned for me to pull over. This was not good. I welled up with anxiety and nervousness. My stomach was in knots. What the hell had I done?

The officer exited his vehicle and came to my car window. Suffice it to say our skin colour was diametrically opposed. With a deep, rough Irish brogue, he asked for my driver's licence, vehicle ownership, and insurance. Before he had a chance to view any of these documents, he started in on me. "What's your name? Where are you coming from? Whose car is this? What school do you go to?" Then it got real nasty. "You guys think you're hot shit! You're all a bunch of fucking criminal assholes!" He berated me for several more minutes, ending with this infamous and truly disgusting racist statement: "Nice place, this Canada, eh?" This was a sarcastic remark filled with vile connotations. It implied that the only reason for my not working picking cotton in the fields of Alabama or digging yams in continental Africa was due to the liberal attributes of the Canadian government. Based on his accent, he was clearly also an immigrant.

He had classified me as Negroid. He associated me with criminality and hypersexuality. He already had a preconception of where my Blackness ranked against his whiteness given that he was part of a dominant race imbued with the authority of the law. With disgust and all the venom he could muster, without looking at them, he tossed my documents into my lap and left. What happened here was a total emasculation of this young Black man who'd woken up with a smile and good intentions and ended up embarrassed, humiliated, saddened, degraded, disillusioned, and robbed of all sense of self at that moment. The officer had done this in front of my girlfriend, and I was completely impotent to do or say anything. I was scared and intimidated. He had power and authority over me. His whiteness combined with the authority vested in him by the Province of Ontario by way of the Toronto Police Service gave him power to treat me the way he did. It was obvious by what this officer was saying that he was not happy or in favour of what he saw in that vehicle . . . a young Black man with a young white woman.

I spent many sleepless nights replaying that encounter over and over in my head. He had the power and I didn't. I never wanted to be in that position again. My goal from that day forward was to join the ranks of a police service and be sworn in as a police officer. I wanted the authority and privilege of being on the inside, intuitively knowing that I could provide a level of policing that would incorporate character, decency, respect, and fairness that this man and others like him would not provide. It was about policing the right way.

Attending college for me was a completely new discipline in learning. In high school, I was a very poor student. My grades were borderline at best. The high school environment was not conducive to my learning style. I needed more attention in the form of one-on-one follow-ups from teachers to ensure that I understood the material. I didn't know how to learn well. That all changed at college. I committed to investing the time and effort required, not only to comprehend the material, but also to be able to retain and deliver the course curriculum during testing. I felt no discrimination during my time at the college. My fellow classmates were all awesome, a fantastic group of young people who were plotting out their futures with clarity and direction. We had a collective vision of making a positive contribution to society while serving our community. We had a real sense of togetherness. Although I had a wonderfully rich experience in college, I still ponder to this day why I was the only Black student out of dozens as part of this particular course. Being from Rexdale, where the number of Black families was increasing daily along with the growth of minorities throughout the Greater Toronto Area, it surprised me that the interest was not there. Although I will contend that without the benefit of that nasty encounter with the officer at the CNE, I too might have been absent from this course.

The facilitators were mostly former police officers, which intrigued me; I felt as if by hanging on every word I could glean some added advantage that I could use in the future. They seemed very curious to hear some of my perspectives on certain subjects they were teaching and my thoughts on how my community viewed law enforcement. In one of our classroom debates, a discussion around people putting themselves in positions of forcing the police to become physical was trending towards most of the class seeing the police as the good guys, having never had a negative encounter with the law. I, on the other hand, viewed law enforcement quite differently. My argument was, if you happen to occupy a body with this skin colour, then one of the last things you want is to be singled out by police and directed to submit. There is usually an ass-whooping or something worse coming your way. We had some dynamic and often sobering discussions, which spoke volumes as to the different worlds we occupied in the same space and time.

At some point during my first year, one of my classmates, Randy Martin, came to me and said that the York Regional Police (YRP) were hiring. He and another classmate had gone to two district headquarters the day before and had picked up two applications. His advice to me was to go after class and get an application. I did exactly that. My experience was somewhat different from theirs. I approached the front desk and asked the officer for an application. He told me, in a stern voice, that there were no applications, and that the service was not hiring. I responded by saying that I was aware of two people who had dropped by the day before and had picked up applications. That didn't go over very well. He snapped at me, repeating that York was not hiring, so there were no applications and I should leave.

Back at school the next day, I recounted the story to Randy. He was rightly pissed and called out the bullshit. Although aggrieved, I felt that

I did not have the time or energy to complain. Besides, I really felt that my complaining to the service would have effectively blocked any hope of me being a successful candidate in future endeavours with YRP. The follow-up to this account was that Randy was successful in his bid to join the service and left the college that year to become an officer. Many years later, I would end up working as a fellow officer with Randy.

One of my lingering memories as it relates to my college days was a field trip to Detroit organized by the course faculty. Over several days, our group visited the Wayne County Sheriff's Department as an introduction to American policing. Three events that formed the framework of my experience are worth relating. I remember the tour through the station, given by a commander who took us to a locked and secure property room. He proudly showed us an area containing firearms, tagged and secured. "Here we have eighty-seven firearms that were used in crime last week," he said, proudly displaying the confiscated materials. What? High-powered, homemade, brand new, old and decrepit — you name it, and it was there.

Next, part of the sheriff's department duties, at the time, was to serve as jail guards on a rotational basis. We were provided an opportunity to tour the jail facility. First, we entered the female lock-up section. The women were in their cells as we paraded down the corridor, providing them with a chance to welcome the baby students to their current abode. Several of them filled cups with urine and flung them at us while we passed. I was one of the fortunate ones who escaped the wet treatment, but not without a combination of the Ali shuffle, James Brown electric slide, and the Jackson 5 moonwalk. On the way out, we passed by an open elevator with two guards and a female inmate. The inmate was bent over, holding one of her eyeballs in her hand. Ouch!

Finally, we attended a court where a young white man was on trial for killing an older Black man. The Judge was Black, the court stenographer Black. The prosecutor? Black. All members of the jury were Black. The man was found guilty immediately, receiving a sentence of life with no chance of parole. Holy shit! Could this really be the case? It certainly was.

Even on the big screen or on television, I had never seen or heard of such a situation.

During my years in college I was still an active member of the militia. My final summer came as every other, with several of us signed up for full-time training and as support personnel on Base Petawawa. This particular training was a three-week operation where troops were in the bush under semi-combat conditions. We did have tents, sleeping bags, and a field mess, but that was the extent of the luxury. The days were long and hot. There was all manner of insects that didn't care if you were Moses himself— they were coming for you with bad intentions in mind. The tasks were hard, pushing you to the brink of exhaustion. We set up massive water purification systems in order to drink and shower. We constructed trails and roads through the bush. We trained in rapid route denial (the placement of anti-tank and anti-personnel mines denying the enemy access). Then the gruelling war games — seek and destroy potential enemy strongholds, usually at dusk or early morning.

I think you get the picture.

A week and a half into this training, my troopmates Uton Wilson, Daniel Simpson, and I had had enough. We were tough, but the black-flies and mosquitos were veteran combatants who wanted their woods and swamplands back. They were relentless and showed no mercy. We just wanted to get the hell out of there. We devised a plan where I would get a hold of one of our Jeeps in order to make it back to base, make a phone call home, and return to the field before being noticed. The plan was flawless. I phoned my sister Monica and pleaded with her to come up with a way to get me back home . . . and also to get a hold of the contacts Daniel and Uton had provided and relay the same message. The next day, the command got an urgent message that I was required home due to a job offer that could not wait. This was enough for me to be released from training and sent home. Both Uton and Daniel were also relieved of duty for medical emergency reasons.

Well, the plot turned out to be a *real* job offer. My sister had somehow arranged for me to be employed as a child care worker at Warrendale

Youth Centre in Rexdale. I started a few days after returning home. Warrendale was a secure facility that housed delinquent youths who were in need of a behavioural assessment prior to having a pretrial in court or an adjudication meeting. My job was to secure them in the facility, monitor them, protect them, and provide a written assessment of their behaviour during the period that they were assigned to the unit.

Two years later, I ended up at 311 Jarvis Street, Toronto, at the York Detention Centre. This was a Ministry of Community and Social Services–run secure facility for juvenile offenders, now referred to as young offenders. The unit housed some really troubled young people. These folks had committed or were on their way to committing real adult hardcore crimes. We housed a number of individuals who had committed serious assault, arson, sexual assault, robbery, child molestation, prostitution-related offences — the list goes on. The staff used to participate in recreational activities with the youth; I'm pretty sure this doesn't occur now. We would play basketball, floor hockey, dodgeball, and badminton. We would even weight-train with them. The young folks absolutely loved these mixed activities. I believe to this day that the value of those interactions had a profoundly positive impact on those kids.

Experiencing human behaviour in young adolescents who are saddled with real-world crimes and confined to a locked, secure facility, is an invaluable lesson that no textbook can adequately replicate or prepare you for. Those clients were a tinderbox of emotions — combined with their need to belong and receive the care they deserved, it made for very interesting shifts. Being a secure facility, the staff worked days, evenings, and night shifts. My permanent partner was Alice Whiteneck, an absolute gem of a person with a flamboyant sense of humour matching her genuine care and servitude for the young residents. For handling volatile situations, we had a nice balance of good cop, bad cop that worked quite nicely for us. Alice could and often did handle herself in physical altercations. She was a brown belt in the martial art of judo (she should have been a black belt but never went for her grading). She would be the first to jump between combatants but never did so with excessive force, not once during our five years together. I saw the consummate professional in her. She definitely earned my respect.

Worth mentioning were the two directors of the facility. They were an elderly English couple, Mary and Jimmy Daimer. I would say that both were in their seventies, and they were two of the nicest people that I have ever met. Mary was the motherly, caring, protecting, and soothing matriarch who was truly a miracle worker when dealing with these troubled youths. With a calming and disarming English accent, she would convince them that they were in a safe environment that respected and valued them. We housed some severely troubled individuals, and often there was no other option than physical restraint until we were able to sort out the fight or rage, which presented real harm to residents and staff alike. Mary would wait for the right time not only to sort out the conflict but to put a perspective on the situation that would ease and guide the youth to reflect on their actions with some clarity and, most often, remorse.

Jimmy was the same way. He was a soft-spoken man and an absolute pleasure to be around. We spent many hours chatting about his time spent in the British army and many of the battles he'd endured as a young man fighting in World War II. I didn't have the presence of mind back then to record some of our sessions; a regret I feel today. I was truly blessed to have worked with both of them, who without a doubt shaped me to a significant degree into the person I am today.

I recall the masterful way the Daimers cared for a troubled transgender youth known to us as Leo Black. Leo worked as a prostitute in the Parkdale area of Toronto under the alias Lisa Janet Black — despite being born with a male body, she identified as a woman. Leo was a regular client of the unit and in crisis most of the time. The Daimers paid special attention to her in a parental way that provided some peace and fleeting stability in this young person's life. On March 2, 1987, Leo was murdered by her roommate over an alleged bad drug deal or for informing on robbery suspects. The facts are still in dispute. What is clear was the care, devotion, sympathy, and empathy, along with engagement tied to tangible results, that were demonstrated constantly by the Daimers.

After my five years spent at the institution, the York Detention Centre was closed. The ministry was seeking to consolidate their secure facilities as a cost-saving measure, leaving me seeking employment elsewhere. I landed at the Syl Apps Youth Centre in Oakville, which at the time was a level four (maximum) detention facility for young offenders. I was considered casual part time, which meant I was given a number of hours of work per week that did not add up to full-time hours and my schedule was subject to change at any time. I needed more than that, so on a day off I drove to Milton, Ontario, and literally walked through the front doors of Maplehurst Correctional Centre. I told the front desk operator that I was looking for a job and I would like to speak to someone there who could help me. As luck would have it, there was a high-level supervisor in the booth at the time. I have tried in vain to remember his name, but it has eluded me. He asked me a few quick questions, then gave me an application to fill out. He motioned me to an area of the lobby and requested that I do the best I could when filling in the required information. After I completed the application, he brought me into a room and conducted a full interview. I was hired on the spot. Several days later, I received a phone call to start employment as a correctional officer in the newly established young offenders wing of the facility. I was fortunate to end up working in the adult units as well.

For those who have never worked in a closed facility that houses criminals, the best way to describe it is a world unto itself. There are rules and codes that to everyday folks make no sense, but in lock-up they are the law of the land. For instance, cigarettes were king. That was the currency of the day. The inmates were given what was known as canteen money provided by the government while they resided in the institution. It wasn't much, but the items they could purchase, such as chocolate bars, toothpaste, and of course tobacco, were at significantly reduced prices, making them affordable. The tobacco was cheap stuff and needed to be rolled in paper, but was top of the pecking order as far as commodities were concerned. One could buy or trade almost anything from a fellow inmate with tobacco. Another oddity was the word *goof*. This one derogatory jailhouse slang denoted an insult that, when uttered at another inmate, was enough provocation for a full-on fist fight. Sometimes words within the confines of an institution take on meanings far from the original definition, as this one seems to have done.

Within the unit there was always one alpha who ran the wing. He was the person the guards would petition to get things done if persuasion was necessary. The alpha was for the most part the toughest inmate or the most notable in terms of outside influence in the criminal world. I remember one incident where my unit was receiving a new inmate from one of the other units. Funnily enough, I remember his last name. It was Bell. The unit was buzzing with the anticipation of Bell. He had quite the reputation throughout the institution. On his arrival, there was a palpable tension in the air. Bell was a large, chiselled, powerful-looking biracial dude who didn't say a word on his arrival. Within a couple of hours, the guards were assisting the former alpha out of the unit to seek medical attention. He was busted up bad. Well, there was no guessing what happened. As guards, we knew that from now on we would deal with Bell, petitioning him to get things done when persuasion was necessary.

As a correctional officer, I perfected the art of quiet persuasion, which is the gentle way of leading. The inmates respected strength but hated being told what to do in an aggressive manner. Some of the guards never learned a better way of getting the job done. While inmates were in my custody, I never let them feel less than, only part of. You see, if you engage the system as the bottom line of their situation while in the institution, then appeal to the roles that we each play along with the rules and regulations that govern the institution, chances are you will get compliance without any significant resistance. I did not rule by fear; instead, I showed no fear. I treated them fairly but firmly.

During one evening shift at Maplehurst Correctional Centre, there was a nervousness in the air on the wing where I was working. The high tension permeated the walls and ceilings, clinging to anything and everybody that moved. Something was about to happen, and it had the smell of a full-scale riot. I had not experienced this type of event before but, on two separate occasions, I had come on shift immediately afterward and had seen the devastation and heard about the injuries that resulted. One of the more reasonable inmates had passed information to me stating that "if it kicks off, it's gonna be bad." Feeling that I had enough of a rapport with the inmate boss of the unit, I met with him in the rotunda and asked if there was anything I could do to possibly prevent the riot from occurring. He told me that the inmates had a list of grievances starting with wanting the removal of a specific inmate from the wing. Overstepping my authority slightly, I made immediate arrangements to have that inmate moved to a different wing within fifteen minutes. This brought me immediate credibility among the inmates, and I was invited to sit with several of them and discuss their concerns. At one point, I suggested the inclusion of my supervisor at this sit-down, but they weren't having it. I did not come as the enforcer, only someone concerned about their well-being. This turned into a situation where I had positional authority over the inmates but, more importantly, personal authority that had been earned and given by the inmates. The result was a stand-down order by the wing boss preventing that evening's planned event.

I need to give a big shout-out to those who serve as correctional officers: it's a tough and thankless job rife with danger and little reward. It is extremely difficult to get up each day to attend the same institution, sometimes for years, and deal with all the situations that happen in a place like that. The word *anxiety* is a real thing for many officers. I've done it and I know.

WHY AM I HERE?

In 1980, I graduated from Humber College Institute with a diploma in Law and Security Administration along with an Advanced Police certificate. I felt I was ready to meet the challenge of becoming a police officer. I set about putting in my application to the Peel Regional Police. I was soon called for testing. I passed. I was then summoned for an interview. I passed. The next phase was a background investigation that was positive, advancing me to the final stage: to appear before a selection board committee. This was really happening. I went out and bought a dark blue, badass three-piece power suit complete with wide pinstripes. Yeah, there was a bit of a flare going on at the bottom of the pants, but it was still professional. I topped it off with a crisp white shirt and dark tie. It was the '80s, so platform shoes were the choice of the day. Understanding the conservative nature of the service, I opted for moderate soles that were not too high but would keep that soul groove going. And let's not forget the afro. Nice and tight and rounded to perfection.

I arrived at police headquarters early and positioned myself outside an office. When my time came, a sergeant brought me into the boardroom. Have you seen the old western movies where the gunslinger walks through the saloon doors and the whole place comes to a halt? The music stops, the card games stop, and everyone stares at the newcomer? Well, that's the best way I can describe my experience. Four senior officers were sitting at a table side by side, with a chair in front of them. When they saw me, their chatter immediately stopped. I remember the instant cold looks of surprise on their faces. It was obvious that no one had told them I was Black.

There was no hello or greeting of any kind. I was told by the sergeant to take a seat, the one in front of the panel. Four older white men — all senior officers — and me. They all had English, Scottish, or Irish accents. I sat up straight and ready. I had prepared extensively and was not about to foul up this opportunity. Without the benefit of an introduction or lead-up, the first question directed to me was "Why are you here?" My careful response was that I have had a burning desire to serve in the capacity of a police officer working with the community contributing to the betterment of the—

My answer was cut short by the same interviewer restating the question: "No, why are *you* here?" Oh, okay, I got it now. I stated that the Peel Regional Police was one of the premier police organizations in the country and progressive in their approach to policing, that I wanted to be part of an institution that was making a positive contribution to its citizens—

"No! Why are *you* here in front of *us*?!"

Oh, *fuck*. Did he just say that? Yes, he did. At this point, I was lost. I started to say something about working hard and preparing for the selection board interview but was immediately dismissed, sent away from their esteemed presence. The same sergeant led me out of the room to sit in the same waiting area outside the office.

The whole interview had lasted approximately three to five minutes. A short time later, the sergeant emerged from inside the boardroom and told me my interview had not been successful. I thanked him and said I understood that if one is not successful after this stage of the process, one would be able to try again in a year's time, and I would do exactly that. His words still haunt me to this day. He said, "The board has decided that you are never to apply to the Peel Regional Police Service again." I felt an immediate pain in my stomach. I left the building and located my car in the parking lot. I sat in my car, unable to move. The tears flowed down my face uncontrollably, I couldn't stop them. The pain was so intense. I hurt. I sat in that car for more than forty minutes, trying to make sense of what I had just experienced. No matter what my vision was, no matter what plan I had put into place, no matter how prepared for the opportunity, the hue of my skin was a little bit too "rich" for their liking.

Racism 1, optimism 0.

I eventually pulled myself together and decided not to allow those bastards and people like them to determine my future. From that day forward, I doubled down on my tenacity and perseverance, understanding that the times were against me but losing was not an option. It was six years and thirteen police departments later, including major services such as Toronto, Durham, Halton, Guelph, Waterloo, Niagara, and the RCMP, before I was eventually hired as a police officer with the York Regional Police.

The year was 1986. York was my preferred choice of services, as the department had real growth potential, which would give me the opportunity to advance within the organization. I was twenty-eight years of age, married to my beautiful, intellectually astute soulmate and life partner, Cheryl Dawn Merith. We lived in Mississauga, Ontario, at the time.

The job came about after a nine-month application process, which I believe was somewhat standard for the time, culminating in a selection board interview in front of a number of senior commanding officers. However, a hiccup during the process almost derailed my success. While in the background investigative stage, a recruiter told me to report to 1 District station to get my picture taken and then attend a scheduled doctor's assessment immediately after. The doctor's office was a short distance away. A time had been given to me, and I made sure I was at the station early. As I approached the front desk, an officer pointed to the corner of the counter and told me to sign the book. When I looked at the book, it was for people on recognizance (required by the courts to report to a police station as part of their release conditions). I said to the officer, "No, no, wrong person. I'm here to have my photo taken as part of the recruitment application to join the service." He was not pleased, to say the least. He ordered me to take a seat in the lobby area and wait. So, that's what I did. Ten minutes later, I went back to the counter and spoke to that same officer and told him I was also scheduled to see the YRP doctor within the next thirty-five minutes. He barked at me, telling me to take a seat and wait. Twenty minutes had now passed, and this officer had not so much as looked in my direction. Now very concerned, I convinced myself to make another approach to get an idea of when I could expect my photo to be taken. Not hiding his annoyance with me, the officer said that he had contacted the Identification Bureau and it was up to them to come and get me. I sat back down in distress. I was fully aware that promptness is a virtue respected by police organizations, and being late for my next appointment would be frowned upon. Several minutes later, a sergeant came out of one of the rooms and was passing by. I found the courage to ask him if he could help me get my picture taken due to my circumstance. His words to me were, "Sure, come with me." He walked me into the building, down some stairs, and introduced me to the identification officer, who had no idea I was here but knew someone was scheduled. He had never been notified that I was waiting at the front desk. He immediately took my picture and walked me out of the station. I just barely made my next appointment on time. I remember going home and telling my wife about what had just transpired, wondering if this was another indication of what I would be exposed to when — not if — I'd be hired by a police service. What the hell was I getting myself into?

∞

On September 28, 1986, I reported for duty at the old 28 District head-quarters, located in Richmond Hill, Ontario. A week prior, I had received a phone call informing me that I had been hired by the York Regional Police and that I needed to fill in some forms and pick up my uniform and equipment. I remember the surreal feeling having gathered my equipment and immediately heading home to put everything on: shirt, tie, pants, hat, utility belt complete with an empty holster. Man, what a feeling. I had really made it. I was a cop. Well, not quite — there was the matter of being sworn in — but that to me was a minor consideration. Stand back, world, a new sheriff is in town.

I had dreamed of what to expect but of course, it didn't quite match the reality I faced. I was thrust into a world of "you're it!" You are tasked with dealing with situations that you have just heard about or seen on television (and not very accurately depicted). My new world was dealing with people, *real* people in a real world that operated simultaneously like the one I knew and like one that was entirely new to me. The learning curve was particularly winding and incredibly steep. What I suspected and ultimately faced was an organization that didn't know who I was and why I was there. Their world was seriously impacted by this invasive species that could be malignant but had not been diagnosed as of yet. The question facing them was, was there a need for the organization to change, or did I need to conform? Clearly the answer for me was conform or feel the wrath. Or more accurately, the established ones would run things around there either way; the wrath would just be part of the equation.

My initial path within this organization was disjointed and unusual. In October 1986, I was part of a contingent of YRP officers that attended the Ontario Police College for thirteen weeks of training — a prerequisite to being authorized to operate as a police officer in Ontario. The college was located near Aylmer, Ontario, some 170 kilometres from my home. I drove up on a Sunday in preparation for a Monday start. This old institution has been around since World War II and was originally a training facility for soldiers. The interior and exterior were built to last, consisting of solid brick and mortar with no frills attached. It is configured in units that house several pods that are basically self-contained, including individual rooms, a common shower facility, and a common lounging area. Men and women were housed in separate pods. The college was a central point for provincially mandated police training, including the accreditation of new recruits. Members of police services and other governmental services attended the college for a variety of courses, each of which carried a specific length of time for completion.

I entered the halls of the Ontario Police College. I, and many others, approached the front desk, where we were assigned our rooms and instructions as to how we were to start our program. In the early morning, we were commanded to gather in the auditorium, three-hundred-plus students from multiple police services across the province. As I scanned the theatre, I located two other Black male officers out of the hundreds. Well, I thought, things were looking up.

After we were dismissed, I wandered the halls for a bit, getting oriented prior to the day's planned activities. That's when I saw them. Not one but *two* Black female student officers. My heart skipped a beat. This was not possible! But it was true. There they were, Sonia Thomas of the Toronto Police Service and Ingrid Berkeley-Brown of the Peel Regional Police Service. And yes, they were the only two. As our time at the college progressed, we bonded, forming a kinship that morphed into a genuine friendship that has strengthened over the years. Both officers rose to prominent positions within their respective organizations. Sonia, after her promotion to inspector in 2010, became the service's first Black female senior officer and the highest-ranking Black female officer in the country. Ingrid would eventually surpass that title in 2018, as she became the deputy chief of her service. Both appointments were monumental in Canadian law enforcement history.

The college course unfolded in a haze of long, interesting, fascinating, and revealing days. The fact that I was implementing my vision of becoming a police officer, the fact that I was among over three hundred other recruits from all over the province training together, and the knowledge that I and four other officers were anomalies spoke volumes. At the age of twenty-eight, I was one of the older recruits, and it showed. Some of the others struggled with being away from home — operating in group settings with limited life experience caused undue stress. For me, it was quite the opposite. The college was not a struggle . . . except for one part: swimming. From the first splash, I was immediately assigned to the Rock Club. And so was every other Black student. We often met in the pool, commiserating about this extracurricular activity that we had a slim chance of succeeding in. The goal was to make it into Guppy, one level above Rock. I spent hours in that pool trying to keep the water from going up my nose and drowning. I eventually passed, but barely.

Now that services were slowly infusing visible minority officers into the ranks, the old-timers needed to ask themselves: Do we need to be careful? Naw! We, the established and anointed members, replete with nepotism, run things around here. That's how it was for many years. To give you a jarring picture of what it was like in those days, imagine going into a Criminal Investigative Office (CIB), one of the premier offices in the department, made up of senior constables and detectives, and the common vernacular of the day was *nigger, spic, wop, Jew* (used pejoratively), *Paki, raghead, chink* . . . you get the drift. This was the language of the day — derogatory terms were commonplace. There was no hiding the ugliness, and why should they? There were little to no repercussions or, for that matter, visible minority members within the organization to warrant any redress.

Ezra (Tony) Browne was the only Black officer on the service at the time I started. He told me of a physical altercation he had with one of the detectives in the CIB office. Tony was recounting an investigation to another officer when a particular detective told him to "keep the fucking noise down, you fucking nigger." Tony immediately confronted the detective, and both had to be separated. The situation was escalated to the unit commander, and his response was "What do you want us to do? Other guys in the office are going to repeat it." Meaning this was commonplace in the office and basically condoned. The only resolution offered — which was *not* discipline — was by way of an apology from the detective. Oh, how times have changed. Or have they?

UNDERCOVER

After graduating from the police college at age twenty-eight, I was assigned to the Morality Squad as an undercover officer, bypassing the prerequisite of doing uniformed police work. The usual path was for the graduating officer to be assigned a coach officer to perform uniformed patrol duties for a period of three months. They would be joined at the hip, working side by side the entire time. In my case, I was provided with a unique opportunity to do what most police officers and law enforcement officials have not done and never will. My task was to make connections with street drug pushers, identify the dealers, infiltrate organized groups, purchase drugs, root out the suppliers, collect evidence to support arrest and criminal charges, develop a case against them, and assist in the prosecution through the court system. This was accomplished by assuming a fake identity and becoming one of them, a drug dealer.

During the late '80s the region was experiencing a rise in illicit drugs flooding the streets. Investigators soon realized that their efforts required another dimension in the form of undercover operators to provide intelligence and create situations where perpetrators could be arrested and charged. As a young Black man, I was an anomaly within our service, and senior command felt that I would be able to fit in and penetrate the organized world of the drug business. In my mind, this was the height of stereotyping. I can only assume that in their minds a Black man equates to a familiarization with drugs and street knowledge. For this assignment, my skin colour had a purpose. I went along with it, feeling that this was a special assignment and an opportunity that should not be missed. I was now tasked primarily as an undercover operator.

In order to connect, I had to fit in, so a new identity was required. Welcome, Ishack Washington! A friendly, badass drifter who made his income buying and selling drugs. This role took me through the underbelly of street life, which shaped my understanding of who and what a lot of so-called criminals were about and why they did what they did. The unintended consequence of being undercover was that I also got to know the true colours of the officers who did not know who I was, and some who did.

Armed with the fact that I was a police officer — a newbie at that — the prospect of exploring the underworld from this perspective was exhilarating, even intoxicating. Being relatively new, I hadn't had a great deal of exposure to other officers and the general public, so my anonymity was relatively secure. Add to this a physical-appearance transformation that enhanced, as much as possible, the separation from any connection to policing. Three significant changes were initiated immediately. I remember that prior to my assignment date, I went to the barbershop and had lightning bolt designs etched into both sides of my hair. That was pretty radical for those days, but I needed the added assurance that my appearance was street and tough. The next step was to have my ear pierced. In the late '80s, having an earring (and only on the left lobe) was cool. I went a step further and had two piercings on the same side. The final part of the transformation was the purchase of all-new funky clothing. This was what I called the trifecta.

Entering the world of undercover work was strange in the sense that all the personal attributes essential to the police service were detrimental to operating in an undercover capacity. In order to be successful, one must lie, cheat, overindulge, be a con man, exaggerate, steal, brag, infuse coarse language into most conversations, drink alcohol, and talk shit, along with the macho garbage of viewing women as objects to be ogled and used.

The best way that I can describe the work would be as that of an actor. In fact, there should be an Academy Award for the successfully accomplished role of an undercover officer. On top of this, it takes a great deal of courage, in certain situations, to create the outcomes that you hope will materialize. No training of any sort was provided to me during the three years I spent in this capacity. There were many times, I will confess, that I feared for my life, but somehow I got through it.

∞

One of my first assignments as an undercover operator was an investigation into a bad cop, one of our own. I was summoned into a small office at the 2 District headquarters by Inspector Mennie, who at the time was in charge of the Professional Standards Bureau. I remember him being quite older than me, very stately and pleasant. He brought my attention to a uniformed patrol officer by the name of Terry Martin. Terry, at the time, was alleged to be dealing drugs and running girls out of the Pro Café in the town of Vaughan. My job was to infiltrate his circles and purchase narcotics from him directly. By the time I had received this information, surveillance teams had already conducted surreptitious observations and investigators had a rough idea what establishments Terry frequented and with whom. I must admit, I was extremely nervous about this assignment, for all the apparent reasons. This dude is a cop, and although I didn't know him, he's one of us. But it's true that there are certain behaviours within our benevolent organization that are not sanctioned in any way, and that would be police officers who align themselves with the criminal element.

This particular task would require a special type of fortitude from the investigative team and me to catch him in the act and have enough evidence to remove him from service. Well, the game plan was to first attempt to connect with the working girls that Terry was supposedly managing. For a week or so, I attended the Pro Café adult entertainment joint every day. This establishment was the typical seedy stripper bar adorned with a worn-out centre stage, dim lighting, cigarette smoke, and a DJ announcer introducing the upcoming featured performer in an exaggerated deep, rhythmic tone. Prior to this, I had never set foot in a strip bar in my life. The whole experience was daunting. I felt a bit repulsed at the dehumanization that I witnessed hour after hour, day after day. I watched as the same men entered the bar at approximately the same time each day. It appeared each man had a favourite woman who would pay special attention to him by way of entering his personal space and touching him every now and then. I watched as these men reached into their pockets and showered the women with money, paying for each individual lap dance.

The shallow proposition of paying for attention rubbed me the wrong way, and the fake admiration that contributed to the unholy transaction was so disingenuous that I truly felt disgusted. I held myself up as morally superior to this display of human degradation, which I didn't quite understand at the time. At this stage of my life, I no longer have those judgements in my heart. Now that I have years of lived experience and the benefit of maturity, those excessively critical points of view have been erased.

I managed to make contact with a young woman who was in touch with Terry. When I felt the time was right, I asked her if I could score some cocaine from her. She immediately shut me down, wanting to know why I was inquiring and telling me to go ask someone else. That was the end of that. She never spoke to me again. Dead end.

Moving on, the team decided to target some other possible associates. With the intel we possessed, we centred on an area in the Thornhill district known as the Bay Hill Mews plaza. We kept up our observations until we located Terry meeting with a man whom I would later come to know as Coretta. He now would become my secondary target. From this point forward, I was outfitted with a wire. The intent was to capture conversations in order to build a case for the prosecution. After several days of watching Coretta's movements, I found the opportunity to make a cold approach and engaged him in conversation. This led to many more conversations, most of which focused on my request for weed from him. As it was, Coretta introduced me to several of his acquaintances, which ultimately led to me purchasing a quantity of hashish from one of them.

One day, I was in a vehicle with a suspect known to me as Gary. I expressed concern about being caught by the police and declined to smoke up with him. In his state of elevated bliss, he told me that Coretta had a friend who was a cop. This cop didn't bother Coretta and his friends despite knowing that they bought and sold drugs. Gary told me that the cop was cool, that he wasn't interested in police work, just the money and smoking weed like them. Then he told me the officer's name was Terry. Boom! I was in the group now. Gary, Coretta, and other associates came to trust me enough to both sell me stuff and say things about their criminal enterprise that they wouldn't ordinarily divulge, including names of group members and their hierarchy. In my world, that's a good thing. It wasn't long before Terry started showing up at the Country Style donut shop located in the plaza.

I eventually took up residency at the donut shop. I visited as often as possible, becoming a familiar entity there. On Saturday, April 18, 1987, I was sitting at the front counter of the shop and in walked Terry Martin. Oddly enough, he approached me and said, "I think I know you!" I responded that I didn't believe so. He then somewhat apologized, saying he had made a mistake, and moved to a stool nearby. This was my opportunity to make the connection, so a short time later I walked over to where he was and engaged him in conversation. We were in sync right off the bat. He told me that he worked at a gravel company, and after a hard day's work, he liked to "smoke" and mellow out. I believed that this was his way of testing the waters as to what level of involvement he would have with me. At some point in our conversation, Terry invited me to his car, where he had a bottle of alcohol. The vehicle was parked in front of the convenience store located in the plaza. We ended up sitting in his vehicle, sipping on peach schnapps while chatting like two long-lost friends just reunited. The topic of marijuana came up again, and Terry told me that he had enough on him for a joint. He produced a cigarette container with what looked like green plant-like material (police jargon for weed). He then proceeded to roll a joint. As soon as he completed the joint and put it in his mouth a marked police cruiser entered the parking lot; that was one hell of a coincidence. Anyway, Terry immediately announced that we were going for a drive. Terry pulled out of the lot and headed northbound on Yonge Street. Chuckling about the bad-luck police interruption, he proceeded to light the spliff, and after a couple of deep draws, he handed it to me.

The following is what I wrote in my notebook documenting my next move. "Due to the fact that we were driving at a high rate of speed and the suspect seemed highly unstable, I decided that it would be in everybody's best interest to play along until I had the opportunity to effect an arrest. I took the joint, squeezed the end making the smoke unable to pass through, and then held it to my mouth. The joint was slightly under my bottom lip and I pretended to smoke it. This occurrence happened approximately 3–5 times." I don't know what was happening to him, but he was driving like a maniac. He was racing down the street, completely ignoring road and speed signs. I believe by this time he was suspecting something wasn't right. He started accusing me of not smoking the joint. I snapped back that he was full of shit. My thoughts at this time were, *I have the evidence in my hand, and I need to keep it somehow, some way.* Fortunately, by this time Terry had slowed the car down to watch me a bit closer and retrieve the joint. As he reached for it, I slapped his hand away, at the same time grabbing the door handle. Terry threw a Mike Tyson left hook that just grazed my nose. I answered him with a barrage of one-two combinations followed by the elusive uppercut. Well . . . perhaps it wasn't quite as dramatic as that. I'm not sure the attempt at the uppercut actually reached him, or even if it was part of the series of blows. Nevertheless, it got absolutely crazy in that car. We were both screaming and jostling, attempting to gain control of each other. While the car was still moving, I managed to pull the door handle. The door immediately opened as I tumbled out onto the roadway, complete with a face plant and full body roll. Terry immediately jammed on the brakes, yelling at me through the now-open passenger door, "What the fuck are you doing?" With all the authority vested in me and with the adrenaline surging through my veins, my simple but iconic response was, "Police, you're under arrest!" Yes, those famous words, just like on television.

It was at that point that Terry Martin completely lost his mind. I can't even imagine what was going through his head. He was a currently active police officer, albeit on one of his days off. An undercover officer had set him up with evidence that attested to his drug usage. He knew where there was one copper there must be others, and his career was about to end. The only thing he could think of at the time was to run, and that's exactly what he did. Terry took off as fast as his vehicle would allow him to. What he didn't know was that there was indeed a team of plainclothes officers in unmarked vehicles following his every move. After I got to my feet, Morality cover team officer Ray Mather, who was right behind Terry's vehicle at the time of my premature departure, immediately picked me up. The vehicle radio was alive with the crackle of voices in rapid succession, announcing that officers were in pursuit of a vehicle driven by an off-duty police officer travelling northbound on Yonge Street north of Benson Avenue. Ray entered the pursuit and announced via radio transmission that he had the UC (undercover officer) onboard.

My first police high-speed pursuit! I was so jacked up that I didn't have the presence of mind to be of any help at all. I was like a child in a car seat waiting for my parents to make the next move. My adrenaline was at maximum capacity, making macro-perceptions as the lead contributor to the events at hand. The pursuit intensified, and uniformed patrol vehicles joined the chase, which now had come off the main road and danced through the various side streets that formed the egress into residential areas. Police vehicles were everywhere, lights flashing and sirens blazing. Terry was in full-blown flight mode, driving erratically and extremely dangerously. I believe his only objective at that moment was to get away. What was daunting for all involved was that we had no idea if he was armed with his service pistol. And if so, was he prepared to use it? One way or another, we would soon find out.

We were now in hot pursuit of a possibly armed and potentially dangerous person. Terry had no intention of being caught or surrendering. The jeopardy that he faced was severe: dismissal from the service with the possibility of incarceration. For a former officer, being locked up was a terrifying proposition, making flight the only option at the time, although not the rational choice when one took the time to evaluate the situation.

As we weaved through the side streets, the complexity of this type of police apprehension was extremely apparent, in that the excessive speed of the vehicles along with the untold number of situational possibilities made it extremely dangerous for not only suspects and apprehenders but also any citizens in the immediate area. The one major advantage the police had was the use of the car radios. No matter how fast and reckless the suspect drove, he could not outrun the police radios. As his desperate attempt to flee was broadcast, several cruisers took alternate routes to cut him off. And that's exactly what happened. He was eventually boxed in and forced to stop. I was right there when this occurred. My heart was racing to the point that I felt slightly dizzy but strangely excited. An arsenal of handguns and several shotguns were focused on the suspect's vehicle. Just like on television, Terry was ordered out of the car with his hands in the air. He was placed under arrest by Detective Sergeant Eugene Kerrigan, handcuffed, searched, given his rights to counsel, and cautioned. Once he was placed in one of the cruisers, it was the last time I ever saw him.

Whatever happened to Terry Martin? The truth is, I don't really know. Very soon after his arrest, Terry resigned from the service. As far as I know, the police didn't move ahead with the multitude of charges. I can only assume that some type of deal was struck providing him with a way of not proceeding to trial. I was never called to provide testimony as to the events in question, nor was I part of any further dealings involving Terry. I will say, though, that this experience was my very first investigation into police corruption, and included my first high-speed chase. I'm still extremely proud of my instrumental role in this investigation oh so long ago, an investigation that was legendary at the time but has fallen to the annals of history, which seems fair and proper as time marches on. I recently attended a retirement affair of one of my service friends, where I ran into now-retired Superintendent Tony Cusumano. He brought up the Martin investigation and recounted that he was in one of the surveillance vehicles that eventually boxed in the suspect vehicle. We had fun reminiscing. Tony is one of a number of officers whom I admired and respected, and who truly was an inspiration to me over many years.

∞

I remember one time when I was undercover and met an individual at a bar who took a shine to me and developed a trust. I later purchased several grams of weed from him on multiple occasions. Eventually, I asked him for a large quantity that I knew he could not deliver, requiring an introduction to his supplier. We arranged to meet at a farmhouse in a rural area of my region. This was strategic on his part, as the area was vast and wide open, and the inhabitant had a clear view from all directions of vehicles and people coming into it. This presented a big problem for my cover team (a group of officers responsible for keeping me safe during my encounters): there was no place nearby for them to hide. I assured them that I would be fine, so they stayed back out of sight. I drove onto the property and was directed to park near a barn at the rear of the old farmhouse. My contact walked with me to the barn, and two other men met us. The greetings went well, and all four of us chatted for a bit, shooting the shit. At some point, we started to talk business. There were several questions posed as to quantity and price. I wanted to start with a pound of weed to check the quality and perhaps at a later time have them as my supplier. As we sat around a table chatting, one of the individuals brought out some small baggies, tossed one over to me with some rolling papers, and told me to roll a joint. My immediate response was that I'm a businessman and don't engage when doing business. He insisted, and I told him to kiss my ass.

At that point, his buddy got up from the table, walked over to the barn doors, and closed them. He then took a hatchet from a block of wood and violently embedded it into the wooden table that we were all sitting at. He looked directly at me and demanded that I roll the joint and smoke it. And that's what I did. I had spent many hours at the office practising how to roll joints and was pretty good at it. During an expletive-laden diatribe of "this is bullshit," I built a three-paper solid work of art in record time. I lit the spliff, took several puffs then tossed it on the table. The mood in the barn immediately changed as one of the men picked up the joint and took his own puffs, passing it on when satisfied. We all joked and laughed, and eventually they sold me the pound I had requested. A short time later, I left and met up with the cover team. The point of this story is that I had put myself in a potentially dangerous situation that could have gone sideways very fast. I was alone with dealers who had a lot to lose and wanted me to understand that this was no longer a game . . . it was for real. I got the message.

∞

In another instance, the Morality office had received a Crime Stoppers tip about a house in the Jane and Finch area of Toronto, which had a lot of criminal activity surrounding it. The tip made mention of illegal cigarettes being sold from the premises. Our background checks and preliminary investigation produced an individual known to us who we suspected was conducting illegal drug operations in our region. We decided that a good way to make contact with this individual was for me to do a cold knock on the door and attempt to purchase several cartons of cigarettes. This area of Toronto, at that time, was notorious for gang activity, and an extremely dangerous place to be if you were not connected. Although the notion of a cold contact was a shot in the dark, I'd had some success with this technique based on a variety of circumstances that presented themselves or were created. On this day, the whole scheme went downhill from the start. It was a little after the lunch hour when I jumped in the back seat of an unmarked vehicle and was driven to the area by two members of my cover team. Both were white men, which was an important factor in how this scenario played out.

I was lying down on the back seat, hidden from view, while these officers drove to the drop-off area, which was a parking lot across the street from the housing complex. In hindsight, this was one of the worst spots for me to have been dropped off. Several hundred metres away was a small bridge that extended across the roadway. At the time, we did not factor in the bridge. As it happened, there was a spotter on the bridge watching for any anomalies, and sure enough, he saw a Black guy coming out of the back seat of a standard plain car that contained two white men. I was a marked man from that point on. The spotter was on a bike. I saw him but pretended I didn't. I made my way across the street and into the complex. These townhomes comprised a complex weave of pathways and courtyards not conducive to crime prevention, which is considered in today's urban planning schemes. As I made my way through this maze, individuals on bicycles would suddenly appear and glare at me, then ride off. It was never the same person, and some were bold enough to, in the Jamaican vernacular, "suck their teeth at me."

Several minutes in, I decided to abort the mission and get the hell outta there. By this time, a group had formed, and the chatter was now audible. Having a Jamaican background, I could understand what was being said. They suspected that I was working for the police in some capacity and deemed me as a "Bumboclaat infaama!" (snitch). I needed to be taught a lesson, and they were coming after me. As they slow-walked and pedalled towards me, I hastened my pace, rounding several corners into alleyways, then ran through the complex out onto the main roadway northwest of where I entered. The pack was in hot pursuit, but they had lost sight of me due to my lead time and distance I had on them. I manoeuvred my way up the street, ducking in and out of any building that offered concealment. My heart was pounding so hard it felt as if it were coming out of my chest. I was struggling to breathe as a result of the auto-response adrenaline dump that my body had initiated to keep my ass alive. There was no way I could make it back to the parking lot where my cover team was waiting for me. I don't know how, but I had the presence of mind to use the cellphone I carried to call a friend who lived in the immediate area and seek refuge at his apartment. He met me in the lobby and brought me to his home. From there, I contacted the cover team and made arrangements for a pick-up. This shit was for real — that gang had bad intent with my face on it.

∞

Her name was Deborah Boogaard. After a brief meeting at the Fifth Avenue Tavern in Markham, Ontario, I had described her in my notes as female, white, twenty to twenty-five years old, black wavy hair, approximately five-foot-six, slim build, around 110 pounds. She was in the company of several individuals whom I had met previously in my capacity as an undercover operator. It was Thursday, March 31, 1988. I was in the tavern in an attempt to purchase illegal substances such as marijuana, hash, or cocaine. She entered the establishment with Donny Matheson, who was a subject of our investigation, and sat with the group sitting on the far west end of the tavern. I remember how friendly she was. I liked her immediately and wondered internally why she would be here with these guys. I had no real issue with the other folks but was actively working to infiltrate their suspected drug operation. To clarify, this was no big drug operation, but more of what I would·call a small group of dabblers in the business.

What you are about to read are the entries in my notebook dated Friday, July 1, 1988:

Weather: Warm, bright and sunny, dry roads
8:50 a.m. Reported for duty 19 Morality Unit, paperwork
10:30 a.m. 10-8 Newmarket
10:50 a.m. 10-6 Headquarters, met with Det/Sgt Shaw
10:51 a.m. 10-8 with Detective Powell and Detective Burness
10:55 a.m. 10-6 York Central Hospital, attend morgue
11:00 a.m. Witnessed autopsy performed on Deborah Boogaard, performed by Dr. Warberton and assistant Dave Kay
11:58 a.m. Completed, leave area

Outside the door of the morgue, I put some Vicks VapoRub in and under my nose to cover the smell that often accompanies any autopsy, a tip I had learned from some of the seasoned detectives. I went through the door and was struck to my core. There was Deborah on a metal table on her back with no sheet over her. She was still. *So* still. Not a flinch or a breath; nothing. The environment was sterile and quiet. Both the doctor and assistant were in the room. There was some conversation between the doctor and the detectives, but I was too lost in my confusion to have taken that in. I couldn't put the pieces together. I had spoken to Deborah on Thursday morning of the previous week, and now it was Monday. I was wondering why she wasn't moving. I started to tear up. It couldn't be helped. The unnecessary, reckless, and sudden loss of life of this beautiful young woman was too much to comprehend. As the autopsy commenced, I found myself repulsed yet totally compelled to see, feel, and hear all that was going on. The doctor was as empathic as one could be under the circumstances and took great care to respect the work that he was doing. Being that I was the rookie in the room, he directed most of his comments to me, explaining the procedure and what was or was not of concern. This was the first of several autopsies that I would attend over the course of my career. The impact of this event on that day has been absorbed into my DNA. It was life-altering in revealing how fragile life really is. Some decisions we make have real-world consequences that are not reversible. This was one of them.

Now the rest of the story. On June 29, 1988, our office had received a Crime Stoppers tip about a suspected drug pick-up involving Donny Matheson, Deborah Boogaard, and Blair Arthur. We were provided with the approximate time, area, and vehicle that they would be travelling in. At approximately 11:00 p.m., we observed the vehicle in the Newmarket area. We stopped the vehicle and arrested the three occupants, Donny, Deborah, and Blair. They were subsequently transported to our 1 District headquarters for processing. The trio was totally shocked and confused to see me as one of the arresting officers. They were separated, processed, and placed in individual cells. A few hours later, Deborah started to complain that she was not feeling well. An ambulance was immediately called to provide emergency care and transport to the nearby hospital. On their arrival, I noted the urgency of the paramedics and attending uniformed officers. I watched as Deborah was wheeled out of the station on a gurney and placed in the ambulance.

The team arrived back at the Morality office around 4:15 a.m. that morning. Within an hour's time, we were notified by the hospital that Deborah's condition was deteriorating rapidly. They asked if we were able to confirm whether she had ingested something, and if so, what exactly was it? Detective Mike Fleming asked me to accompany him back to 1 District to interview the two parties in custody. According to my notes, we arrived at the station at 4:15 a.m. Donny Matheson was brought to the sergeant's office, and both Mike and I advised him of the critical nature of Deborah's rapidly declining medical condition and asked if he could provide us with information about what she might have ingested that evening. His response was that he had no knowledge of her taking any drugs that day. Both Mike and I pleaded with him to be honest, as Deborah's life was in danger. After relentless beseeching and imploring, Donny finally relented and stated that there was a possibility she had taken some cocaine, but he didn't know for sure.

Detective Fleming and I then attended the cell holding Blair Arthur. After several minutes of questioning, all that Blair would say was that he didn't give her anything. We were desperate now, understanding that Deborah was on borrowed time. We decided to give both Donny and Blair an opportunity to speak with each other in private with an appeal to tell us what they knew. They were both placed in the same cell for a few minutes. Donny told us that it was very possible that Deborah had taken approximately three grams — an eighth of an ounce — of cocaine from someone, but not from them. This information was immediately passed on to the hospital.

Deborah didn't make it. She passed away sometime that day. I've carried her death with me for the past thirty-five years. Her death was so needless, so unnecessary, so tragic, so unjust. How could this have been her destiny? Why should her decision to be with these individuals at that time of her life have cost her so dearly? Who was she? Who cared for her? What impact did she make in her short time on this earth? These questions and an awful lot more will possibly never be answered. I do know that she has been a part of who I eventually became and who I will always be. In a very real way, the impact of this event worked its way deep into my core by removing the false covering and pretense of a "game," revealing that what I was in fact doing, as part of my job, contained an element of life and death. What seems standard and routine might not be. What seems innocuous and simple can potentially have dire consequences. Expect the unexpected. Always keep the human perspective close, and never fail to enact it when required.

Rest in peace, Deborah.

· PART TWO ·

RACISM 101

"IT'S NOT ALWAYS RACIST . . . BUT SOMETIMES IT IS"

I had just been transferred from the Morality Bureau into a uniformed officer's position. On my very first day during the parade — the daily inspection by a supervisor — I had an encounter with an acting sergeant who will remain nameless (I very much remember his name) because he would probably not remember our encounter and would be unable to defend my claims, which would be unfair. After the parade, he stood at the doorway waiting for me to pass by. He then engaged me in conversation about where my placement had been prior to the transfer. Of course, he knew very well where I'd come from. He asked me how it was possible that I would have gotten the position of a drug officer straight out of police college. He said, "For that matter, how did you even get hired?" I responded that it had taken me a long time to be hired as a police officer, that it had not been easy. As for the position in Morality, it was a decision that had been made by senior management, not me. Then, once again, I was hit with that denigrating and completely repugnant phrase, "Nice place, this Canada, eh?"

Some weeks later, while in the officers meeting room waiting for the supervisor's daily briefing, several officers including myself were complaining among ourselves that we were sick and tired of car wash detail. Each Sunday, an officer was assigned to wipe down and mop out the interior of the cruisers at the district. The talk was that we are cops, not car detailers, and the service should hire people to look after the vehicles. I was no more vocal than the other officers, who were demonstrating the same amount of passion and resentment. At the end of the parade, we all dispersed into our respective patrol zones. Some hours later, I was summoned off the road to see the divisional inspector, Donald Kirk. The inspector was a hard, tough, respectable old-school cop who knew the positional and personal power he wielded. His door was slightly ajar; I knocked. "Close the door," he said. I did after entering. I was standing and he was sitting. The next words out of his mouth were: "Who the *fuck* do you think you are!" He then proceeded to blast me with expletives that I would be hard-pressed to repeat in this book. This was a take-no-prisoners, full-on frontal assault the likes of Iwo Jima or the D-Day beaches of Normandy. This man was a master at stringing along every adjective, predicate, verb, adverb, noun, pronoun, and consonant in the English language in the most vicious and vile way. He spared no spittle or breath in letting me know exactly how he felt. The more I tried to protest, the louder he snapped. In his rage, he inadvertently mentioned the officer who had named me as the agitator. You see, all of this invective, turns out, was about the car wash detail. I had been pointed out as the agitator who had instigated the rebellion — the young upstart who had come from the drug squad and thought he was special. The officer who had identified me was the same acting sergeant who'd had that conversation with me at the door of the parade room. Under the unrelenting barrage and savagery of the inspector's words, tone, and aggression, I had become convinced that I was about to be fired.

As the berating continued and my defensive, wimpy interjections were met with louder, more vulgar, and more denigrating grenades, I started to tune out, fading into a cloud in my head that enveloped me. The volume of the rant was now less loud. The cloud quickly faded to grey, diffused in the office, obscuring both the room and the antagonist. The sound now was light and muffled. I heard him spit, "Who the *fuck* do you think you are?" again. I faded to black. This event disrupted my mind, sending me to a place of kinship with those who suffered the unjust fate of being treated as a commodity more than four hundred years ago as part of white supremacy. The vision I shared at the beginning of this book flashed through my mind. My rage was off the charts.

The light in the room re-emerged. The voice of the inspector grew louder and louder. The cadence of his words, tone, and inflections slashed into my skin like the lashing of the massa's whip. The sting brought back the many injustices that had been inflicted upon me in recent years, growing up in Canada at the hands of so-called "Canadians" who were simply lighter-skinned immigrants. The bullshit I'd put up with in grade school. The interview with the Peel Regional Police. The unnatural and racist challenges I had to endure being hired and accepted in a police service that for the most part didn't want me. The bigoted, unjust behaviour of my fellow officers and my superiors. Yes, the baggage I brought into that room that day was too heavy. Yes, that huge chip on my shoulder was a burden on my soul. Actually, this was no chip — it was a boulder on each shoulder. "My cup surely runneth over." Some years prior, I had made a promise to myself that I would never be put in a situation to be humiliated by anyone, especially one who was white and in uniform, ever again. I meant it to my core!

The last words I heard of the inspector's rant were that I would be assigned every car wash detail on every Sunday that I worked until he said otherwise. The rage within me would not let this man berate me like this anymore, especially when the accusation was not true. In a fit of fury, I raised my voice and told him "I don't give a shit! Fuck you and this bullshit job!" Silence. More silence. To my complete and total surprise, he shuffled in his chair, smiled at me, nodded his head, and told me to get out.

At this point, some may want to defend the actions of the inspector, speculating that he might not have brought a racial component to the situation he was dealing with, that instead I had grafted my own perspective onto the situation. His fury could have been more about dealing with the so-called insurrection that he was convinced I had plotted and incited. On the other hand, I saw him in that moment as another white man with power and authority over me, scolding me for an accusation brought to him by a racist officer. There was no dialogue other than his ranting, his "let's get 'em, boys" bullshit. Just like in so many cases, there was little in the way of investigation and certainly no justice. I was just sick of this unbalanced, unfair treatment and was prepared to fight one last time and leave the job if required.

Well, for whatever reason, I don't remember doing another car wash detail. Oddly enough, the inspector and I had a very warm and respectful working relationship going forward. I really believed that my last gasp and final desperate act of standing up for myself in his office was something that he admired. He was old school, and to him, strength was a virtue. When we met or had dealings with one another after that day, he was pleasant, cheery, and respectful, and usually had a smile on his face. I grew to really like and admire this man. He was eventually promoted to superintendent and has since retired.

In her book *It's Not Always Racist . . . But Sometimes It Is*, Dr. Dionne Poulton, educator, diversity and inclusion consultant, conflict mediator, and a very dear friend of mine, stresses that there is a fundamental difference between racism and racial bias. Judging others based on race is normal, she says, just as it is normal to make judgements based on age, height, weight, beauty, ability, and so on. Trouble arises when negative perceptions go unchecked. I totally agree with her. When someone in a seat of power, capable of making or skewing the rules, has unchecked assumptions, then we, collectively, have a serious problem. With the weight of history on your side, do you consider race when going about your day-to-day as it relates to your position of authority? Should you consider race? How does that influence your job performance and the best outcomes for the organization? How does that affect the subordinates under your command?

It's not always racist . . . but sometimes it is! There is an inherent danger in calling out racism for every incident that is suspect in the mind of the accuser. Where does that leave the accused, who has done or said something with no thought of race or discrimination whatsoever? The person whose implicit bias (unconscious thought acted out) has been interpreted or exaggerated as an issue of race when it clearly was not? There are times where people are falsely accused of being racist when their actions are void of malicious intent but result in an adverse impact. This is further complicated when that person is in a position of power, having authority to take away your liberty or permitted to use force in certain circumstances, as granted by the laws governed by provincial and federal jurisdictions.

What is unfair is not always racism. As for me, there were times I had to check myself and deconstruct the incident with an honest assessment or even role reversal to get to the most probable conclusions. People make mistakes, and poor judgement can cause erroneous perceptions.

Let me give you an example that occurred later in my career that I believe gives real context to this type of situation. It's about an experience I had with an officer of equal rank. We were both staff sergeants at the time, each managing our respective platoon. I was in line for a promotion to the rank of inspector, and I felt that this person was deliberately attempting to undermine my leadership abilities. As platoon supervisors, we were responsible for the overall proper functioning of subordinates, which were three sergeants and twenty-five to thirty officers. More specifically, we were responsible for the booking and releasing of prisoners along with checking all reports, including Crown briefs (documents provided to the courts regarding specific incidents, along with charging offences) having to do with the platoon, ensuring that they were validated and entered into the system for processing. Just these two tasks alone ate up most of the shift. On a busy shift, it was not uncommon for the staff sergeant to hold back one of the road sergeants to assist with these tasks. There were four platoons in rotation, which meant there were four staff sergeants per district. Booking prisoners and the Crown briefs had to be completed prior to the changing of shifts, but there were occasions where some of the general reports were left over. We all understood and had no issue with picking up the slack when necessary: all but one of us. This individual's platoon followed mine, so he was my relief. On the occasions where work was left over, he would take it upon himself to complain secretly to the divisional inspector and the superintendent. He knew very well that he himself was guilty of doing the same thing, along with the other managers. He would also undermine aspects of my platoon, ranging from how service calls were handled to my competency in managing my officers. This was told to me by the other two staff sergeants over a period of time. I was taken aback because I felt we had a good working relationship. We'd never had anything other than polite professional conversation. No animosity, or so I thought. To my knowledge, he did not complain about any of the other staff sergeants.

Now, the textbooks will tell you that the proper way to handle this situation is to have a conversation with this person as soon as possible, and if you are unable to resolve the problem, then you should involve your supervisors. I chose to put everything I had into ensuring that no work was left over and mitigate, to the best of my ability, anything he could complain about. I felt I just had to prove myself once again. Big mistake! It got worse. The underhandedness continued, and my rage built up. One evening shift, I was told by an officer who had been in a meeting a few days prior with several folks, including the inspector, superintendent, and staff sergeant, that this individual was callously disparaging me to the point of personal destruction. I was on a twelve-hour shift that evening, and I raged the entire night. I was close to losing my mind knowing that I would see him in the morning, as he was the relieving officer. I was well beyond any anger-management techniques acquired throughout my career. All I could think of was what I knew to be true: that some people don't want to see a Black man as their equal and certainly don't want him to be their boss.

Well, the moment finally arrived when he walked into the office and said good morning. I responded with: "We need to talk in the boardroom." This room was a fair distance away from the platoon office, which I knew would be empty at that time of the morning. I was shaking the entire walk. Once in the room, I closed the door and started yelling what no mother should ever hear coming out of her child's mouth — or anyone's mouth, for that matter. My rage was full and complete. I had hate in my heart and venom in my veins. As he backed away, I advanced. If he had resisted me in any way, I am sure we would have ended up in a physical altercation. I said my piece and stormed out of the room.

As I left, I encountered several officers outside of the room who looked stunned, trying to figure out what the hell had just happened. Neither the staff sergeant nor I exchanged a word with each other for the next six to eight months. However, he never mentioned my name in any meetings going forward. Nor did he ever make a complaint against me, which he had every right to do.

I have deconstructed this incident time and time again over many years. In my mind, there was no question that this staff sergeant was acting in a discriminatory manner against me. I truly believed that it was racially motivated. What was missing from this incident was the communication piece. This staff sergeant did not speak to me directly about any issues he had with me or my performance. I had very little to work with other than past experience and the organizational culture as reference points, leading me to assume and suspect that his indirect complaints stemmed from a position of racial bias. The unfortunate outcome was that it perpetuated ignorance on both sides. On seeing him that morning, I didn't take the time to process my thoughts or emotions before acting, so I reacted based on how I felt. With the clarity of hindsight, had we spoken with the intent of listening to each other with mediation and perhaps reaching a better understanding, this would have turned out quite differently. As it was, we were both left with uncertainty regarding the actual issues and no plan to work towards a positive resolution.

My reaction that day was completely wrong. It was not the best of me. The story is worth recounting to advance the notion that, as good a leader (having the right attributes and emotional maturity) that I felt I was growing into, there were times when I did not measure up. This certainly was one of those times. I did not exemplify the qualities of someone aspiring to lead at a higher level within the organization. It was a highly charged emotional reaction that could have been very costly. I used it as a lesson to myself as I matured in the various portfolios I would eventually occupy.

∞

Racism had permeated my life in many ways to this point. I had been battered and bruised: the Black Sambo comment in England; the cop pulling me over at the CNE; the constant repetition of "Nice place, this Canada, eh?"; the persistent messaging that I should be more grateful for things than my white colleagues; the accusation of rape on the army base. This bruising became an open wound the moment it started affecting my children.

My first of two daughters, Jasmine, was born in March 1988. Brianna came two years later, in May 1990. There are no words to describe the feeling of fatherhood and the depth of love I had and continue to have for my girls. I still maintain that I will do everything in my power to protect them from outside forces that may want to harm them. When Jasmine was five, I was unable to deliver on that sacred oath that a father makes to his daughters. Although it wasn't my fault, the failure was one of the most painful experiences that I have encountered in my entire life. My wife and I thought that we were doing the right thing when we enrolled Jasmine in a summer day camp not far from our home. I had the responsibility of dropping her off and picking her up. Jasmine was excited and eager to attend camp. She was a bubbly extrovert with long braids with beads on the tips, great energy, and a fondness for other kids. The first day of camp, I delivered her to the camp counsellor, who greeted us in the outdoor play area. Jasmine was so excited she immediately made herself welcome on one of the swing sets. A number of other children her age were playing there as well. The kids immediately gravitated to Jasmine, as she was so friendly. Seeing that she had settled in right away, I returned some hours later to pick her up. Jasmine was waiting for me at the same spot where I had dropped her off earlier, with the same counsellor. Her demeanour was somewhat subdued, which I noticed right away. She jumped into my arms and gave me a nice hug and smile. I asked her how her day was. She replied that she'd had a good time. Not as enthusiastically as I had expected, but okay. I questioned her on the drive home and got pretty much the same response.

Day two, I dropped her off to the same counsellor and came back for her at the required time. Something was definitely wrong. Jasmine was trying really hard to smile and act as if she was fine, but I knew that she was not enjoying the camp. I asked the counsellor how Jasmine's day had been and if there were any issues. She told me that all was good and Jasmine had been well behaved. I wasn't sure what, but I knew that something was not right. I asked Jasmine if she wanted to continue going to camp, and she said she really wanted to continue. When I picked her up on day three, Jasmine was not smiling this time, and folded into my arms. I sat her in the car and turned my attention to the counsellor. I asked her what was going on. She would only say that everything was fine. I knew it wasn't. I was persistent in finding the cause by appealing to her sense of parenting. "If she were your child, wouldn't you want to know what was going on?" She finally relented and said to me that the other parents had told their kids not to play with Jasmine. I asked her why. She told me that my daughter was the only Black child and was therefore different, and the parents didn't want their children exposed to her. I was completely and utterly crushed. The ugly, venomous, and vile demon of racism had touched my child. She was only five years old, as innocent as one can be. But that didn't matter — only the colour of her skin did.

Did I really fail my daughter, or did the world fail us? What would compel adults to see a five-year-old, beautiful, dark-skinned girl bubbling with effervescent joy and deem her not worthy to play or mix with their children? My understanding was that this was a collective agreement between the parents that had not been called out by the staff. Why did my child have to suffer at the hands of bigots when she had played no part in what they objected to? It seemed her Blackness was the only offensive criteria. We collectively hurt to this day as a family at this vicious attack on our dignity.

Sadly, this was not the only wound inflicted on my girls as they ventured into this unfair world. But I also know that good people are found anywhere and at any time, even in the face of something as ugly as racism. When Jasmine was about eight, there was a McDonald's restaurant near us that had completed major renovations, including a large indoor area for kids to play. One day, we as a family decided to treat ourselves to a McMeal and let the girls play on the equipment. Jasmine asked if her best friend, Jonah, an absolutely wonderful young Jewish boy whom we adored, could come with us. Of course he could. We sat and ate our food, and the kids were eager to get to the play area. I remember the restaurant was quite full, partly from the novelty of the restorations. It didn't take long before a young boy confronted Jasmine and called her a "nigger." The boy's apparent mother or guardian was right there and did nothing. To be fair, she didn't get a chance: Jonah immediately stepped in front of the boy and launched into a dressing-down worthy of a Nobel Prize for Humanitarian Efforts. Why was this young boy able to see the ugliness of the word and actions and find it within himself to defend my daughter the way he did? He was truly offended and did what he could to protect Jasmine. Where did the other boy get that word from, and how did he know how to use it and to whom? (Obviously this is a rhetorical question, as we all know the answer.) As I write this book, Jasmine is thirty-five years old and Jonah is still one of her best friends.

∞

I am a Black man, who, during the earlier years of my career, did not find being Black to be advantageous. I desperately wanted to effect positive change from the inside. I felt that my relationship with fellow officers and commanders, along with my wholesome, honest treatment of the citizens with whom I came in contact, would somehow drastically change or at least assist in improving the service. I truly didn't have a good under-standing or appreciation of the depth of what that meant. My core spoke to me, but there was no guidance, road map, or mentorship. Nor were there any support mechanisms that I could tap into to make the appropriate impact. Although somewhat prepared for the fight, I deeply underesti-mated the baggage that I brought with me that at times skewed my vision and perspective on a few dealings with my fellow officers and commanders. I believe one of the best examples of this was the length of time that it took for me to trust any white officers. For many years, I just couldn't get there. I had distrust in most of what they said and demonstrated. By the very nature of the work we were doing, you had to have comfortable working relationships with your partners to be an effective officer. The job was multifaceted, and there was not one person who knew all there was to know, so you were bound to work together. For the most part, that brought us together as brothers and sisters for the cause. At some point, I realized that there was a genuineness to their rapid response to my calls for backup and the extent to which they assisted me in the job. Eventually, I connected with several officers above a superficial level, creating a few meaningful partnerships. The few who I put my trust in did not disappoint me. I still consider them friends to this day.

PINPRICKS AND
MICROAGGRESSIONS

After working undercover in the drug world for three years, it was time to move into another area of the service. I opted for the uniformed patrol role, as this was where I had originally wanted to explore and experience the visual and hands-on aspects of policing. My new assignment was 4 District, located in what was then the town of Vaughan (and would later become the city of Vaughan). Finally, I had the chance to put on that new uniform and equipment I'd received three years earlier.

My second day, while in the change room getting dressed, I received a page from the front desk that there was a phone call for me. I stepped out of the room, went down the hall, and answered the phone. A few minutes later, returning to the change room, I was unable to locate my four belt clips that secured my outer belt to an inner belt. They had been stolen. Could this be possible? Stolen! I have no idea why someone would take the clips or what message they were trying to send to me. Was I in for a rude awakening! Talk about the start of a bad day. I made my way to the parade room and sat among several other platoon members for our daily briefing — yes, just like *Hill Street Blues* or *Brooklyn Nine-Nine* — my uniform pressed, armed with my service revolver, and notebook in hand. The sergeant entered the room and began the briefing.

"Folks, we had a robbery of a convenience store overnight; four culprits described as male niggers who, when caught, need to do jail time and be shipped back to Africa."

What?!

Now, once again, I ask you to imagine this scenario: Keith Merith, a proud young man who happens to be Black and fought like hell to get hired as a police officer, is finally sitting among his peers in uniform, thinking he is part of this new world that he longed for, and then . . . this. In a room of white officers, I was being sent a message loud and clear: You don't belong. You are a nigger, and you need to go back to Africa. Another piece of me crumbled and fell to the floor that morning. I felt lost, ashamed, humiliated, and angry. My internal pain was paralyzing and debilitating.

At the conclusion of the briefing, on my way out of the room, Steven Patrick, a tall country boy who enjoys the simple hunting and fishing life, put his arm around my shoulders and said, "That guy's an asshole; you are part of the team, and we'll look after you." That man resurrected my soul. I will be forever grateful for that single moment, the empathy, kindness, and strength of character demonstrated that day. We worked on the same platoon for approximately two years. To me, that one simple act set him above the rest. He did not know how much it meant to me. In fact, Steven's inclusion of me extended outside of the service. He had me out on his boat on Lake Ontario, fishing for salmon (I do have a true story about the monster fish that got away that day, but I'll reserve it for another time). Steven also invited my wife and me to his hunting camp deep in the bush of "who knows where." This was in the middle of winter, and colder than the polar ice cap. We had a blast. Thank you, Steven, for everything.

∞

Close your eyes for a few seconds and imagine with me a time when you were stuck by a pin or a tack and remember the immediate shock of pain and realization, and your instant reflex: you rub the spot, quickly soothing it while making a mental note to not do that again. That pinprick hurt a bit, but it was certainly bearable. Now, can you think of a time when you pricked yourself over a dozen times in one day? Most of us can't. But what if it were not self-inflicted? It was done to you at random, unannounced, recurring over many days, weeks, months, and years. I ask because that is how I perceive the realm of *implicit* and *explicit* biases along with microaggressions experienced by many Black people. Implicit biases are prejudices that turn into an action that is unconscious. Explicit biases are prejudices that you are aware of but act them out anyway. Both of these constructs require examples to get a better perspective on them.

A man goes into a major hardware store wanting some information on a building project and the tools to accomplish the job. There are a number of attendants, some of whom are female. The customer intentionally seeks out the male attendant. He may not even realize that he's done this (implicit). On the other hand, he may have done so deliberately, believing that the male attendant would be more familiar with the trades (explicit). Either way, his biases manifested into action. It's important to understand that implicit bias can turn into an explicit bias once it's recognized and acted on, but an explicit bias can never be implicit. I'm going to say something that I think is quite profound that might take some time to sink in, but when it does, it will make sense and perhaps provide some insight into the essence of this chapter.

A bias is defined as a preference for or a prejudice against a person or a group. Implicit biases operate outside of our conscious awareness. We don't know that we have them, although we now have the tools to be able to test for them. We also know that they often run contrary to our conscious beliefs. Dushaw Hockett, founder and executive director of Safe Places for the Advancement of Community and Equity (SPACEs) noted during a TED Talk on September 18, 2017, that a law enforcement officer who is deeply committed to the motto inscribed on his/her service vehicle ("To Serve and Protect") can be the same officer who leads the organization in the rate of stops-and-frisks of young Black men or people of colour. Consciously, they are deeply committed to the principles of protecting and serving; unconsciously, their behaviour is inconsistent with that. It could also be said that they believe targeting and incarcerating young Black men *is* serving and protecting, that their racism leads them to equate the two, so they don't see the contradiction.

Chester M. Pierce first coined the term "microaggression" in the 1970s as a way to describe the subtle insults and put-downs that African Americans experience regularly. Many such incidents can be classed as unintentional acts of prejudice. There is no harm meant, but harm is felt. Yet again, it goes to intent versus impact.

Now walk with me as I demonstrate some of the pinpricks and micro-aggressions that I felt during many of my shifts spent in a uniformed capacity at 4 District in Vaughan.

Regardless of shift, it's customary for me to arrive early and be greeted by some members of my platoon: "Morning/afternoon, Keith." But others acknowledge me with a "Yo bro!" (Pinprick.) Sitting on parade, I am the only officer of colour in the room and most often in the entire station. (Ouch.) When we are paraded by the sergeant, often there is a mention of Black people or other racial minorities related to crime and to be on the lookout for them. We are told, those Black people might be planning a festival, party, or an event that could possibly require police intervention. (Pinprick.) Rest assured that there will be a racial joke to accompany that information. (Another jab.)

An officer notices the shine on my boots and asks if I could do theirs for fifty cents. (Pinprick.) "Merith, you're assigned the 420 car," the shittiest vehicle in the fleet. (Jab.) Someone purposely removes my submitted report and I get called out by the staff sergeant as derelict in my duties. (Poke, jab, and punch.) I overhear officers referring to members of our visible minority communities in disparaging ways. (Pinprick.)

On patrol, I encounter the shock and sometimes indignation of a few folks who are not used to seeing an officer of colour, or feel that this is a reflection of the state of things to come and they don't like it. (Pinprick.) Others are shocked and surprised when I speak with proper grammar and word formation, with no accent. (Jab.) In conversation at service calls, I get the "where are you from?" question. (Another jab.) Woven into several conversations is a denial of individual racism, as in, "I don't see colour" or "I have friends that are Black." (Poke.)

When I'm using the car radio or portable radio, other officers squawk it, meaning they depress their microphones, effectively cutting me off. Accident? It happened too many times in the earlier days for it to be such. (Pinprick.) On occasion, while dealing with a matter that was my call, an assisting officer moves from assisting to interfering, feeling that their whiteness is an asset. (Jab.) If a group of white kids is loitering around a convenience store, the call would be for a group of youths; if, on the other hand, it is a group of Black youths, the officers or dispatch would announce them as Black and the response would be different, with more responding officers than necessary and more sense of urgency. (Ouch.)

An invitation to grab lunch or dinner by some officers turns into a joke at my expense, with them telling the server I'll take fried chicken with a side order of watermelon. (Sword thrust.) If, by chance, I encounter another Black officer in the station or on the road in the presence of white officers, those white officers inevitably make a comment about "Black brothers" banding together or forming a posse. (Pinprick.) Filling up the patrol car with gasoline elicits a comment about me seeking secondary employment. (Jab.)

I'm not being overly sensitive; I'm just merely pointing out that being outfitted with Black skin often brings out certain biases and microaggressive behaviours from peers and from the people you serve — not just once in a while, but all the time. What may be a "joke" to them is hurtful to us, piling up throughout the day until we're covered in tiny wounds that begin to fester.

The world of policing was, and still is to some degree, the bastion of men who are predominantly white, so imagine the reality of women officers who enter into the service seeking equality and fair play. The women had it *hard*. The misogyny and workplace harassment never stopped. It was ever-present and underreported. Now add the fact that a small number of these female officers were Black. I would call that the perfect storm. Against all odds, some Black women set a tone and standard that was impeccable and unimpeachable. With their achievements, they sent a message across the country that Black women are a force to be reckoned with. Their accomplishments spoke to the fact that the seemingly impossible is indeed possible.

∞

The type of work police are involved in is not a good mix with these pinpricks and microaggressions, which have real negative consequences. If left unchecked, they can turn into real threats, causing real trauma. The adverse affects often cling to one's chest and metastasize in the mind, causing irreparable damage. I was involved in one such incident that was directed at my partner by an unknown member, and it opened a wound that has never healed.

On December 8, 1988, seventeen-year-old Michael Wade Lawson, a grade eleven student attending Erindale Secondary School in Mississauga, was an occupant in a stolen black Nissan Maxima in a residential area of the city. At 7:45 p.m. that evening, Officers Anthony Melaragni and Darren Longpre of the Peel Regional Police fired six shots at the back of the vehicle. One of those bullets found its way through the back window and into the head of Lawson — he died fifteen hours later. The officers were subsequently charged. Anthony Melaragni was acquitted of second-degree murder and Darren Longpre acquitted of two counts of unlawfully discharging his firearm. The killing of this young man was fraught with controversy, including the type of bullet that the officers had fired that evening. At the time, the standard-issued police rounds were .38-calibre. The bullets fired that night were hollow points, which were not issued by the force and certainly were against regulations. This breach was significant, as these types of bullets inflict a more lethal wound pattern and have what is known in the industry as more stopping power.

I say all of this to introduce Ezra (Tony) Browne, a member of the Morality Bureau and a constable at the time, who from day one adopted the duty of being my guide, mentor, coach, and friend — he was also Black. It was an extremely rare event in those days to have two Black officers working in the same specialty unit. A few weeks after the killing of Lawson, Tony and I were in the office, sitting face to face at a desk, chatting. As I remember it, Tony was going through a stack of mail. He got to an internal mail envelope and dumped the contents on the table. It contained a single item: a hollow-point bullet. The same type of bullet that had killed Lawson. The envelope was addressed to Tony, so there was no mistaking what this was. It was a message in the form of a threat to his life. Tony had had absolutely nothing to do with the Lawson investigation. In fact, the homicide had happened in the jurisdiction of the Peel Regional Police. This was no outside threat; this was an internal message. The *why* is still undetermined. As if synchronized, we both became short of breath and tears welled up in our eyes. We felt the blunt edge of that bullet pierce our soul. A piece of ourselves was excised in that moment.

Together we discussed what we should do. We decided that due to the gravity of the incident, Tony would go in person to police headquarters and speak with the executive command. With weak knees and a broken heart, Tony left the office. On his return, Tony advised me that he had met with Deputy Chief Robert Wilson and had a conversation with him. The deputy was extremely sympathetic and advised Tony that he would do the best he could to look into the matter, and that included transferring Tony out of the unit. Yes! A transfer out of the unit! A little while later, the unit commander of the Morality Bureau came into the office, quite disturbed and extremely pissed off. He turned to Tony saying, and I quote, "And you, Tony, keep your petty complaints to yourself!" Those nine words were forever seared in my mind, and haunt Tony to this day. A few days later Tony was transferred out of the unit. The matter has never seen the light of day since it happened. The department had failed us — instead of putting resources into tracking down the perpetrator, Tony was transferred away from a unit he'd grown accustomed to, as if *he* were the problem. Institutional ignorance of the effects of this type of conduct permeated the service. It severely limited the proper responses, at the expense of members such as Tony and myself.

Dealing with pinpricks and microaggressions is exhausting and painful. They can have dire consequences if left unchecked, often evolving into more constant, intensified, and potentially serious actions on the part of the offender. Why should anyone be subjected to this type of behaviour by virtue of being part of society? We should not have to live like this.

RACE RELATIONS

F our years in uniform patrol had passed, and it was time to make another move. A position had opened in the Training and Education Bureau. Kevin Smith was the service guru for our Defensive Tactics program, and he reached out to me to see if I was interested in joining the unit as a Use of Force instructor. Yes, of course I was! Years spent in this particular unit turned out to be some of the best ones I had as a member of the York Regional Police. (I will explore more about these years in a later chapter.) Having the opportunity to interact with almost every member of the service by way of Use of Force training provided me with an opportunity to participate as a facilitator in the academic section of our in-house training. Besides instructing on topics such as the Canadian Criminal Code, Provincial Offences Act, annual requalification, and recruit training, along with service rules and regulations, I was given the task of facilitating our Race Relations and Employment Equity Policies training.

It was during one of those Race Relations courses that my day turned to a night that lasted for several months. Sergeant Denyse Ross, a wonderful young white female officer, was my co-trainer in the class. Sergeant Ross was bright, competent, and very opinionated. She, in my judgement, was never given the respect that was due to her. We worked closely together, giving me an insight into her true personality, which I appreciated and admired. She should not have had to fight as hard as she did to stay afloat in this male-dominated organization. It was extremely unfair and, without a doubt, diminished her heroic contributions to the service.

There were approximately two dozen officers in this particular class in early 1995. After some instruction on the who, what, and where of racism, Sergeant Ross instructed the class to form small groups to conduct a joint tabletop exercise. The task was to use a flip chart and write out thoughts on how stereotyping affects police work. If memory serves, I believe that they had around ten minutes to come up with written answers to present to the class. When the time came for the group containing Constable Randy Porter and Constable Brent Stitt along with four other officers to present, Randy volunteered to read the group's contribution. This is what was presented, written out, and stated aloud to the class: "Closed minded. Not accepting. Insensitive. Gives bad attitude. Gets people upset. Exaggerates reality. Relates differences. S.I.U." So, innocuous on the surface, right? Well then, Randy proceeded to draw our attention to the formulation of an acronym (the first letters of each word). Let's you and me (the reader of this book and the author) spell that out. Here we go: C.N.I.G.G.E.R.S.

Are you serious?

This is what the dynamics of the class looked like so many years ago. You have a young Black officer and a white female instructor facilitating a race relations class to a group of all-white police officers, who for the most part don't want to be there. Who certainly don't think they have an issue with race, and hate being accused or labelled as maybe having a problem. Two of these officers decided they were going to send me a message that, uniform or not, instructor or not, "You are still a nigger." (The other four members in the group voiced during the formulation of the exercise that they wanted nothing to do with what was being planned.) I was embarrassed, humiliated, hurt, angry, and badly wounded, but tried to keep my dignity and resurrect the class. Sergeant Ross was indignant and immediately came to my rescue. She stopped the class in its tracks and proceeded to blast those two officers. She did not for one second hold back. Her exact words escape me now after so many years, but I do know that she eviscerated them with everything in her. I am forever grateful to Sergeant Ross for standing up for me that day.

Inspector Rick McCabe, the officer in charge of the unit at the time, was notified immediately and he came straight to the class prior to any students leaving. I had already left the room, so this part is hearsay backed up by eyewitnesses. I was told that the inspector used language fit for a sailor and threatened to take both officers out back and kick the living shit out of them.

Five days later both officers were charged with breach of procedure 70, a lawful order of the chief of the York Regional Police. Procedure 70 was created by the service to address discrimination and harassment by governing the conduct of members. It defined harassment as "unacceptable conduct or comment that undermines the employment relationship or that should reasonably be expected to cause offence or humiliation to any member."

Both Randy Porter and Brent Stitt ran to the York Regional Police Association for leverage and financial support, seeing as they needed personal lawyers to advance their not-guilty pleas. When officers are charged under the regulations or procedures, they are entitled to a trial adjudicated by a hearing officer who, for the most part, is a trained police officer at the rank of inspector or above. The association granted both officers' requests for financial support. This meant that my contributions to the association by way of dues was supporting the defence of the two officers. It also meant that any other officer who disagreed with Porter and Stitt's behaviour was also contributing to their defence. Suffice it to say, I attended a few of the association meetings protesting the course of action and stance taken by the group. Some officers who knew of me or worked with me agreed and vehemently voiced their opposition at several loud and contentious meetings.

The association, led by Detective Paul Bailey, had entered into deep waters and had no clue how to deal with this new dilemma of internal race relations involving officers of colour. They concluded that they needed to defend their white officers at all costs, or else situations like this would come up more often. They hired a private investigator to look into my background to find anything they could use to discredit me.

Yes . . . this really happened. Not only was I paying for the defence of these two officers but my dues were now *also* paying for a private investigator to investigate me. I was *livid*. I made several requests to the association to provide me with all communications, memos, and recordings where my matter was discussed at the executive meetings. They refused and immediately stopped voice-recording their meetings so as not to incriminate themselves.

The membership stood up and eventually voted down the financial support for the officers. The association quickly tried to explain the private investigator thing and took a shellacking. They backtracked, danced, and skipped their way out of that mess. Porter and Stitt eventually went to trial but were acquitted by Durham Regional Police Inspector James Adams, cutting the four-day hearing short. He decided he did not need to hear the defence's case to make his ruling, citing there had been no misconduct. What happens in the classroom stays in the classroom.

∞

I am a big believer in the practice of risk management, not risk aversion. Own your positional authority; use it to its maximum capacity and make decisions. These words were put to the test on the evening of November 11, 2006. I was the staff sergeant in charge of "D" Platoon working out of 4 District headquarters in Vaughan. My role was to manage the station's operation, which included booking prisoners, signing off on officers' reports, and scheduling and ensuring proper running order of the officers under my command. District senior officers, inspectors, and superintendents work primarily day shifts, so in the evenings the staff sergeant is in charge of the station. Most evenings and night shifts there is a duty inspector charged with the overall command and control of the entire service. Their responsibilities end at 4 a.m., then they are replaced by regular senior officers who start their shifts around 8 a.m. On this particular evening, Constable Ryan Venables was assigned front desk duties, which meant that he was answering the phones and attending to people walking into the station. This was a rotational position, and it just so happened to be his turn this day. Ryan was just a rookie, having around two and a half years on the job at the time. I knew him as a go-getter, loving the action and not afraid to get involved when it came to getting the bad guys. I would describe him as pleasant, likable, smart, and tuned in to this relatively new world of policing.

That evening, several members were working at the front desk, so when Constable Fred DeWine needed an escort to complete a detail, Constable Venables volunteered to assist him. Once they were on the road, a decision was made to pass by a traffic stop initiated by another officer to ensure all was well. This was not out of the ordinary, but what happened next was definitely an aberration. Constable Derrick McNamee had arrested a suspected drunk driver. Constable Kevin Partridge assisted him. The officers charged the suspect with refusing to provide a roadside breath sample. They handcuffed the suspect and placed him in the back of Constable McNamee's cruiser. Constables DeWine and Venables arrived on the scene while the paperwork was being completed. Constable Venables then approached the cruiser and asked the now prisoner if he was Russian. The prisoner replied that he was. Constable Venables then called him a "fucking drunk Russian" and punched the prisoner on the side of his head, resulting in the prisoner sustaining injuries in the form of a chipped tooth and a cut and swollen lip. When Constable Venables returned to his own cruiser, he remarked to Constable DeWine, "I hate Russians."

At approximately 2:45 a.m., I received a phone call from Constable McNamee, who was level-headed and sober in his demeanour but was extremely upset, stating that a person in his custody had just been assaulted by another officer. He then went on to detail the events that had occurred and asked me what he should do. I instructed him to stay in place and I would have the sergeant attend the scene. I immediately contacted Sergeant Mark Ruffolo, relayed the information as I understood it, and instructed him to find out what had happened and report back to me. Sergeant Ruffolo attended the traffic stop, investigated the occurrence, then returned to the station. Mark advised me that the assault had happened in the same manner as described by Constable McNamee, and that he had ordered Constable Venables to return to the station. On confirmation, my responsibility was to notify the duty inspector, who would then take charge of the investigation and manage next steps according to organizational policies and procedures.

When I contacted our Commutations Bureau and requested the duty inspector, I was advised that he had already completed his shift and had gone home. That now left me as the person in charge of this situation. I had to make a decision. Understanding the nature and gravity of what had occurred, I was determined to make the right pronouncements, utilizing the full extent of my authority. My thought process went something like this: A police officer under my direct command had attended a call that he was not detailed to. He had assaulted a handcuffed prisoner, who was contained in the back seat of a police cruiser. He had uttered a racial comment while assaulting that prisoner. There was no concern of a continuation of the assault, as the officer and prisoner were separated, but I did have a concern about the state of mind of Officer Venables as it related to him and the general public. I also had to keep the best interest of the organization and the reputation of the service as part of the equation. In addition, I needed to ensure that the other platoon members knew that I was prepared to confront any wayward behaviour in the swiftest manner.

I concluded that I was not prepared to allow Constable Venables to complete the end of his shift and potentially interact with the public with the authority of an active police officer. My next step was to summon Constable Venables in the presence of Sergeant Ruffolo and suspend him right then and there. We took away his use of force equipment along with his badge and warrant card. He was then escorted out of the building with the direction to report to the inspector's office on the upcoming Monday morning, seeing that we were now into Saturday and the senior officers were off for the weekend. By this time, it was around 7:30 a.m. Due to the seriousness of the incident and the drastic measures initiated, I contacted my station inspector and superintendent via phone at their homes. I then contacted Inspector Karen Noakes (officer-in-charge of Professional Standards) and provided her with all of the details as I knew them to be.

Later on that morning, I was on a conference call with several senior officers, including the chief, where we discussed the occurrence in detail. Joining me on my end was Sergeant Ruffolo. We both listened in dumb-founded amazement when the conversation revealed that the chief did *not* support my actions. His take was that I should not have made the decision that I did but should have deferred to the divisional superinten-dent — who, by the way, was at home sleeping, I assume, seeing that it would have been about 5 a.m. His contention was that I was just a staff sergeant and didn't have the authority to suspend the officer. I defended my actions by stating that I had the authority by virtue that the duty inspector had gone home, so I in fact was the acting inspector during any major occurrence in the district. I also fought back by suggesting that the real course of action was that I should have arrested Constable Venables for assault causing bodily harm, as the attack met all the criteria for reasonable and probable grounds for that action. The only senior officer on that call to defend my actions was Inspector Karen Noakes, who showed courage in the face of the chief's assertions. Sergeant Ruffolo did the same, voicing support for all the actions taken.

It was around a month later, after an in-depth investigation by our Professional Standards Bureau, that Constable Venables was arrested for assault causing bodily harm. On May 2, 2007, Constable Venables pleaded guilty to the Criminal Code offence of assault. He received a suspended sentence and eighteen months probation subject to terms.

Constable Venables was now subjected to a disciplinary hearing and faced several very serious charges under the Police Code of Conduct.

Constable Venables pleaded guilty to two charges of discreditable conduct and one charge of unlawful or unnecessary exercise of authority. An agreed statement of facts was submitted. In addition, character evidence was presented on behalf of Constable Venables. In his acknowledgement of wrongdoing, Constable Venables said he had been frustrated after a previous call that evening; he'd never intended to punch the prisoner; he didn't recall making the ethnic comments but was embarrassed that he had; his conduct was out of character; following the incident, he had attended anger management courses and had registered for a course on racial sensitivity.

The hearing officer acknowledged the mitigating factors, which were an essentially clear employment record, guilty plea, apology to the victim, and a sincere expression of remorse. However, in his view the serious, reprehensible nature of the misconduct outweighed these factors. The hearing officer observed that the assault had damaged the reputation of the service, jeopardized public trust, and raised serious issues of police accountability and integrity, especially given the overtones of ethno-racial intolerance, which could undermine community outreach initiatives in the multicultural population served by the York Regional Police. The hearing officer concluded that the appellant's rehabilitative potential was outweighed by the seriousness of the misconduct and the potential damage to the reputation of the service if he were to remain on the force. He then imposed a penalty of dismissal from the service failing resignation within seven days. Constable Venables opted to resign.

I will mention one other thing related to the incident, which illustrates some truly disgusting behaviour by members of the platoon. A number of officers felt that Constable McNamee had broken the thin blue line and that he should never have reported the incident but rather should have worked with the other officers there to cover it up. Several officers were on scene that night but, of course, none of them had witnessed the assault. A couple of weeks after the incident, Constable McNamee requested to speak to me in private. Derrick was just a rookie himself, trying to manage the steep curve that the world of policing places on young officers in the early phase of learning the job. He was extremely sombre and spoke in a soft, aching tone. He was on the verge of tears, which made me feel real pain regarding what he was about to tell me. Without giving any names, he told me that members of the platoon were treating him like a pariah. Folks had not only stopped talking to him, but they had abandoned him to the point that he felt completely alone and unsafe. He requested a transfer out of the station and if possible to be moved to 1 District, which is located in Newmarket.

This broke my heart into many pieces, to think that this bullshit code of silence extended into my platoon, especially due to the nature of the event that unfolded that evening. Derrick, without an inkling of doubt, emphatically did the right and only acceptable thing that he could and should have done. I was ashamed of those officers who had participated in this conduct to the point that I needed to address this head-on.

First, I needed to honour Derrick's request for a transfer. Within a week the transfer was completed. With that done, I went on the platoon shift parade and spoke my mind. I expressed all the concerns I had with the occurrence and the subsequent behaviour of members of my platoon. The final note was a promise that I would come down without mercy on any officer that crossed the line of what was expected and called for as their duty in the service of the community.

Working within systems and organizational culture makes for interesting outcomes when dealing with rogue officers who exercise their racial biases. In the case of Porter and Stitt, the victim was Black, a police officer, and a good man. The system challenged the assertion that what had occurred was in fact worthy of the proper adjudication. In the end, the poor behaviour of the officers was systematically condoned. In the second example, the victim was white and was the subject of a hate crime. The system for the most part worked the way it should by ultimately holding that officer accountable and delivering the proper course of action with his dismissal. But the organizational culture, as demonstrated by the platoon officers, was almost dismissive of the crime while emphasizing the culture of not crossing the thin blue line. My thoughts are that in both incidents the service strived to do the right thing in holding officers accountable. Even ten years *later*, the gaps were still glaring.

A PLACE AT THE TABLE

Infused throughout the York Regional Police 2011 Annual Report is a set of shared values that all members of the service are expected to adhere to. The values are non-negotiable and speak to how business will be conducted as the service continues to work towards its vision and mission of making a difference in the community and ensuring citizens feel safe and secure through excellence in policing. These shared values are as follows.

> **Our People:** We foster a work environment of respect, open communication, empowerment, and inclusivity.
> **Community:** We engage our citizens and are dedicated to providing quality service.
> **Integrity:** We are ethical and respectful in all we say and do.
> **Leadership:** We are leaders in policing and all lead by example.
> **Accountability:** We accept responsibility for our actions.
> **Competence:** We are committed to excellence, professionalism, learning, and innovation.
> **Teamwork:** We succeed by working together and in partnership with our community.

So how was this organization pulled so far down a rabbit hole as to imbue the wrath of the Black community to the point of being labelled a racist police service? This is how.

Constable Dameian Muirhead was a young Black officer whom I would describe as a bright, astute achiever with a great disposition — a truly competent officer. I really liked Dameian. My impression of him was that he would be on the list of successors in terms of advancement within the organization. What happened to Dameian was an abject failure of an organization that thought it was on the right track but clearly was sideways and didn't know it. What happened to Dameian destroyed a good officer and caused irreparable damage to the trust and validation of many of the remaining Black officers working there today. What happened to Dameian was inconceivable but true.

On May 21, 2011, Constable Dameian Muirhead and several other uniformed officers responded to a domestic assault complaint that occurred at a private party in the town of Aurora. The party was held outdoors at a farmhouse situated on a large property. There were a number of people at the party, all of them white. According to Dameian and several other officers who were present, the patrons were uncooperative and hostile to the point where a male party-goer said he would "love to see that guy (Dameian) hanging from a tree." Dameian interpreted this comment to be a racial slur referring to lynching him because he was a Black officer. In order to gather information, Dameian continued recording licence plates of a number of vehicles parked on the property. He came across a motorcycle that had a jacket obstructing the licence plate. He moved the jacket, laying it on the seat of the bike, and it slipped off and fell to the ground. At that time, the owner of the motorcycle started yelling at him, ordering him to "pick up the fucking jacket, you fucking pig." The situation was described as very hostile towards the police. Officer safety had become an issue, Dameian would later claim, so he did not respond verbally or bend down to pick up the jacket, believing that he would be attacked. The investigation continued and police eventually cleared the scene.

Four days later, on May 24, 2011, while conducting regular uniform duties, Dameian stopped at a gas station in the town of Aurora for an unrelated matter. While he was in his cruiser, the same motorcycle owner approached. This man, quite by coincidence, happened to be at that gas station and had recognized Dameian. He demanded a business card, claiming that he was going to lodge a complaint against Dameian for dropping his jacket on the ground. Dameian gave the man his information verbally, and directions to the station where he could make his complaint. The man began walking away and stated he heard Dameian call him a loser. He then called Dameian a punk and stated, "If you didn't have a gun and a badge, I would kick your ass." Dameian interpreted that comment as a threat and arrested the man.

As a result of the arrest and subsequent complaint, an investigation into both occurrences was commenced. Detective James McRobbie of the Professional Standards Bureau was the lead investigator and alleged that several breaches of the Code of Conduct under the Police Services Act by Constable Muirhead had been identified. His recommendation was brought before a Discipline Review Committee (DRC). Here are the charges laid against Dameian:

Count #1. Insubordination: Constable Muirhead had not obtained voluntary or informed consent prior to moving the complainant's jacket to see the license plate. The DRC deemed the search was not intrusive and it was done in good faith, but ultimately amounted to minor misconduct. The chief believed that this should be dealt with by way of training.

Count #2. Discreditable Conduct: The DRC deemed that Constable Muirhead had not acted in a respectful manner by failing to acknowledge the complainant after dropping the jacket on the ground, that he did not accept responsibility for his actions in dealing with the complainant, and did not reflect the York Regional Police Professional Code of Ethics. The chief believed that this misconduct should be dealt with by way of a forfeiture of hours as well as training. And get this one:

Count #3. Neglect of Duty: The DRC deemed that Constable Muirhead did not properly investigate an allegation he'd made in his arrest report that connected the complainant to a person making racist remarks. The chief believed that this misconduct should be dealt with by way of a forfeiture of hours.

Yes, you understood that correctly: Dameian was charged for failing to investigate racial slurs against . . . *himself*. Who in their right mind would come up with charges such as these taking into consideration the described circumstances? How the hell did Detective McRobbie arrive at his conclusions? Where was his immediate supervisor, who would have been a detective sergeant? How could that person have let those charges stand? Where was the detective sergeant's direct supervisor, who would have been the bureau's officer-in-charge, an inspector? How could that person let those charges stand? Where was the bureau commander (superintendent), who at any time could have made a decision that those or any charges against Constable Muirhead were unwarranted? The Discipline Review Committee typically consists of the chief of police, one or two deputy chiefs, a superintendent or two, an inspector, and the officer in charge of the investigation. You mean to tell me that all of these officers sat around a table and agreed to this nonsense? They didn't have the wisdom or foresight to see the inevitable critical fallout by making the decisions that they did?

This is a great example of why being in the room with consciousness, influence, and courage is necessary. It is often said that we as Black folks need to be at the table where decisions are being made. I say that's not enough. We need to be at the table in numbers, with influence and the intestinal fortitude to speak up about what we see, what we know, and what we will not accept. To have charged this officer in the first place was disgusting, but to charge him for failing to investigate racial slurs against himself is an abomination. When have you ever heard of a white officer charged with failing to investigate a racial slur hurled against them?

Needless to say, the general public was outraged and did not mince any words in calling out this organization for its perceived racist behaviour. Because Dameian refused to accept the charges and recommendations by the chief, the process escalated into a Police Act Tribunal. To make matters worse, the organization, in its infinite wisdom, assigned Superintendent Robertson Rouse, a Black officer, to adjudicate the matter. To the Black officers and the Black community, this appointment was seen as a way to placate them and was insulting. Dameian still had to defend himself at the tribunal. Under this air of distrust, the only outcome that would be accepted by the Black community was complete exoneration. Rouse's appointment was viewed as a corporate fix. The superintendent had loyalty to the service, which put him in a position stuck between being a corporate servant or a Black justice liberator. I can only suggest that at this point, the organization was trying to save its hide, and Superintendent Rouse was operating on the premise that he would do his best to make a determination on a resolution in a fair and balanced manner. The trial, as expected, was an absolute shit show, with both prosecution and defence at each other's throats. Partway through the trial the York Regional Police discontinued the case against Dameian.

This certainly was not our finest hour. The organization took a beating from the media, special interest groups, the citizenry, and members within the YRP. This is a prime example of intent versus impact. I'm assuming the intent was to demonstrate that the service took complaints from the public very seriously and would hold any officer accountable for their actions. They failed miserably by missing the sensibilities at play. They completely missed the interconnectivity of the racial overtone of that Black officer doing his job under adverse conditions, which was far deeper than they could have imagined or experienced. They failed to understand that diplomacy, in many occasions, works and should be employed as a tool in the adjudication process of sensitive matters that are outside the scope of regular occurrences.

If I had been the chief of police at that time, what would I have done? My first reaction would be to ask probing questions as to what level of investigation had been conducted. Is the assigned investigator the right person to investigate this type of allegation? How competent was the investigation? Were all of the witnesses interviewed on both sides? Did the officer act in a reasonable manner based on the circumstances? Now that the investigative details are in front of me, including the incident's racial overtone, do I have all the perspectives that I need to make a determination? Are charges necessary and why? What would be a better way of resolving this matter? And here is the crucial outside-the-box move that I would have made: I would have delayed my decision until I had spoken to or brought in several senior Black officers to get their thoughts, opinions, and perspective on the matter. I am confident that no senior Black officer would have condoned these or any charges. Why? They have what was *not* in the room: a relatability to the notion of being Black in uniform in the presence of a hostile white crowd and a comment directed at you regarding lynching. It also would not have been a huge stretch for me to summon the officer and have a one-on-one with him regarding the occurrence. Looking back at this incident in hindsight, I am confident that I would not have charged this officer and would have found alternatives that made sense for all involved.

THE SPACES THAT SQUEEZE US

In 1990, the premier of Ontario, Bob Rae, came out with an edict that, in essence, stated that police services in the province must be reflective of the people they represent. He was speaking directly to the executive officers of police departments who were almost exclusively white: this is not *your* police service; it belongs to the people. This was at a time when services, primarily the larger urban ones, had made an effort to slightly diversify the hiring of both sworn officers and civilian members. What was at the core of the disparity was the system that limited the hiring of visible minorities. At the heart of that system was a paramilitary hierarchy that gave the respective chiefs an enormous amount of power and autonomy to enact their will and shape the departments to their liking. Yes, there were some governances in place in the form of a Police Services Board, to which the chiefs reported, but the chiefs would construct the messaging to the board justifying the operations of the service. On the surface, the systems seemed fair, equal, and applicable to all. But what is built into the system under the surface is the "space."

The space is where people find loopholes or leeway. In my experience, people in privileged positions use the space to keep marginalized people on the margins. It's the wiggle room that allows people to take advantage of others in order to maintain the status quo that keeps them in power. It allows the system to operate in the way it was designed. So, let's examine the concept of the space with some examples.

If someone wants to join a police service in Ontario, they need to first apply. There are criteria they must meet in order to be eligible, such as age, education, Canadian citizenship or permanent residency, along with being mentally and physically able to perform police constable duties. If you have these qualifications, then you're on your way. The application is received and screened. There was a time during my career when all applications had to be hand-delivered by the applicant. There was no assurance that the receiver of the application would do the right thing and submit the application according to procedure. This is the first example of space — that individual could choose to pass on the application, or they could use that space to dispose of it if the applicant didn't suit their idea of what one should look like. In my service, the individual recruiting officers did the initial screening. They had the power to accept or reject the application. If the candidate made it through the pre–background assessment, they advanced to an interview stage. During that interview process, the interviewers had the authority to not advance the candidate based on their assessment of how the interview went or was scored (space). Then came the background investigation and a number of other considerations (space). Now, please don't get me wrong: there must be processes in place to ensure that services hire not only qualified candidates but, more importantly, the right candidate. However, for many years, whatever police services were doing in their hiring processes was not working for minority candidates. We need to question why. In my case, I can tell you that the degree of latitude granted to individual officers was a barrier.

Let me give you more examples of what I'm getting at. As noted earlier, I spent three years as an undercover operator entrenched in the world of drugs and organized crime. If you check my history with the service, you will not find a single training course specifically for drug investigations during the time I spent in the unit. Why? Well, it came down to the space — in this case, the latitude given to the unit commander to authorize who would or would not attend courses. So, while others in the unit and in outside units such as Intelligence were receiving drug-related courses, I was denied. The unit commander had the space within the system to place a barrier before me because there was nothing in place telling him he couldn't.

Why did this happen? I have a theory that has been validated over my many years working within the department. It has to do with building a strong portfolio for advancement within the organization. Throughout police services in Ontario, courses are seen as qualifications worth acknowledging and become credits towards advancement. Right or wrong, I saw the denial of courses, the choice of courses provided to others, and training events that I should have had but that weren't granted to me as a denigration of my creditable service. I would spend two years in the Training and Education Bureau teaching Race Relations and Employment Equity yet was denied every course that I put in for — the very students in my classes were being given the opportunities I'd been denied. I again refer you to my personal history record. You will not see a single course relating to race relations provided by or sanctioned by the service (space). When I was promoted to the rank of staff sergeant and was assigned to manage the Training and Education Bureau, there was an annual budget line approving the attendance of a specific training course for managers in this position, which four staff sergeants prior to me had attended. This course was denied to me by the inspector of the unit, who could not provide me with a reason other than "Because I said so." You see, the system had a hard enough time with someone like me operating on their level and certainly could not stomach me as their equal or boss. The space within the system allowed the superiority imbued within the system to operate. Now, for clarity, I'm not saying that every action of denial was racially motivated. Some had to do with nepotism, favouritism (hockey buddies), and one hand washing the other, but I can truly say the colour of my skin played a big part in some of the decision-making.

Being an anomaly in a system with space created a research-and-development scenario. The guardians of the system were somewhat uncomfortable with this stark degree of change. The introduction of colour, at that time, was uncharted territory and had them a bit unhinged. You see, we as a small number of minority officers were smart, educated, confident, articulate, and athletic. This was no ordinary foe. This internal invasion could only get worse. The tide was shifting where the talk of equal opportunity for all was truly manifesting into reality. The service was changing. Many of the white officers had confided in me that they'd had very little exposure to minorities other than arresting them. Through general conversations, I gleaned that they knew maybe one Black family and they'd grown up with few or no Black people in their neighbourhoods or high schools. Many of them grew up with the enjoyment of white privilege that they didn't even know they had.

The number of officers hired in the early and late '80s who played ice hockey shocked me. That seemed to be a common theme throughout the organization. Another was the suggestion that it helped you get hired if you were a member of a Masonic order. I could never confirm if this was true, but it was a common rumour. Add on the large contingent of nepotistic hires. So many officers were related to one another either directly or by a few degrees of separation. Then the buddy system of being able to hire your friends despite their not being the best candidates. A system had been established, but with the arrival of officers like me, it now became about "Who are these invaders? Who the hell let them in? Are they qualified or competent? Were they hired because of some affirmative action? Does that mean fewer white officers will be hired in the future because of the pressure to hire minorities? Was the testing lowered for them to be able to be hired?" Believe me, the directness, coyness, and subtleness of these and many more questions were intrinsic to how we were dealt with. The testing of the boundaries of what could be done to keep us in our place, so to speak, was daring, bold, and often reckless. The space in the system allowed the established order to practise a degree of implicit and explicit bias to advance the majority and hold back the few. There were genuine nervous rumblings of the dreaded replacement theory as white officers started to worry about being replaced by officers of colour.

The space also allowed the system to change the rules that advantaged them. An example would be the creation of a promotional system that favoured a larger number of white officers. Certain prerequisites were instituted that severely limited officers of colour because we had a lot of catching up to do in terms of numbers and time on the job. Since a larger number of white officers had been officers longer and had the opportunity to take courses, they were in an advantaged position.

The lesson here is that the space is no accident. The unfair application of the room inside systems has been, and will continue to be, detrimental to some and advantageous to others. I call this out to draw attention to some aspects of what on the surface seems level but on closer examination is truly uneven. Addressing the inequities within systems and implementing checks and balances will allow for positive revisions that move us closer to a more even, cohesive existence.

RACISM AS A CONSTRUCT

et me start with Johann Friedrich Blumenbach. He was a graduate of the Friedrich Schiller University of Jena and the Georg August University of Göttingen, Germany. As part of his medical degree, he wrote his thesis, *De Generis Humani Varietate Nativa* (On the Natural Variety of Mankind), which was first published in 1775. At the time, it was considered one of the most influential works in the development of the concept of human races. Blumenbach divided the human species into five races: Caucasian, or the white race; Mongolian, or the yellow race, including all East Asians and some Central Asians; Malayan, or the brown race, including Southeast Asians and Pacific Islanders; Ethiopian, or the Black race, including sub-Saharan Africans; American, or the red race, including Native Americans.

Blumenbach did not consider his work racist; in fact, it is said that he developed the thesis that all living races are varieties of a single species. Moreover, he concluded that Africans were not inferior to the rest of humankind "concerning healthy faculties of understanding, excellent natural talents, and mental capacities." But other scientists of his day used his work to advance the notion that Africans were an inferior race and that Caucasians were surely the dominant class (scientific racism).

Next up we have Gomes Eanes de Zurara, a Portuguese chronicler during the Age of Discovery (the fifteenth to seventeenth centuries). According to American author, professor, antiracist activist, and historian Dr. Ibram X. Kendi, Zurara was "the first race maker." In a book commissioned by the king of Portugal, Zurara lumped together all the peoples of Africa, referring to them as a distinct group that was inferior and beastly, despite pre-colonial Africa being composed of some of the most sophisticated cultures. The question is, why would he have written such a book? It had everything to do with the generation of wealth. Several years prior, Portuguese explorers had effectively pioneered the Atlantic slave trade. They were the first Europeans to sail the Atlantic directly to sub-Saharan Africa to capture slaves. Other countries quickly followed suit. Zurara stated the Africans captured and sold into the slave trade were heathens and needed religious and civil salvation. By dehumanizing and diminishing the life and existence of the darker foreign entity, it was easier to justify the slave trade and thus make more profit. This train of thought was wildly pervasive throughout Europe to the point of being fact. This mindset gives you a little insight into how and why systems were developed to ensure that the white race would reign supreme for all times.

I remember being taught in social studies class that humans were categorized into three distinct races. They were Caucasoid (Caucasian, from all or parts of Europe); Mongoloid (Indigenous peoples of East Asia, Southeast Asia, and the Arctic Region of North America); and Negroid (Indigenous peoples of Central and Southern Africa). How things have changed. According to the international Human Genome Project, a research effort to determine the DNA sequence of the entire human genome, completed in April 2003, the classification of race is anthropological nonsense. The project concluded that genetically we humans are 99.9 percent the same. The term *race* is a social construct that has seeped into our everyday lexicon, with diabolical results.

Learning this history should shift how we understand and relate to each other and process why things are the way they are. So, is race real in terms of its application socially and politically? If so, we have a sound understanding of how it was constructed. Therefore, we should have the fundamental concept of how to deconstruct it.

When we speak about racism, we need to see it as a system, not an event. We need to have a fundamental understanding of what that means. Racism is not only a prejudice, attitude, beliefs, and stereotyping directed at a group of people, but most often it includes the power to do something with that prejudice, leading to discrimination. Practised racism perpetuates the notion of superiority or dominance over individuals, or one group over another.

Let's see if we can make sense of that. If we were to speak to the ways white racism adversely affects Black people, we could come up with an extensive laundry list: state-sanctioned kidnapping resulting in four hundred years of enslavement, torture, rape, and ruthless abuse; segregation and bans on voting and interracial marriage; lack of health care, employment, education, housing, social services, policing, financial wealth, transportation, and government representation; gerrymandering and an unfair justice system. Broken down a bit more, these factors relate directly to personal growth, unequal pay, mental illness, depression, adverse family interactions, cultural degeneration, generational trauma, human rights violations, sports, films, literature, language, dehumanization, subprime mortgages, redline districts, mass incarceration, school-to-prison pipeline, disproportional special referrals and punishment, testing, tracking, school funding, historical omissions . . . you get the point.

Racism exists to limit access to opportunities, power, money, and resources along racial lines, supporting the supremacy of whiteness. Now, let's talk about the ways that Black racism affects white people adversely as a group. Since it is rare that Black people in general are at the seat of power in North America, it's difficult for me to come up with adverse effects. So, by that definition, Black racism towards white people does not exist. In other words, where Black people might certainly dislike white people or mock them in stereotypical ways, it doesn't result in the white race being disempowered. What many experts have concluded is that the root of Black racism is fear. Yes, fear of the Black man. The bigger and darker, the deeper the fear. That begs the question: why?

Historically, Black men have been perceived as a threat, ripe with criminality and hypersexuality, exuding primal aggression and predatory behaviour, which they have difficulty controlling and which needs to be tempered by those in power. Exhibit A: various systems such as the justice system, correctional system, and even the political system have been structured and built around this premise. Exhibit B: the police have functioned as agents of the state. They have been complicit in the degradation and outright abuse of Blacks, based on the systems by which they have been programmed.

While performing uniformed duties in the city of Markham, considered one of the most diverse areas of the region, I was part of a number of incidents that spoke to this reality. One evening we received a noise complaint having to do with a house party full of Black people. The police response was outrageous. I was one of the attending officers because it was in my patrol zone. There were over a dozen officers there. It was a reggae party with approximately twenty to thirty people attending. The officers were making a big deal out of what amounted to a noise complaint, which we would normally handle with two officers. There was no unruliness, no fighting, drunkenness, or incidents other than the music being a touch too loud for this residential neighbourhood. The officers circled outside but were hesitant to go in. You see, some of the folks had locs and spoke with heavy Jamaican accents, so the police deemed them dangerous. I grabbed one of the officers, and the two of us entered the house. I spoke to the homeowner and asked him to turn down the music. He was very apologetic and immediately complied. Even so, it took a long time for the officers to clear — way too long.

Another time, I took great offence to an officer calling Markham a ghetto. You see, in his view there was a fair number of Black residents, and that made him uncomfortable. He made this statement in front of a new recruit who was riding with me for the day. We had just finished dealing with a domestic matter and were in a parking lot, finishing off our notes, when a cruiser pulled alongside us. We engaged in small talk, then he turned his attention to the rookie. He said, "Welcome to the ghetto," and without missing a beat added that a lot of foreigners lived there. I was pissed — his comments were a direct indicator of how he really felt about the residents of this community, and he had no problem contaminating this young recruit with his vile shit. Many in the area were non-white and a good portion of them Black. To him, his whiteness denoted superiority. I lit into him with a barrage of aggressive questions to which I knew he could not offer suitable responses, starting with, "Why is this area different from where you live and why do you think that is?" He knew immediately he had stepped into shit and found a way to get the hell out of there in short order. By the way, there is not a single area in Markham that is anywhere near what one would consider a ghetto.

Even the conditioning received in North American schooling contains subtle and not-so-hidden underlying currents of white supremacy. If one were to examine the curriculum, both past and present, there is a design in place to downplay the atrocities committed and emphasize the momentous achievements that denote superiority. Where would you like to start in terms of examples? History? Okay, there was a time when it was said that the sun never set on the British Empire. They systematically conquered lands around the world and laid claim to its possessions. We were taught about exploratory prowess and discoveries of "new" lands. We were taught about the civilized ways to eat your meals and address your elders. We were conditioned to accept the Christian values premised on the King James version of the Bible, which, by the way, was engineered to suit their dominance. But the absolute carnage that accompanied those partially denoted history lessons was never mentioned, nor were the valuable contributions of hundreds of thousands of Black, brown, and Indigenous people who have significantly helped enhance mankind.

I was asked by a dear friend of mine how did I, as a Black officer, deal with the power vested in me when dealing with race? Having been the victim of racial bias all of my life, there was never an issue of unfair treatment of anyone by me along those lines. I went on to further explain that there certainly was a disproportionate amount of discretion used based on the type and seriousness of the offence and the culprit. I saw a person who passed a bad cheque one way, and a child molester another — they are certainly not going to receive the same treatment from me. Outwardly, the processing of the situation would likely be similar, but my attitude and demeanour would be quite different.

Where are we now in our current state of affairs as it relates to our known history? Four hundred years of existing under conqueror rules have left us bitter and irritable. Who can blame us? I would just as soon live my life without the hang-ups and baggage, but I can't; society won't let me. The reminders are everywhere that there is still an imbalance, with corrective measures slow to come about. As I look around and assess my contribution to the greater good, I am concerned that I have not made the impact that I, as a young man, had thought I would. Sometimes it feels like an exercise in futility. Then again, I'm still in the fight, so there must be some measure of success. I hope.

WHEN WAS AMERICA – OR CANADA – EVER GREAT FOR BLACK PEOPLE?

"Though the colored man is no longer subject to barter and sale, he is surrounded by an adverse settlement which fetters all his movements. In his downward course he meets with no resistance, but his course upward is resented and resisted at every step of his progress.

If he comes in ignorance, rags and wretchedness, he conforms to the popular belief of his character, and in that character, he is welcome; but if he shall come as a gentleman, a scholar and a statesman, he is hailed as a contradiction to the national faith concerning his race, and his coming is resented as impudence. In one case he may provoke contempt and derision, but in the other he is an affront to pride and provokes malice."
— Frederick Douglass, September 25, 1883

Have you heard of Wilmington, North Carolina? It was only recently that I came across a story about the Wilmington massacre of 1898. All my years of engaging in the struggle for human rights and emancipation and against anti-Black racism, I had never heard about this event before then. Interestingly enough, there are several iterations of how to classify this massacre. The white press in Wilmington at the time described what happened as a race riot caused by Black people. As more information came to light and the facts became hard to dispute, it turned out to be a mass riot carried out by white supremacists. In the end the true version was that it was a *coup d'état*, the violent overthrow of a duly elected government, by white supremacists.

In 1898, Wilmington was the largest city in the state, comprised of around twenty-five thousand people, with a majority Black population (approximately 55 percent). This thriving city provided opportunities for many Black freemen and women — formerly enslaved — who had elevated themselves to be considered part of the rising middle class. This middle class included skilled labourers such as plumbers, craftsmen, watchmakers, butchers, and tailors. In Wilmington, Black people were intricately involved in local politics, with three of the city's ten aldermen being Black. A Black man was part of a five-member constituent Board of Audit and Finance. Black people occupied positions as architects, financiers, and real estate agents. One gentleman became the appointed collector of custom at the Port of Wilmington. They took up positions ordinarily excluded to them, such as councilmen, magistrates, policemen, coroners, restaurant owners, and so on. The city even had one of the few Black-owned newspapers in the country, the *Daily Record*. From all accounts, Wilmington had more than two thousand Black professionals with some sixty-five Black doctors, lawyers, teachers, or professionals in other fields where they were not excluded from competing. As racial tensions in the state festered and intensified, Black people in this town were moving forward at a rapid rate, growing economically strong, politically astute, and socially engaged.

Alfred Moore Waddell, a former Confederate colonel and former congressman, vowed to end "Negro domination" in state legislative elections in the city of Wilmington. The idea was to topple the multiracial government. The raid was a completely orchestrated coup plotted by white politicians and businessmen designed to prevent Black citizens from exercising their constitutional rights. It was the culmination of a month-long white supremacist campaign designed to strip Black men of the vote and remove them from public office. White supremacists had gone so far as to persuade the white police chief to fire the ten Black police officers prior to the massacre. They also sounded the tried, tested, and guaranteed racist death rattle for Black men by declaring the safety of white women would be in jeopardy if nothing was done.

On November 9, 1898, Waddell assembled approximately eight hundred white citizens and produced the "white Declaration of Independence." It reads as follows: "We the undersigned citizens . . . do hereby declare that we will no longer be ruled and will never again be ruled by men of African origin." The next day, November 10, 1898, Waddell led a throng of people — some say as many as two thousand armed men — to the building occupied by the *Daily Record* and burned it to the ground. The massacre followed. Aided by the police along with white supremacist soldiers of the state militia, the mob hunted down and killed around sixty Black men.

As a result of the coup, Black men holding political office were killed and those who were not killed, along with white political allies, were forcibly removed from office and replaced by coup leaders.

Prior to the massacre, 126,000 Black men were registered to vote in North Carolina. Four years later only 6,100 were registered. It wasn't until the passage of the Voting Rights Act of 1965 that Black voters returned to voting in any significant numbers.

According to a July 2020 article by David Zucchino in *Time* magazine, after the coup, no Black citizen served in public office in Wilmington until 1972. No Black citizen from North Carolina was elected to Congress until 1992. No one was prosecuted or punished for the killings and violence. President William McKinley ignored pleas from Black leaders to send in federal marshals or U.S. troops to protect Black citizens.

In June 2020, three Wilmington police officers were caught on tape using racial slurs and making derogatory comments — Officers James Gilmore and Michael K. Piner and Corporal Jesse E. Moore II were fired as a result. The conversation, partly about the Black Lives Matter protests that were taking place around the country, had so inflamed Officer Piner that he believed a civil war was coming, adding that he was going to buy a new assault rifle. He felt martial law would be declared and said, "We are just gonna go out and start slaughtering them fucking niggers. I can't wait. God, I can't wait." Piner further said he felt that a civil war was necessary to "Wipe 'em off the fucking map!" The conversations these officers engaged in were so repugnant, yet, unfortunately, are far more common than you might think.

I'm going to pause here to fill you in on the impact of what I have just recounted. There is a movement stemming primarily out of the United States about not subjecting its white population to the notion of critical race theory (a divisive discourse borne out of an examination of how laws, societal acceptance, and politics are shaped by race and ethnicity). A certain sector of the population does not want to hear about the barbaric past of their ancestors — they believe it'll make white students feel bad — so instead they argue that history should be suppressed or subject to revisionist retelling. I have two points of contact with this history: First, I completely identify with my ancestors as to the sinister way they were treated, for I am of the same stock. Having had my genealogy researched through my DNA, I discovered that I am a direct descendent of enslaved Africans. At a different date and time, those events could have happened to me or any of my relatives. Secondly, I spent thirty-one years of my life associated with an institution that was, and still is, complicit in the abuse of my people. To know that some have taken that sacred oath of being gatekeepers of our life, liberty, and well-being and, based on racist hate, are willing to do us harm with no just cause plays heavily on my psyche. I am fortunate that I'm able to work through this contradiction, but it's still close to the surface.

By the way, Canada was not and is not immune to the scourge of racism in all its nasty forms (as I've already shown through the many examples of racism that I've encountered throughout my life here). I bring your attention to Africville, so aptly named by both residents and observers alike. Africville was a small community on the southern shore of Bedford Basin, Halifax. This area consisted mostly of formerly enslaved African Americans, Black Loyalists, and their descendants, who were determined to plot a course of self-respect and provide a family life worthy of living. There was also a contingent of Jamaican Maroons, who had rebelled against slavery in Jamaica and had been deported to Nova Scotia by the British. Africville was founded around the mid-eighteenth century and was prospering quite nicely, to the point that its inhabitants were able to buy land and construct a menial infrastructure as deemed necessary for a flourishing economy. The City of Halifax taxed the residents but refused to provide the services one would expect, such as running water, sewage, police protection, garbage collection, or even paved roads. Around 1854, the government expropriated the land and homes in Africville and constructed a railway extension right through the village. If that wasn't enough, the city began a ruthless campaign of locating undesirable services in and around the area. These consisted of what were called night soil disposal pits (human waste pits), a prison, an infectious diseases hospital, a garbage dump, a slaughterhouse, and a fertilizer plant. As these atrocities continued, it was only a matter of time before many white people in proximity to Africville pronounced it a slum. The Halifax city council in 1947 rezoned the area as industrial land and moved against the residents by appropriating homes and land. They bulldozed homes, and owners relocated to dilapidated housing in the city, thereby effectively rendering Africville non-existent.

∞

Examples of white supremacy at work in North America aren't just relegated to the eighteenth century. On January 6, 2021, members of the "Stop the Steal" movement invaded the Capitol Building in Washington, DC. This was nothing short of a coup wrapped up in an insurrection on top of a mass takeover of the seat of power in the United States of America. Let's just take a step back and have a topical look at what happened and why.

A five-year escalation of racial tensions and divides started the day Donald J. Trump rode down the escalator in the Trump Building in New York and announced his run for the presidency of the United States. He was not the cause, but he definitely poured fuel on the fire. He emerged onto the political scene with the stains of racism on his sleeves. Back in the '70s the U.S. Justice Department sued the Trump Management Corporation successfully for violating the Fair Housing Act. Evidence revealed that this organization was keeping Black people from renting their units. They lied to prospective tenants, claiming that units were not available, and outright refused to rent to them. In 1998, Donald Trump took out a full-page ad calling for the death penalty for four Black teenagers and one Latino teenager who had been falsely accused of raping a jogger in New York City. His action was akin to a public lynching. This case, referred to as the Central Park Five, was later re-adjudicated and the boys found completely innocent after spending seven to thirteen years in prison. In 2016, Trump repeated that he still believes that the boys were guilty regardless of their exoneration, including a confession from another man and DNA evidence proving his guilt.

One of his early platforms was to accelerate the racist and divisive conspiracy theory about the illegitimacy of Barack Obama as president, which has been referred to as "birtherism," by claiming that Barack was not born in the United States and therefore was not the legitimate president. Never in my lifetime did I think I would bear witness to the inauguration of the first Black president. For millions of people, it was a marvel of epic proportions. Yet, due to the colour of this man's skin and his unusual name, he was denigrated.

Trump rode on the slogan "Make America Great Again," which was a not-so-subtle revisionist call for the better days (Jim Crow) when white people were in a dominant position to affect the lives of racialized people as per their vision. As odd as that may seem, he received a lot of support for this nonsense from many citizens, media sources, and members of the existing Republican Party at the seat of power. As he gained momentum, Trump upped his rhetoric, slanting his comments on the side of bigotry, which he noticed was growing his base. He called Mexican immigrants criminals and rapists. He promoted the idea of building a great wall that will keep out migrants who were seeking to enter the U.S. as a means of escaping an assortment of life-mitigating circumstances. By the time he won the election, Trump was fully attached to this form of governing and had firmly locked in a certain percentage of hardened supporters, who formed an unwavering allegiance that followed him to the end of his term and beyond. What the world witnessed was the uncloaking of the American psyche, in that the underpinnings of racism, bigotry, and discrimination were alive and well. Trump enacted a ban on Muslims entering the country. He enacted the policy of separating families at the border with no vision of reuniting them after due process. The program to date has led to more than five hundred children unable to be reunited with their parents. This form of dehumanization resonated with some of the entitled citizenry. He stated that a judge should recuse himself from a case due to his Mexican heritage.

Trump appointed Steve Bannon, co-founder of Breitbart News, an alt-right website, as his chief strategist and senior counsellor. He installed Stephen Miller as a senior advisor for policy to the president. Miller's politics are described as far-right and anti-immigration. White supremacist groups came out from under the sheets and willingly exposed themselves with little fear of repercussion. They were endeared by the president's rhetoric and actions, feeling a kinship of sorts. Near the end of Trump's term in office, his administration was almost exclusively white, which in no way reflected the cultural diversity of America.

Trump systematically dismantled everything he could that had Barack's name attached to it, regardless if it was beneficial for the American people or not. The bigotry was palpable. He told his followers that mainstream media was the enemy of the state, driving many to alternative platforms that supported his view of what America should look like and how it should operate. Trump called countries that were primarily Black "shitholes" and stated a preference for immigrants from Norway (a primarily white country). The Trump administration delayed the replacement of the twenty-dollar bill that would depict Harriet Tubman (an abolitionist who was instrumental in leading enslaved peoples into freedom via the Underground Railroad) in place of Andrew Jackson (a populist slaveowner). The plans for this bill started under the Obama presidency and were slated to be rolled out by 2020. Trump's treasury secretary, Steven Mnuchin, declared that there were technical difficulties that would not make it possible to produce the bill until long after Trump left office. Sure.

White supremacists rallied in Charlottesville, Virginia, in a "Unite the Right" parade, marching down the street with tiki torches chanting that the Jews would not replace them. The president defended them, stating that there had been good people on both sides of the confrontation. David Duke, the former head of the Ku Klux Klan, applauded Trump's comments. Trump denied knowing who Duke was, despite photographic evidence to the contrary. He continually refused to explicitly condemn white supremacist groups who looked at his xenophobic, bigoted, racist rhetoric as an endorsement to continue, even escalate, their deplorable agenda. To me, this one act put my life and those of Black people in North America more sharply in the crosshairs of danger. There is little difference in core beliefs between hate groups in the U.S. as those in Canada. To them, Black or Jewish people need not take up residency, because we are not wanted.

The president directed federal agencies to end all programs for employees related to diversity and inclusion. He deemed them divisive. Trump made appeals to women in his base that he would keep undesirables (racial minorities and the poor) out of suburbia (there was no ambiguity as to whom he was referring to). He demonized Black Lives Matter, a movement that protested the abuse and killing of Black and brown citizens at the hands of police, and labelled them a terrorist group. His direction to them was, "When the looting starts, the shooting starts." Utilizing an overwhelming force, Trump ordered federal agents along with National Guardsmen to attack and clear Lafayette Square of peaceful Black Lives Matter protesters, who were there to draw attention to the killing of George Floyd. They were met with chemical agents and rubber bullets so Trump could cross the street for a photo op at a church holding a Bible . . . upside down!

The alt-right were delighted, licking their lips and unable to contain their joy. Finally, they were at the seat of power — not just any power but the highest occupancy in the country. During the first 2020 presidential debate, Trump refused to denounce the white supremacist group Proud Boys, instead issuing directions to the group to "stand back and stand by."

And here is the dupe: he touted himself as the law-and-order president. This nonsense also took hold to the point that the Fraternal Order of Police, the largest police union in the United States, endorsed him. So, just to be clear: During the run-up to the next election, Trump was endorsed by white supremacists (who have been deemed by the Federal Bureau of Investigation as the most lethal and persistent terrorist group in America and have killed more Americans since 9/11 than jihadi terrorists). Groups that lined up in support included the Boogaloo Movement, Proud Boys, neo-Nazis, the Ku Klux Klan, the Nationalist Social Club (NSC-131), the Oath Keepers, Super Happy Fun America (SHFA), the Three Percenters, and some members of the *police*.

The visuals of the storming of the Capitol Building were surreal. It was truly disturbing on every level. The Capitol Police were engaged in a full-on battle with these domestic terrorists and easily overrun. Their lack of preparedness was obvious and somewhat suspect. The terrorists, almost exclusively white men and women, chanted that they wanted their country back. Leading the charge were white supremacists, many identifiable by articles of clothing that they had no issue flaunting. What cannot be ignored and certainly took front and center was that a hangman's scaffold with a noose was erected outside the grounds — meant for Mike Pence, who they believed should have been helping Trump overturn the election results — and the flying of the Confederate battle flag in the rotunda of the Capitol Building. It was like Wilmington, North Carolina, on a grander scale.

Some active and retired police officers were complicit in the insurrection. Should we really be surprised? After all, the policing group is, in a sense, a microcosm of the world around us. There are good, bad, saints, and racists among us, which is truly reflected in the policing environment.

According to Anti-Defamation League CEO and director Jonathan Greenblatt, his group came across a data leak that revealed the membership list of the right-wing group the Oath Keepers that had participated in the storming of the Capitol. Using open-source techniques, public records, and social media, his group reviewed every single name from that data leak. What they found was shocking — among the membership were hundreds of active and retired law enforcement members, ten chiefs of police, eleven sheriffs, a few dozen active members of the U.S. military, and eighty people who were running for public office.

Speaking for most officers, Canadian or American, Black and white, association with these militia groups is simply deplorable. We officers serve the greater good, not the fringe elements who anoint themselves keepers of their version of democracy. We serve all, not some. Don't tarnish the uniform in this or any other manner. Many of us have invested sweat equity both individually and as a collective to right the historical and current wrongs, hoping that we can repair some of the systemic and isolated damage associated with law enforcement. I am deeply troubled when I hear of brothers and sisters in blue eroding public trust. It's so hard to repair. As I consumed and digested as much information that I could glean from media sources, it became abundantly clear that the very same people who stormed the Capitol were the ones trying to drown out Black Lives Matter protests by posting "Blue Lives Matter" all over their Facebook pages. Yet they fought with police officers who were valiantly fighting for their lives defending the democracy that is America. Also, 150 sisters and brothers in blue were injured on that day. Brian Sicknick of the Capitol Police died of injuries he sustained that day. In my mind, it is not possible to reconcile this attack with any idea of making America great again. In fact, it served to reveal the truth of what's under the surface that, once agitated, is almost impossible to tame.

White rioters marched on the Capitol and subsequently stormed and occupied the building wanting their country back, according to them. Back from what? I believe that what they saw and felt was the erosion of their whiteness and privileges. The invasion of Black and brown people in what they referred to as "their country" was an issue to them. How the hell was it possible for a Black man to have become the president of their country, they mused. The insurrection included a sinister component that was orchestrated and planned, creating an opportunity to seize control with the intent of keeping their supreme leader, Donald J. Trump, in office — a leader who thinks like them, who is not afraid to expose his bigotry, who had the power to restore the good times when white men were in charge, who had the ability to influence lawmakers and government institutions in their favour. Yes, we must keep him in power — that was their intent. And some police officers were in that crowd.

∞

There is an old saying utilized by some in this country, and it goes like this: "If Americans sneeze, Canadians catch a cold." Everything that happens in the United States affects Canada in some way, shape, or form. Many Canadians, especially Black Canadians, are truly frightened by American politics. We understand the dire consequences of being on the receiving end of hate. The zealous rhetoric of Christian Nationalists, the professed superiority of the alt-right, the white supremacist militia groups, and the amplification of these ideas and elements by Fox News media and other media platforms scare the shit out of us. We have seen the rapid alignment of these ideologies festering in our politics with the subtleties that only Canadians can muster.

In Canada, in early 2022, a movement that came to be known as the Freedom Convoy began to percolate. The original intent was for Canadian truckers to take their concerns to the country's capital and protest what they saw as restrictive COVID-19 vaccine mandates, arguing that those mandates inhibited their cross-border business. Their chosen form of protest was to form a convoy of trucks from different points in the country, ultimately converging on the capital city of Ottawa.

On January 29, 2022, the truck convoy situated itself in the city along with thousands of pedestrian protesters, who felt that this was the right opportunity to voice their concerns regarding Canadian vaccine mandates. With the convergence of the hundreds of truckers and the thousands of protesters, the city was effectively shut down. They claimed that they would occupy the city until the COVID-19 restrictions were repealed. The blockade was now in full swing. The initial intent of the movement morphed or was subverted by many who now saw the protest as a Canadian Unity rally with the goal of removing the current prime minister, Justin Trudeau, from office and dissolving the government. The police response was a massive concentration of officers from around the province of Ontario, including a large contingent of Royal Canadian Mounted Police (RCMP). During the three weeks of the occupation, police clashed with protesters using pepper spray and stun guns, ultimately arresting 191 protesters.

And there it was, amid all of this turmoil, the Confederate battle flag. White supremacy had reared its ugly head at a freedom protest in our nation's capital. As described by Peter Sloly, Ottawa's police chief at the time, there was a significant element of American involvement in the organization and funding of the convoys. And he was absolutely right. American right-wing personalities and commentators had lent their support and voice to the occupation. Canadian government officials elevated concerns that some protesters had connections to far-right extremist groups, including those advocating for violence. Near a blockade in Coutts, Alberta, weapons were seized and four men charged with conspiracy to commit murder of RCMP officers.

Some of the donors participating in the protest's GoFundMe campaign were from the United States, and many used false names or remained anonymous. A website set up to elicit donations for the cause was compromised, and information on its donors was released to journalists. It revealed that of the $92,845 in donations, 55.7 percent came from the United States. Of the Canadian donors, some were members of the Ontario Provincial Police, causing that organization to initiate an internal investigation.

∞

Canadian police officers engaging in white supremacy is, sadly, nothing new. In 1995, the RCMP launched a whole-scale investigation into Canadian police officers who, on an annual basis, attended a notorious racist police picnic in southern Tennessee. Known as the Good Ol' Boys Roundup, it attracted whites-only police officers from all over North America. Agents of the Bureau of Alcohol, Tobacco, and Firearms (ATF) operated the picnic from 1980 until 1996. It was established that the founder of the event was ATF Agent Raymond Eugene Rightmyer, who from all accounts was deemed to have racist tendencies.

Attendance for officers outside the ATF was by invitation only. The cost for attending was between seventy and ninety dollars per person. It was truly an outback affair, with tents, trailers, and motorhomes and, of course, beer trucks. By the time the picnic was investigated, the number of attendees had grown to around 350. How bad could this so-called benign gathering be? Well, let's see. On entering the event location, one was met with the sign "Nigger Checkpoint Area." Vehicles were then scrutinized for Black people, a process affectionately called "Checking cars for niggers." At one point, a sign read "Any niggers in that car? 17c/lb (seventeen cents a pound)."

After an initial greeting and a few beers, if one were so inclined, one could venture over to the vendors section and pick up an array of souvenirs, such as a nigger-hunting licence, or perhaps T-shirts depicting Martin Luther King Jr.'s face in sniper crosshairs. Not to your liking? How about a shirt with Black men sprawled across police cruisers with the phrase "Boyz on the Hood." Or can I interest you in this O.J. Simpson head-in-a-noose depiction? Also available were T-shirts with a drawing of the head of the character Buckwheat from the old television show *Little Rascals* as if he were stuffed in the small pocket of the shirt, and the words "Good Ole Boys '92" written on it.

Now, what would a picnic be without some live entertainment? They offered skits with white men in blackface being sexually assaulted by an officer in a white-robed Ku Klux Klan outfit. According to the executive summary of the Department of Justice Office of the Inspector General's 1996 *Good O' Boy Roundup Report*, in 1990 officers from Florence and Boone County, Kentucky, and a civilian from Ohio performed a skit as part of the Redneck of the Year contest in which a dog was traded for a man in blackface who then pretended to perform oral sex on a person in mock Ku Klux Klan garments. Entertaining? Here's another one: A Fort Lauderdale police officer competing in the Redneck of the Year contest performed a skit where he claimed to have found a watermelon, which had fallen off the back of a passing truck, struck it until it broke open, and then pulled out a doll he had painted black. He described the doll as a seed and told the audience that one must "kill the seed when it is young" and proceeded to beat the doll. As part of the ongoing entertainment, music by outlaw country singer David Allen Coe was played at various campsites, including a song titled "My Wife Ran Off with a Nigger." If you were so inclined, you could participate in the official racially offensive joke-telling competition.

I had become aware of the annual Tennessee Law Enforcement Picnic a year or two after joining the York Regional Police. There was talk among some officers about the Roundup, making plans to attend or recruiting others to come along. It was never spoken about as a racist event, just a gathering of cops from all over North America getting together for some drinking and a whole lot of fun. I was never invited and had no interest in it, considering it was called the "Good Ol' Boys Roundup" and was held in Tennessee. To me that denoted a Southern drunk fest that might be uncomfortable for me. Deep down, I knew there wouldn't be many officers attending who looked like me. Some officers spoke about this being an annual event that they had attended over the years.

And then . . . two members of an Alabama militia group, the Gadsden Minutemen, who wanted to discredit the ATF, exposed the goings-on at the picnic. They had attended and surreptitiously videoed the event, and then went to the media with what they had obtained. Included in that video was a Canadian flag draped over a camper. The *Washington Times* picked up the story and ran an article on July 11, 1995. Following the article, several Black ATF agents made complaints that the picnic was a "whites-only event" and was racist.

The deputy attorney general launched an immediate investigation. The Department of Justice Office of the Inspector General and members of the Senate Judiciary Committee emphasized that there must be a full investigation due to the numerous law enforcement agencies involved. Then senator Joseph Biden said, "If it turns out to be as bad as it looks, at a minimum they should be shunned. They should be disgraced out of their badge." Because of the Canadian content, the Royal Canadian Mounted Police were notified and commenced their investigation. When the story broke in Canada, I remember reading an article in the *Toronto Star*: the headline was "Metro officer probed over racist picnic." Written by Philip Mascoll, the first paragraph reads as follows: "A Metro police officer is being investigated by his Force for allegedly attending a notorious racist police picnic three years ago in the southern United States." The story continued: "The *Star* has learned Constable Wylie Sheridan of 51 Division Major Crimes Squad is the officer being probed." A number of articles from various news outlets provided shocking details of what had occurred. I had no idea that such activities were occurring at those picnics until I read it in the media.

In 1989, Wylie was a member of the York Regional Police Morality Bureau, and we worked directly with each other. At one point, we were partnered up to do various tasks. Wylie was a seasoned officer who had left the Toronto Police Service and joined York Regional Police. Prior to the article's release, Wylie had left the YRP organization and returned to the Toronto Police Service. I must tell you, I really like Wylie. He was an extremely talented police officer with a super-engaging personality. He was a pleasure to be around. In the short time we spent together, my learning grew exponentially. During our off hours, as a group the unit would let off steam at several bars around town, with Wylie as the alpha in the pack. To be completely honest, I have nothing negative to say about Wylie. I thought he liked me, since he'd basically taken me under his wing, providing mentorship, direction, and guidance without being compelled to do it. He never spouted any racist shit that I was aware of. The fact that he was named in that article shocked me.

I was called into our Professional Standards Bureau to be interviewed and to provide a statement relating to what I knew regarding this officer and his behaviour towards me. Prior to giving the statement, I was mildly coached by the investigating officer as to how to word the statement and to not make a big deal out of the incident. The truth was I had heard, prior to being interviewed, that the investigator had also, at one time or another, attended the picnic. I gave an honest account. I have no idea whatever became of my testimony.

The truth is there were a number of officers from various police services in Canada that attended the Roundup more than once. If you knew what went on at this picnic and attended, then you are a racist. If you knew what went on at that picnic and you did not denounce it, you are a racist. If you attended more than one time and encouraged others to attend, you are deplorable. There is no getting around that fact. Law enforcement agencies of all stripes were represented at those picnics over the years. You had members of the Treasury Department, Customs Service, members of the FBI, Department of Justice (DOJ), Secret Service, ATF, state police, RCMP, provincial police, municipal police, and so on. I have yet to come across one disciplinary matter as a result. The organizers quickly dissolved the event, and the stories eventually fell into the annals of history. According to then ATF director John Magaw, the event had no overtly racist overtones until 1985. Although, he conceded eight days later that Black people would never have felt welcome at any point. And get this. The Office of the Inspector General (OIG) acknowledged occurrences of racially hostile conduct but found it not to be pervasive or sanctioned. The OIG concluded in their investigative report: "Other than one inappropriate comment by one FBI agent, we found no evidence that any DOJ employee engaged in racist or other misconduct while at the Roundup. Although we found that in certain years egregious acts of racism occurred, in most cases we concluded that the DOJ employees in attendance those years were either unaware of such conduct or had learned that the organizers had taken action to terminate it."

Now to the bigger picture: if you are a racist with the powers vested in you by the county, state, provincial, or federal government, how is it possible for you to do your job objectively, fairly, and with compassion? I say it's not possible. If your core is racist, then you will act that out in some form or manner, whether implicitly or explicitly. Who then pays the price? It always comes down to the diverse community members who are stereotyped, labelled, and discriminated against. Within my service, I knew a number of officers who attended the Roundup more than once. Some of these officers were on their way up the chain of command and years later were the officials managing the organization. Some at the time had already reached the supervisor and management levels. As a Black man who happens to be a police officer in a white-dominated organization, I knew the truth about some of the officers I worked with directly and indirectly, some to whom I reported. How do I now manage my day to day, week to week, month to month, year to year interactions with them, having learnt these truths?

For me and many like me, the fact that a former president of the United States of America — deemed to be the most powerful country in the world, the bastion of democracy, the beacon of light that guides the world to a place of safety and equality — has given tacit approval for far-right, alt-right, white supremacist groups to expose themselves and spew their nasty shit is terrifying. And seventy-four million Americans voted for four more years under his rule . . . four more years! I know some Canadian police officers who approve of him too. All of that frightens me. Most Black folks I know are afraid to fall victim to hate. What is it about white privilege that is so hard to understand? Perhaps it's the fragility of it that has the ability to exploit the disconnect, putting a strain on dealing with what it really is. We are so weary and tired of the everyday struggle just to be. When will this nightmare end? Will it? On Tuesday, November 15, 2022, former president Donald J. Trump announced that he would be seeking a second term as president in the upcoming 2024 elections. Soon after that, he was having dinner at his Mar-a-Lago estate with Kanye West, a devout Holocaust denier and supporter of Hitler, along with Nick Fuentes, a well-known avowed racist, white nationalist, and another Holocaust denier.

There is a resurgence of white supremacy and alt-right groups throughout the globe, and Canadian police services are not immune to attracting and hiring some of these individuals. I don't believe that any police organization here would court or want employees with these tendencies. They would be trouble waiting to happen, but they do occasionally slip through the door.

Then all they need to do is to seek out like-minded officers to wreak havoc on the civilian population, resulting in severe consequences to the service. Just a few of these law enforcement officials can and have caused irreparable damage to the criminal justice system. I've seen it. I've been a victim of it. I continue to fight it every day.

∞

In conclusion to this chapter, I have provided three quotes that I believe speak volumes as to where America is in terms of the current state of affairs.

First, Ron Johnson, a Wisconsin Republican senator who witnessed the storming of the Capitol first-hand, still made these following comments shortly after: "Even though those thousands of people that were marching to the Capitol were trying to pressure people like me to vote the way they wanted me to vote, I knew those were people that love this country, that truly respect law enforcement, would never do anything to break the law. And so, I wasn't concerned. Now, had the tables been turned — Joe, this could get me in trouble — had the tables been turned, and President Trump won the election and those were tens of thousands of Black Lives Matter and Antifa protesters, I might have been a little concerned."

Secondly, a fifty-year-old Texas real estate agent who participated in the assault on the U.S. Capitol on January 6 named Jennifer "Jenna" Leigh Ryan tweeted: "Definitely not going to jail. Sorry I have blonde hair, white skin, a great job, a great future and I'm not going to jail. Sorry to rain on your hater parade. I did nothing wrong."

Thirdly, in the words of Franklin Leonard, an African American film executive: "When you're accustomed to privilege, equality feels like oppression."

VICTIM KINSHIP

I was absolutely mesmerized by what I was looking at. It was the late '70s or early '80s, and I had made my way to an area of Toronto that had a stretch of Jamaican food restaurants. I came out of one of the shops after buying a patty and there on the same side of the street, a few feet away from me, was a uniformed police officer on a majestic, chrome-laden Harley-Davidson motorcycle. He looked surreal in his black patent leather calf-high boots and blue shirt complete with leather cross-strap holster and belt assembly, sitting on top of this imposing machine. But the reason I was frozen in place when I saw him was that he was Black. Until that time, I had never seen a Black police officer in Canada in person . . . *never*! And this dude was on a motorcycle! I stared and stared and stared some more. He pulled away moments later, but he was forever seared into my mind.

On September 23, 1981, at approximately 8 p.m., Constable Percy Cummins and Constable Michael Jones of the Toronto Police Service responded to a disturbance call where they ran into twenty-one-year-old Desmond Everton Peart. During the ensuing struggle, Percy's revolver fell out of his holster and Peart seized it. Peart shot Percy in the neck and Jones in the hand. Eventually, he was shot and paralyzed by another responding officer. Two hours later, Percy had succumbed to his injuries.

This murder of an on-duty officer headlined news media. Percy's picture was everywhere. My heart fluttered when I saw it. I immediately made the connection with the Black officer outside the Jamaican restaurant. In my mind, Officer Cummins looked like my father. He looked like an older version of me. Moreover, he was representing us in the Black community. This to me added a deeper dimension to the death of a police officer because I had mentally formed a kinship with him in those few moments that we'd been on the same street.

Years later, while working on this book, I made some inquiries and came to the realization that Percy was *not* the same officer that I had seen on the street. It turned out that during that period, as best as I could determine, there were four Black Toronto police officers who were riding motorcycles. They were Keith Forde, Chester Harding, Evon Reynolds, and Kenny Trotman. My understanding was that Percy had never been assigned a motorcycle. At the time of his death, Percy had served eleven years as a Toronto police officer after leaving a seven-and-a-half-year career with the Royal Barbados Police. He arrived in Toronto from Barbados in 1970. He joined the Toronto Metropolitan Police Service in June of that same year. By all accounts, he was a good professional officer with strong positive ties to the community. He left behind his wife, eight-year-old daughter, and five-year-old son.

And he looked like me.

∞

"You know, if I had a son, he'd look like Trayvon."
— President Barack Obama

Trayvon Benjamin Martin was seventeen years of age at the time of his demise. He'd become the victim of a neighbourhood watch volunteer of the Retreat at Twin Lakes, located in Sanford, Florida. George Zimmerman observed Trayvon walking through the neighborhood and took it upon himself to challenge Trayvon as to why he was in the area. A confrontation ensued, resulting in young Trayvon being shot and killed by Zimmerman. Trayvon was Black. Zimmerman was a twenty-eight-year-old Hispanic American. As this story unfolded, it was revealed that Trayvon was visiting his father at his father's fiancée's townhouse. Trayvon had left the house to purchase a pack of Skittles and a bottle of iced tea at the local convenience store. He had every right to be where he was. The date was February 26, 2012.

My daughter Brianna was in tears. You see, she had instantly made that victim kinship with this young man. She saw him the same way she would view one of her classmates, her boyfriends, her cousins, or a brother. She saw it as unjust, a profiling that had resulted in the murder of a young man. She intuitively knew that what had happened to Trayvon could happen to any one of her friends or family who fit the profile — young, male, Black, wearing a hoodie. We had numerous conversations as to why this type of hunting and killing of young Black men keeps happening despite the fact that we are now in the twenty-first century. Despite the work of so many to bring hope to the future of those who have suffered through the repugnant course of history, it still does not feel like it has made enough of a difference to change the state of our condition that makes us victims. I felt her pain as she felt mine.

My daughter and I revisited that discussion, including the pain, on December 28, 2016, when we heard about the brutal assault on a Black youth in the town of Whitby, east of Toronto. As a result of the attack, nineteen-year-old Dafonte Miller would be left with a broken nose, a broken jaw, a broken right wrist, and a blinded left eye at the hands of an off-duty Toronto police officer and his brother.

In the early morning, Dafonte and a friend were alleged to have broken into a truck belonging to the assaulter's father, John Theriault, that was parked in his driveway. Both sons gave chase, eventually catching up with Dafonte. At this point, Dafonte was severely beaten by Officer Michael Theriault with a metal pipe. Having jurisdiction, Durham Regional Police responded to the disturbance. When they arrived, Michael identified himself as a Toronto police officer. A responding officer handed Michael their handcuffs to place them on Dafonte and allowed for Michael to search him. The Theriaults are white; Dafonte is Black. Dafonte was arrested and charged with a variety of offences.

In Ontario, it is mandatory that any incident involving police where injuries are more than trivial needs to be reported immediately to the Special Investigations Unit (SIU), an independent body that investigates such incidents. In this case, two police agencies were involved and neither contacted the SIU. In fact, it was Dafonte's lawyer, Julian Falconer, who notified the SIU, resulting in an investigation that commenced some four months after the incident. Officer Michael Theriault and his brother Christian were subsequently charged. Charges against Dafonte were dropped. Michael was eventually convicted of assault and sentenced to nine months' incarceration, while Christian was acquitted. The assault on Dafonte was particularly brutal, causing aggravated injuries and a lifelong disability.

There is a uniqueness about meeting a brother or sister on the street. First is the recognition that we share a similar skin tone. Second, an understanding that we are in the minority in this city, this province, this country, this continent. Automatically there is a kinship, to the point where we acknowledge each other by way of a nod, smile, wave, or a vocal response. Let me try to explain it from my perspective.

Our skin has been demonized over hundreds of years to the point where it often becomes a death sentence for some. There are hundreds of thousands of recorded histories where there was no fault on behalf of the Black victim but conclusive, irrefutable evidence in support of the white perpetrator. Let's remember that the transatlantic slave trade was the largest migration of people the world has ever seen. They were Africans who'd been kidnapped, held in bondage, transported across the ocean, and sold to white men and women to be held as property for their prosperity and pleasure. It can be said that millions of us are descendants of this vile degradation of the human condition. Our forefathers are us. We are them. From birth to death, there is no escaping our heritage, nor our history. For one is intrinsically intertwined with the other. No denial or attempted claim of transformation can ever erase the true inner core of who we really are. Many have tried to do that, in order to cope or to foment an existence of acceptance allowing them to live a menial life within their reality. This is a futile proposition, as those around you will never let you forget who and what you are. Their actions, demonstrated by the enactment of laws and constructed systems that hold you in contempt, tell you all you need to know about who you are deemed to be.

Governmental institutions such as the police and the criminal justice systems were put in place to enforce the laws of the land. The police in North America have been tied to and are indeed complicit in the brutalizing violations of Black and brown citizens.

I would like to take a moment to delve into the George Floyd killing at the hands of police on May 25, 2020. Floyd had been arrested for allegedly using a counterfeit bill at a convenience store in Minneapolis, Minnesota. Floyd was unarmed and handcuffed. He was subsequently placed facedown on the ground with three police officers holding him there. One of the officers was Derek Chauvin, who had his knee on Floyd's neck, restricting his breathing. For several minutes, Floyd begged and pleaded with Chauvin that he couldn't breathe, eventually crying out for help from his mother. Members of the public that were on scene beseeched and implored the officers involved to get off Floyd, explaining that they were killing him. The three officers continued to hold down Floyd; Officer Chauvin's knee continued restricting the breathing of Floyd for nine minutes and twenty-nine seconds.

George Floyd lost his life that day at the hands of the police. With the release of video evidence, the world watched this Black man murdered in plain view, in the middle of the day, by the people who'd sworn to protect him. There was no more questioning the actions of the victim. There was no more deflecting to the criminal background and questionable nature of another Black male. There was no more "He should have complied or listened to the officers' command." Floyd had been murdered, and the world watched it happen on video. Handcuffed on his stomach, on the ground, with three officers holding him down, in daylight, in front of both police and civilian witnesses, on video.

What conditions must be in play in the Minneapolis Police Department and in the United States that three officers were able to kill an unarmed Black man, who was in physical restraints and under control, in broad daylight, on a public roadway, in public with witnesses, *knowing* that they were being recorded? How were they emboldened enough to even contemplate that they would be able to get away with this behaviour? I'll tell you why. Let's have a quick look at Officer Derek Chauvin's file. At the time of George Floyd's death, Officer Chauvin had nineteen years of service (I use the word "service" loosely) and had gathered up a dubious record of twenty-two complaints or internal investigations, including eighteen complaints alone of excessive force — only one resulting in discipline. Officer Chauvin had been involved in three shootings, one of them fatal.

In 2017, Chauvin was investigated for using excessive force against a fourteen-year-old teenager during a domestic assault call. The teen's response to Chauvin's command was not acted upon quickly enough for the officer, resulting in the youth being struck on the head multiple times with a flashlight then put in a similar type of neck restraint applied to George Floyd — this time for seventeen minutes — as the boy's mother pleaded with Chauvin to stop because the boy couldn't breathe. Three other Black people have come forward with similar accounts at the hands of Chauvin. Here is where we must question a system that would allow an officer, with this type of record, to remain on the police service. It's clearly not just the behaviour of one or two officers, but also the construct of a system that would allow officers like Derek Chauvin to operate in this mode with almost complete impunity.

Perhaps this truth can shed some light on the current state of affairs as it relates to the ugliness of police interacting with Black people. In the eighteenth century, primarily in the American South, the business of slavery was vital to the economy. White masters considered enslaved people as property worth keeping. The history of policing can be traced back to the formation of slave patrols contracted by owners to not only retrieve runaways and return them but also to viciously put down any rebellion or insurgencies that cropped up. These slave patrols eventually evolved into policing units, where they were given greater scope of responsibilities as it related to the shaping and maintaining of the social order at the end of the Civil War. The Reconstruction Era contributed to the growth of the number of formerly enslaved people forming African American communities attempting to live peacefully among their oppressors. This was not to be, as the laws of the day restricted and regulated equal rights and general freedoms for the Black population. The police were empowered to control and deny access, which they did with increased levels of violence, which we have come to know as police brutality.

The list of fatal and brutal police interactions against members of racialized groups continues. With these cases and others, with the dismal history of slavery, bigotry, hatred, discrimination, dehumanization, dismantling of families, lynchings, beatings, rapes, and red-zoning of Black people at the hands of white people in North America, how is it possible for us to ever trust the systems that were designed to keep us subjugated and as a lesser people? History has concluded that Black people have suffered exceedingly brutal and lethal consequences when in contact with the police — whether confrontational or not, innocent or not, witness or suspect, compliant or resisting, minding their own business or involved — it didn't seem to matter. I haven't even touched the Civil Rights Movement of the 1950s, '60s, and '70s, when the police were complicit in enforcing the unjust and outright racist laws that prohibited interracial marriage, or Black people from eating in certain restaurants, using certain water fountains, or riding in the front sections of public buses. Public schools were segregated, housing was restricted, business loans were not available to Black people, and employment at any level above domestic help, porter, server, butler, and labourer were not readily available. These realities are recent history. In fact, my mother and father, when they were alive, were subjected to these subhuman existences.

These atrocities past and present are consistently happening. Each time, there is an immediate connection with all people who share that colour of skin, as we share similar characteristics and feelings. Trayvon Martin,

Dafonte Miller, and George Floyd all represent the subjugation of people of African descent. That is our history. It is our story. It is not possible to separate us from our pigmentation. Racism is not only global and systemic; it also envelops hundreds of years, with the common denominator being the colour of our skin. This is how we are physically presented to the world. Our skin colour is a staple ingredient that forever binds us in the collective battle for equal rights and justice. It is the evidence that we know has proven, case after case, to have relegated us to victim status. I am not alone in saying that each time these events occur, I feel a kinship with the victims, knowing that based on my appearance and the appearance of many others around me, we are not immune to suffering the same fate.

LAW AND ORDER

There was a time not so long ago when men of all stripes and colour wore the uniform of the United States Army and were shipped overseas to fight for freedom and country, during the conflict that was crowned World War II. One such U.S. citizen was Isaac Woodard, who happened to be a Black man. Isaac would spend three and a half years in that uniform. Who was Isaac Woodard? Well, he was born in South Carolina but raised in Goldsboro, North Carolina. As were the times, he attended segregated schools for Black Americans with little in the way of adequate funding. At age twenty-three, feeling the need to serve, Isaac enlisted in the army out of Fort Jackson in Columbia, South Carolina. While overseas, Isaac Woodard would go on to earn a battle star, an Asiatic–Pacific Campaign Medal, a Good Conduct Medal, a Service Medal, a World War II Victory Medal, and a promotion to the rank of sergeant. On February 12, 1946, at 8:30 p.m., Sergeant Woodard received an honorable discharge from the army. He was twenty-six years old. An hour or so later, he boarded a Greyhound bus with the intention of going home to Winnsboro, South Carolina, to reunite with his wife and head up to New York to visit his mother and father.

Still in his uniform, he was among other returning soldiers, both Black and white. The bus made a stop at a small drugstore about an hour outside of Atlanta, near Augusta. Sergeant Woodard asked the bus driver if there would be enough time for him to use the bathroom. This resulted in a verbal argument with the driver, who finally conceded and allowed Woodard to relieve himself and return to the bus. The next stop was about half an hour later, in the town of Batesburg, South Carolina, where the bus driver got off, then returned with the local police. He then told Sergeant Woodard to "come outside for a minute." Upon exiting the bus, Sergeant Woodard heard the driver accuse him of drinking on the bus along with causing a disturbance. Without any investigative process, the police took Sergeant Woodard to a nearby alleyway and beat him mercilessly. One of those men inflicting this extreme cruelty was Chief Lynwood Shull. The savagery of the beating — the intentional blows to his face by police officers wielding their own style of justice, using department-issued nightsticks — was so severe that Woodard would be blinded in both eyes. They arrested Woodard for disorderly conduct and lodged him in the town jail. Sergeant Woodard spent two months in hospital and would never see the world around him, or anyone in it, again.

The police chief was eventually charged with the assault against Sergeant Woodard and went to trial on November 5, 1946, before Judge Julius Waties Waring. The trial concluded on that very day, with Shull acquitted by an all-white jury. In the words of Sergeant Woodard, "I spent three and a half years in the service of my country and thought that I would be treated like a man when I returned to civilian life, but I was mistaken. If the loss of my sight will make people in America get together to prevent what happened to me from ever happening again to any other person, I would be glad."

A quick note about Judge Waring. From all accounts he was a good man, even exceptional. In the case of Woodard, he would later write that this case had been a mess, that the prosecution had basically failed to do anything other than interview the bus driver, and that the jury had had absolutely nothing to go on. Judge Waring became an ally to the cause of equality and a champion of civil rights. He concluded that segregation was not just wrong but unlawful. For this and subsequent rulings, he incurred the wrath of his compatriots and his community.

By 1914, Hogan's Alley, as it was unofficially known, formed the nucleus of Vancouver's Black community. The first Black immigrants arrived from California to the Vancouver area in 1858 and eventually settled in the city of Strathcona. They were joined by Black settlers from Alberta whose origin can be traced back to Oklahoma. Many who came to Strathcona were employed as porters by the Great Northern Railway. By all accounts, Hogan's Alley was a thriving working-class neighbourhood at the east end of Strathcona that was alive with music, restaurants, nightclubs, and bootlegging joints, and was an all-around exciting place to be. But as many stories throughout history reveal, it had a sinister side in terms of extrajudicial abuse that speaks to an undeniable history where Black people are concerned.

On August 8, 1952, the *Pacific Tribune* published an article with the headline "Negro Held in Hospital; Beaten by City Cops." The subjects of the story were victim Clarence Clemons and perpetrators Constable Dan Brown and partner Constable Robert Wintrip. First let me introduce you to Clarence. Born in Alberta on January 27, 1900, Clarence ultimately ended up in British Columbia in 1937. Like many other Black people, he made his home in Strathcona. It wasn't long before he found employment on the docks as a longshoreman with Empire Stevedoring Company.

In the early hours of July 19, 1952, Clarence attended the New Station Café located on Main Street with the intention of having a few drinks while waiting for his common-law wife, Delores Dingman. New Station was a popular establishment known for its clientele, who would eat, drink, and be merry, as it were, at all hours of the night. Here is where a drastic divergence of the truth emerges. According to police, Clarence was intoxicated and loitering on the street. When approached by officers, he was resistive, resulting in his physical arrest. On the other hand, witnesses on scene claimed Clarence had been resting, his head on his arms, when he was set upon by the officers. He was not making a scene or being disruptive in any way. In any case, Clarence was severely beaten, arrested, charged with assault, and put in jail. After making it known that he was suffering from some paralysis in conjunction with intense pain, he was ultimately transported to hospital. Clarence was seen by hospital staff and eventually discharged with a diagnosis of "hysteric" (ungovernable emotional excess or temporary state of mind). He was returned to jail and shortly released as a result of Delores posting fifty dollars as bail. Clarence never recovered from that beating. Several days later he was readmitted to hospital, where he eventually succumbed to his injuries. Fifty-two-year-old longshoreman Clarence Clemons died on Christmas Eve, 1952.

Three things of note: While Clarence was at home after the arrest, he told friends that he had been beaten and kicked repeatedly in the groin by officers; Clarence's friends knew of and referred to officer Dan Brown as the "Negro-hating cop"; and Clarence had committed the cardinal sin of having a white wife, evoking the wrath of white men.

Clarence's death certificate listed his death as unnatural, which automatically required an inquest. Prior to his death, no official or mainstream media would pay attention to the circumstances leading to his demise. Black community leaders railed at the injustice and voiced their disdain of the deadly abuse at the hands of the police. The inquest began on January 6, 1953, in a packed courthouse. Police held fast to their account, claiming the arrest lasted close to ten minutes as Clarence violently struggled with them. They claimed that their use of force had been completely justified. A witness provided a completely different account, stating that Clarence had been handcuffed, savagely beaten, kicked, and repeatedly struck with a truncheon.

As in many current cases of police abuse, the authorities introduced the criminal history of Clarence to besmirch his character. All the medical examiners introduced the theory that death was more likely a result of a past injury suffered by Clarence that had resulted in an osteoarthritic condition near the base of his skull. The struggle had aggravated this condition, likely resulting in his death. This same strategy of shifting the cause of death onto the victim was a key strategy injected into the minds of the jury trying the killing of George Floyd, when a medical examiner raised the issue of Floyd's enlarged heart as a possible cause of his death.

After less than an hour deliberating, the jury (all white men, I might add) ruled that Clarence Clemons had died "an unnatural death . . . caused by an old injury which may have been aggravated by his strenuous struggle, while resisting arrest by two Vancouver City Police Officers . . . in the normal course of their duty."

∞

Did you know, according to the records maintained by the National Association for the Advancement of Colored People (NAACP), that from 1882 to 1968, the State of Georgia recorded the second-highest number of lynchings, with 531, surpassed only by the State of Mississippi with 581. Loosely defined, as I perceive it, lynching is the apprehension and subsequent public execution — usually by white people — of the victim, who is usually Black. Lynchings are generally assumed to be an abomination of the historical past. But on February 23, 2020, a modern-day lynching showed us how little had changed.

Ahmaud Arbery was a twenty-five-year-old young Black man who'd had the audacity to enter into a fairly affluent, primarily white area of Brunswick, Georgia, known as Satilla Shores, more than once I might add, and on several occasions entered onto a property that was under construction to look around. That's all it took for several of the neighbours to condemn him as a thief who should be detained for questioning. This despite video recording of Ahmaud on the property and no evidence of him ever taking or destroying anything whatsoever. On this fateful day, Ahmaud was jogging through the neighbourhood and was seen by Gregory McMichael, a resident of that area. Gregory immediately ran into his house and summoned his son Travis to get his shotgun and go after the intruder. Gregory armed himself with a .357 Magnum handgun and both of them got into their pickup truck, the licence plate of which was adorned with a Confederate symbol. The two white men chased Ahmaud down several streets in the attempt to stop him. The initial part of the pursuit was witnessed by another neighbour, William "Roddie" Bryan, who took it upon himself to join in the apprehension of this Black man running in his neighbourhood. William jumped into his own pickup truck and aided in the blockade of Ahmaud. At some point during the chase, Bryan started recording the incident on his phone. By this point, Ahmaud had been running in an attempt to evade the pursuers for around five minutes. At the corner of Buford Road and Satilla Drive, Ahmaud was confronted by Travis McMichael, now out of the truck with a shotgun. He made a decision to fight for his life. Ahmaud was subsequently shot three times at close range, eventually succumbing to his wounds.

In a previous chapter, I talked about the space in the systems that allows room to operate at the disadvantage of the minority, or in this case, the oppressed. Here is a clear example of what I mean. A young Black man who had committed no crime was hunted down in broad daylight and murdered. The shooter's justification was that the victim had been running away and therefore must have done something. *We needed to apprehend him, he got hold of my gun, so I shot him. Self-defence!*

The first officer on the scene saw three white men, two of them covered in the victim's blood, and a young Black man lying on the ground, and understood that the young man had just been shot. He asked the white men if everybody had their weapons up (meaning that the weapons were no longer in play and had been secured). Both father and son responded, "Everybody's got their weapons up." The officer took the perpetrators at their word and proceeded to take pictures of the scene with his phone. He did not secure the scene. He did not render aid to the victim, who was still alive and breathing at the time. He did not control the movements of the men. Why? All I can tell you is I can't imagine an incident involving Black men holding weapons and a dying young white male at the hands of those men where the responding officer would have reacted this way.

Space.

The initial on-scene investigation was shoddy at best. The scene was compromised; the involved suspects were moving around the immediate area; they were not secured. A specific officer was not assigned to manage each suspect. They were allowed to speak with one another, and evidence such as the vehicles used in the crime was not seized. Clothing worn by the suspects was not seized. Greg McMichael's firearm was not seized. The phone containing the original video was not seized. The shoddiness went on and on. The McMichaels and Bryan were not arrested. They spent some time at the station being questioned and were eventually sent home that same day.

At the time, the county's top prosecutor, District Attorney Jackie Johnson, directed to police that Travis McMichael should not be placed under arrest because — wait for it — Gregory McMichael was a former Glynn County police officer and former investigator with Brunswick Judicial Court District Attorney's office. He'd worked for Jackie Johnson.

Space.

The police were in possession of the video showing the hunting down and execution of Ahmaud, but it still took seventy-four days before any charges were brought against all three men.

Space.

Only after the now-infamous video recording was leaked to the public did the Georgia Bureau of Investigation take over the case, and within thirty-six hours it brought down indictments for the murder. The perpetrators had *almost* gotten away with it. On November 24, 2021, all three men were convicted of murder. If it were not for the video entering the public domain, the outcome of this case could have been very different . . . if a case were to be brought at all.

∞

I have one more example that speaks to the repetitious systematic injustice that has plagued the Black and brown people at the hands of police and the justice system. Montreal, in the late 1980s, was the scene of several mass protests relating to the killing of a young Black man by police. On November 11, 1987, at approximately 6:30 a.m., police received a call from a taxi driver that he was in a dispute with a passenger not paying his fare. Constable Allan Gosset and his partner responded to the call. On arrival, a nineteen-year-old man by the name of Anthony Griffin was investigated and arrested based on someone with the same name who was wanted on an outstanding arrest warrant. He was placed in the back of a police cruiser, uncuffed.

The following account is undisputed: On arrival in the parking lot of Montreal Police Station 15 on Mariette Avenue in Notre-Dame-de-Grâce, officers opened the back door, and Anthony attempted to flee. He was immediately ordered to stop or be shot. Anthony complied with the order, stopped, and turned around. Officer Gosset then shot Anthony in the head. Anthony was unarmed. He was taken to hospital, where he succumbed to his injury and was pronounced dead around 11:45 that morning. All of this was the result of a twenty-seven-dollar fare dispute.

Anthony's killing was preceded and followed by so many other young Black unarmed men who have died at the hands of the police. Anthony was not a threat to the officers, who clearly had felt comfortable enough not to handcuff him during transport. Anthony was no threat in his escape attempt, as he was running away and did ultimately comply with the officers' commands. The defence argued that the officer's gun had accidentally gone off. My years of training taught me that there was absolutely no reason for a firearm to have been in play at all. Officer Gosset was charged with manslaughter and eventually acquitted. On appeal, a second trial was ordered and again he was found not guilty.

The question is why are so many officers and vigilantes behaving in this despicable manner? Why are so many people of colour condemned to being at the end of a police firearm or assaultive behaviour just degrees between life and death? What has precipitated the mindset of these officers to condone the assault of Black and brown people by virtue of their whiteness? Why would one think that they could behave in this manner under the authority of their position and think that's okay? Or could it be said that the judicial system, the very same institution that should provide the checks and balances in matters such as these, is also complicit by not taking the proper course of action necessary to adjudicate these cases of racism? Add to this incompetent lawyers and loopholes in the system that validate the notion that policing in this abhorrent manner is acceptable. As for the Arbery case, there were two reasons why this incident ended up in convictions: the video evidence (hard to dispute what was depicted on the tape), and the tenacity of the family in the pursuit of justice. Knowing what I know, if the victims in the four incidents had been white men, none of the brutalization would have occurred. We must challenge the systems that are in place that would allow these travesties first to exist and secondly to continue.

Here is why these stories are important and relevant to me and my community: they speak to the Black experience. Whether it happens in France, England, the United States, or any other country, the issue of police-involved racism — and a justice system that upholds it — strikes at the core of the Black existence. It's our reality. These incidents act as a barometer of our relevance in the twenty-first century. As a Black police officer, scarce as that might be, and even more so as a senior officer, when I speak to family, friends, and acquaintances, it is not out of the ordinary for them to bring up the subject of police abuse — past, present, foreign, or domestic — and ask my opinion as a member of law enforcement. I constantly get phone calls, emails, and texts from people seeking my thoughts on the matter at hand. It doesn't seem to matter if the abuse was right here in Canada or abroad, it forms their interpretation and opinions on police officers. I can personally attest that some are jaded to the point of clouding their judgement when it comes to interactions with cops.

You see, the Black experience, like crime, does not stop at borders. What happens in America directly affects Canadian policing by way of collateral damage. An unjust killing at the hands of police sends shock-waves that pile onto the existing narrative of negative feelings, bringing to light a systemic, intentional, international abuse that is far from being abated. The public will continue to take out their frustrations on the uniform, be it here or abroad. I also found it embarrassing, at times, being painted with the same brush or referred to as "you cops." I made it a point never to defend poor actions by police, not even my own actions. I spoke truthfully and with clarity on how I understood the events from both the perspective of a police officer and that of a person of colour. History, in this context, not only lives with us, it continues to reveal the truth, day in and day out, with what seems to be a reckless abandonment. Learning our history brings a different dimensional shift to how we understand and process events of today. The impact of these occurrences brings forth a sobering realization that the needle hasn't moved very far. For too many years, the call for police reform has seen little change. We are still under the control and covenant of the criminal justice system. Black people are still targeted and abused. What is required is not just words, but urgent action, *now*.

Left: In Grade 7, Elmbank Junior Middle Academy, at age fourteen (1972).

Right: Base Petawawa with troopmate Daniel Simpson, summer of 1974.

Me as a member of the 2nd Field Combat Engineers (1974).

College field trip to Detroit with my Law and Security Administration classmates, visiting the Wayne County Sheriff's Department as an introduction to American policing (1983).

Photos of my mother and father, Ina and Leonard, taken in the early 1950s. My father served approximately five years as a special police constable in Jamacia in the late '40s early '50s.

Me, my mother Ina, father Leonard, and sisters Monica and Shirley in the late '70s.

My younger brother, Carl, and me while on a family outing in Niagara Falls, Canada. This photo was taken in 1971. Carl suffered a fatal brain aneurism three years later and died at the tender age of thirteen.

York Regional Police graduation ceremony with my wife, Cheryl, and my mother, Ina (1987).

THE REGIONAL MUNICIPALITY OF YORK

YORK REGIONAL POLICE FORCE

OATH OF OFFICE

I, _____ Keith Merith _____

(Full Name)

DO SWEAR that I will well and truly serve Her Majesty the Queen

in the OFFICE OF CONSTABLE for the Regional Municipality of York

without favour or affection, malice or ill-will; and that, to the

best of my power, I will cause the peace to be kept and preserved,

and prevent all offences against the persons and properties of Her

Majesty's subjects; and that, while I continue to hold the said

office, I will, to the best of my skill and knowledge, discharge

all the duties thereof faithfully according to the law.

SO HELP ME GOD.

SWORN before me at the Town)
of Newmarket in the)
Regional Municipality of York,)
Province of Ontario, this 6th)
day of January , 19 87 .)

Keith Merith

Judge or Justice of the Peace

York Regional Police Oath of Office, January 6, 1987.

A Morality Bureau drug bust with partner David Jazwinski (1987).

Members of the 1987 Morality Bureau. Top row, left to right: Edward Telizyn, Brent Trask, Eugene Kerrigan, Michael Fleming, Terry Creighton, Edward Bicket, J.C. Penny (RCMP). Bottom row, left to right: Michael Hand, me, Ezra (Tony) Browne, Michael Arbour.

Undercover days in the late '80s.

ONTARIO ID Nº P 945693
Ishack Washington
EXPIRES ON 1992 : 493-644-188
BIRTHDATE

sex	height	weight	hair	eyes
M	5'8"	170	Blk	Brn
date of issue		date of birth		
Sept 06/88		Sept 09/60		

signature

ISSUED FOR PERSONAL IDENTIFICATION AND M.M.I. USE

Graduation photo from Ontario Police College (1987).

Uniform patrol duties while stationed in Markham, providing police presence and security for a street festival (1993).

Instructing on police defensive tactics (officer safety) as a member of the Training and Education Bureau with fellow officer Mark Ruffolo (1997).

Me, Jenny Wenzek, and judo instructor Sensei Bill Kato at one of our judo training sessions.

Competing at the 1994 International Law Enforcement Olympics in Birmingham, Alabama.

Racism charged at picnic for Canadian, U.S. cops

WASHINGTON (AP) — U.S. Senate committee will conduct a hearing into allegations that American and Canadian law-enforcement officials participated in an all-white picnic where racist slogans were displayed.

"I'm very upset about it. I'm upset at the way law-enforcement officers have acted," said Senator Orrin Hatch. "We're not going to sit around and let that type of stuff happen."

The Washington Times reported a former agent of the Treasury Department's Bureau of Alcohol, Tobacco and Firearms helped co-ordinate the gathering of law-enforcement officials — including RCMP officers — known as the "Good Ol' Boys Roundup." It was held May 18-20 in Polk County, Tenn.

The Times, quoting unnamed law-enforcement officers, said the gathering included the sale of T-shirts with the late civil rights leader Martin Luther King's face behind a target and O.J. Simpson in a hangman's noose.

Gene Rightmyer, a retired ATF agent who was host of the gathering, denied racism was rampant at the gathering.

RCMP probes reports officers attended U.S. racist 'roundup'

Police party in Tennessee comes under scrutiny of U.S. senators

WASHINGTON (CP) — Canadian police officers were among about 350 law-enforcement officials who attended a whites-only "Good Ol' Boys Roundup" this May in Tennessee, where a racist skit depicted an African-American being sexually assaulted.

One of the skits portrayed an African-American — a white police officer — being sexually assaulted by an officer dressed in the white robes of a Ku Klux Klansman, the director of the U.S. Bureau of Alcohol, Tobacco and Firearms (ATF) told a hearing yesterday.

"There were video that were cut on that were derogatory. I'm not proud of that," John Magaw told a Senate judiciary committee.

"Clearly, blacks would not feel welcome at this event from the very inception."

Two ATF agents testified at the hearing that this year's annual gathering in Ocoee, Tenn., was attended by off-duty agents and U.S. law-enforcement officers from a variety of services.

"We're still investigating the allegations," he said.

If officers did participate, Magaw said "the next step is to determine what involvement they had in the event." Anyone involved would face a disciplinary review, he said.

"The RCMP does not stand for that type of activity by its members and we don't approve of any racist activities," Moreau said the RCMP should have more information in early next week.

The roundup has been organized by ATF agent Gene Rightmyer, who is now retired, since 1980.

Rightmyer, who has refused to testify, has destroyed the invitation list, said Hatch, who chairs the committee.

SHOWING THE FLAG: A red maple leaf is draped over a camper in this video shot at one of the annual "Good Ol' Boys" gatherings of off-duty police officers. The video was shown yesterday at a U.S. Senate judiciary committee hearing.

Black ATF agents testified that only white officers were invited to the picnic, by organizers who used government stationery for the invitations.

However a few black agents have attended, as guests of white friends.

Magaw said he has learned that items for sale at the roundup included T-shirts depicting blacks on the hood of a police car, and others that had the face of Martin Luther King overlaid with a target.

Controls were held for the Redneck of the Year, and the Ugliest Good Ol' Boy, special agent John Scott testified.

Scott attended with two black officers he had invited — one an ATF agent and the other a Cleveland police officer, Robert Goldston.

Scott said he did not see any racially motivated signs or posters.

But someone yelled a racist insult at Goldston as he walked through the campground where the roundup was held, Scott testified.

And later, "I was approached by four men who were extremely brute that I had invited the two black officers to the roundup," Scott said.

Scott and others dispersed the men, he said.

"If it turns out to be as bad as it looks, at minimum, they should be shunned," Sen. Joseph Biden said of all officers in attendance.

"They should be disgraced out of their badge."

News articles about the investigation into the Good Ol' Boys Roundup (1980–1996), a notorious law enforcement picnic and racist event held in Tennessee.

P2 ECONOMIST & SUN, OCTOBER 11, 1995

Fellow officers 'horrified' by racist term used at seminar

By JULIE CASPERSEN
Staff Reporter

Two York Regional police constables facing suspension were told fellow officers felt "horrified" and "embarrassed" when presented with an acronym that spelled c-niggers, a disciplinary hearing heard yesterday.

Randy Porter and Brent Stitt were charged with disobeying a lawful order 10 days after attending a race relations seminar. The complaint was lodged by Sgt. Denyse Ross and Const. Keith Merith who ran the race relations workshop Jan. 31 as part of a firearms requalification course.

During the first day of testimony before trials officer Insp. James Adams, Ross said she asked the class, divided into groups of five or six officers, to list stereotypical behavior on an easel. The group containing Porter and Stitt came up with eight phrases:
- Gives Bad Attitude
- Gets people upset
- Exaggerates reality
- Relates differences
- Closed minded
- Not accepting
- Insensitive

SIU Ross testified Porter, who joined the force in 1982, pointed out to the class that the first letter of each phrase spelled out c-niggers.

"I was deeply ashamed, for Const. Merith for myself, for the class," she said.

Det. Wayne Cole, a police officer for 21 years, was in the same group as Porter and Stitt. He told Adams that Porter suggested the acronym. "I told him he was a f***ing idiot and backed away from the table," Cole stated.

During questioning from defence lawyer Charles Bourgeois, Cole said he didn't believe the word nigger was directed at any one person.

However, Const. Andrew Quibell who was also in the group with Porter and Stitt, said he felt "embarrassed" by the words on the easel, and apologized to Merith, who is black, after class.

"I didn't think it was appropriate and I withdrew from the group," Quibell said. "At the end of the day...I spoke to Const. Merith and apologized I felt bad about what happened."

The defence is scheduled to begin laying out its case starting Nov. 15 at the Region of York offices in Newmarket.

If misconduct is proven, Adams can recommend the officers serve 20 days' suspension without pay or suspension of five days with pay.

Case dismissed

York cops absolved of charges involving racial slurs/Page 3

York Regional Police Const. Keith Merith (inset), a race relations instructor, testified Friday at a disciplinary hearing that he was humiliated when constables Brent Stitt and Randy Porter (above) used a race relations class last January. The charges against the two officers were dismissed Friday.

News articles about an incident of discrimination during a Race Relations training course involving York Regional Police Constables Randy Porter and Brent Stitt. They were charged with breach of procedure 70 but later acquitted without the defence's case being heard.

Staff Sergeant Tony Browne and I representing for the Association of Black Law Enforcers (ABLE) at the International Day for the Elimination of Racial Discrimination held in Markham (2015).

At the rank of inspector, I was the master of ceremonies at the 2015 York Regional Police Black History Month event.

Receiving my twenty-year medal of service at the rank of staff sergeant (2006).

Receiving a plaque from 4 District platoon members after leaving the platoon due to a promotion from staff sergeant to inspector (2009).

Receiving my bar for thirty years of service (2016).

At home getting ready to manage 4 District "D" platoon as a staff sergeant. I had approximately thirty uniformed officers under my command.

Armand La Barge and his wife, Denise, at one of the ABLE Scholarship & Awards Balls. Armand was a former York Regional Police chief, and Denise a detective sergeant. Armand was instrumental in reforming the culture of inclusion and equity within the York Regional Police Service. His leadership cannot be overstated.

Our amazing female officers representing at the ABLE ball.

The dismantling of a sophisticated criminal organizational responsible for a $5-million insurance fraud was the result of a nine-month investigation dubbed Project Sideswipe.

The complex investigation into deliberately staged collisions also saw 60 people charged with a variety of criminal offences including conspiracy.

Working in partnership, Insurance Bureau of Canada investigators and the York Regional Police Major Fraud Unit identified a disturbing trend in York Region in late 2010. They began to investigate a highly-organized fraud network that recruited drivers and passengers to take part in a series of staged collisions in order to collect lucrative insurance and medical benefit claims.

Six investigators probed the group believed responsible for hundreds of staged collisions in York Region.

Investigators focused on nine incidents where the suspects filed fraudulent insurance and medical claims to insurance companies for services that were not rendered.

In August 2012, investigators completed the first phase of their investigation. Fifty-one suspects were charged with 201 offences including Conspiracy to Commit an Indictable Offence, Fraud over $5,000, Fraud under $5,000 and Obstruct Police. Five months later, nine suspects were charged with an additional 41 offences.

Following the arrests, this criminal organization was completely disbanded, resulting in a significant reduction in the number of false insurance claims being filed.

Insurance fraud costs Canadians more than $1 billion dollars every year and drives up the cost of insurance for all Ontarians to the tune of 17 per cent annually.

Project SIDESWIPE

Speaking at a press conference for Project Sideswipe, a nine-month investigation and dismantling of a criminal organization responsible for a $5-million insurance fraud (2012–2013).

Panel discussion in 2018 with John Sewell (former mayor of Toronto), Mike Federico (retired deputy chief of Toronto Police), and me, moderated by Idil Abdillahi, regarding police officers' use of force surrounding the death of Otto Vass.

David Mitchell (retired Assistant Deputy Minister of Youth Justice Division, Ministry of Children, Community and Social Services, and founding president of ABLE), me, Jay Hope (former OPP deputy commissioner), and Peter Sloly (former chief of Ottawa Police) at a retirement ceremony for Jay Hope (2012).

Receiving the Harry Jerome Community Service Award presented by Mark Beckles (Vice President, Social Impact and Innovation, at the Royal Bank of Canada). The Harry Jerome Awards recognizes and honours excellence in African Canadian achievement (2018).

Me with officers Don Yirenkyi, Tony Browne, and Jeff Martin at the 2013 York Regional Police Black History Month Celebration.

Army troopmate reunion with Daniel Simpson, Uton Wilson, and Carl Davison (2019).

My little girls, Brianna and Jasmine, at Disney World.

Brianna and Jasmine, all grown up, supporting me at an ABLE function.

Group photo with my sisters Monica, Hazel, and Shirley (2023).

My older brother, Dennis. A kinder, nicer person you cannot find. I owe him a debt of gratitude.

My wife of forty years, Cheryl, is my number one supporter and the best thing to ever happen to me.

After retiring in 2017 from thirty-one years of service, one of my greatest rewards is spending time with my grandchildren, Dash and Nova.

NO ROOM TO FAIL

For the most part, police organizations in North America operate within the framework of a paramilitary organization. This is defined as a top-down pyramid structure with a staggered step-down lineage of authority. The concept is quite simple: there is one individual at the top, holding all power and control, with a small layer of commanders just underneath them, reporting upwards. The reporting structure below the commanders consists of managers, who again are reporting up. Directly under them are lines of supervisors who ensure that subordinates below them are doing their jobs according to the decree of the individual with all the power.

In the case of most Canadian police services, the number one in the pyramid is the chief of police. They are served by up to four deputy chiefs. Reporting to the deputies will be, in most cases, staff superintendents, a rank that has been phased out of most services, which now utilize just the title of superintendent. Reporting to the superintendent should be the inspector, who would have the staff sergeants and detective sergeants reporting to them. The sergeants are the supervisors for the constable core.

There is no ambiguity about your place in the structure. Your roles and responsibilities are clearly defined, and there is no colouring outside the box. Often the future leaders are individuals who exhibit early signs of leadership traits. There is no doubt that good leadership skills and abilities can be learned, but for the most part those exceptional leaders have something innate that sets them apart from the rest of us from the beginning. You don't have to be an outstanding leader, but you absolutely have to be a competent one.

During my policing career, I was put into positions of leadership that came with several promotions. To be clear, leaders lead regardless of position, title, or station, but there are times when this detail is thrust upon you, whether or not your state of mind or acumen is ready for the tasks at hand. My first promotion came sixteen years into my employment. I was working a joint forces operations posting with the Ontario Provincial Police Provincial Weapons Enforcement Unit, at the time as a constable. While chatting with several of my counterparts in the office, I received a phone call from my service. The voice at the other end of the phone advised me that I had been promoted to the rank of detective. Although I was aware that there was a promotional process underway, the surprise was real, especially since I had not put much faith in the possibility of being successful. The promotion didn't mean much in the job that I was currently doing. It did not change my stature or influence within the unit at all. Unit members still reported to the detective sergeant, and senior detectives still ran the show. Another year would go by before my tenure expired, requiring me to report back to my department.

Just prior to leaving, while I was having lunch with some of my mates, my cellphone rang. It was Chief Armand La Barge on the line, informing me that I had been promoted again to the rank of staff sergeant and would be taking over the management duties of the Training and Education Bureau. Being promoted twice in little over one year is almost unheard of in the realms of police work, especially in Canada. It has surely happened before and after me, but it is definitely a rare occurrence. The chief told me on the phone that day that he believed I had been overlooked for several years, and he was correcting the disparities that existed. That took real courage and leadership. So, in 2004, I now had positional authority by virtue of the rank I held. Adding to this, I occupied one of the premier portfolios within the organization. The weight of leadership had been thrust upon me in an abrupt and concentrated manner that left no time to prepare. Under my direct command was a staff of four sergeants, fifteen constables, and three civilians responsible for providing Academic Instruction and Use of Force Training to the entire service. Positional authority would remain with me for the rest of my career, spanning the next fourteen years.

What did I learn during those years, in terms of the elusive leadership qualities, about guiding subordinates and ultimately having them grow in the talents they possessed? Working within the confines of rising through the organization, conscious of the eyes and ears waiting to prove certain points — *he only got the position because he is Black; the organization needs to appear like it is complying with social lobbyists* — I had to work even harder to outperform my peers and prove that I deserved each position I was in. Operating in the realm of a senior commander meant there was no room for mediocrity. All eyes were on the anomaly, which meant stepping up and getting this leadership thing right.

I was tested at every turn of my supervisory and management appointments. I wish I could say differently, but I felt that for the most part, I did not get the specific job training that should come with elevated positions. It felt like there was a brotherhood within a brotherhood. I watched as other officers were groomed and coached. In fact, the steps that I took to hand off my positions to my replacements most often were not taken for me by people I replaced. With only two other officers of colour holding supervisory positions at the time of my promotion, there really was no room for any of us to fail. Intuitively, I knew the key to success was owning every position, being bold and fearless, and most importantly, developing an unimpeachable personal authority. Mustering all of my worldly and policing experience, being laser-focused on the road ahead while building up personal credits from my subordinates and managers, was the formula required to survive in this environment filled with landmines.

I have never considered myself a follower. Leadership was always part of my personality. Even when I was a child, the thought of being led by others conflicted with the fierce independence in the depth of my core.

But we all are led in some way by someone at some point in our lives. This is not necessarily a bad or dubious concession; on the contrary, one could argue that being led to a degree is essential to the advancement of personal traits, along with experiences that formulate and shape the more enhanced you. Regardless of my race and skin colour, which was often a barrier, I felt like the capacity to lead was within me, and I led accordingly.

I had spent very little time as a sergeant; my real supervisory experience was as a staff sergeant. Talk about a significant change in my stature within the organization. Many of my peers were now under my direct or indirect supervision. A number of my former supervisors could now only claim equal or subordinate status. Some who had wronged me before now avoided me entirely. Some pretended to embrace me, their obvious animosity mixed with resentment. In the established police culture, you don't speak your mind to the person you resent due to the ramifications for being honest. So other officers had to keep their thoughts to themselves or complain in a confidential manner to their buddies.

I was not overly concerned about their negative opinions, but as a pushback, I became determined to prove them wrong. It was customary to receive congratulatory notes from other members after a promotion. I received many, so it was quite telling when no notes of congratulation came from officers who one would expect to be among the first to acknowledge the promotion. That to me told the real story. When I ran into some of them, it was obviously painful for them to extend a hand and utter the word *congratulations*. After all my encounters throughout my life, it was easy for me to spot the glitch in their behaviour that perhaps was undetectable to them. Now, having positional authority, I was acutely attuned to the reactions of my subordinates, peers, and managers as I journeyed along. But I had a responsibility as well. I never forgot to show the well-earned respect to senior constables and sergeants who absolutely deserved it. I showed them deference and sought their advice on a variety of matters. It was more of a peer-to-peer relationship that the officers appreciated and valued. Some officers tested my authority and quickly understood that I was not one to play with. At this time in my career, I had zero tolerance for nonsense and dealt swiftly in taking the wind out of their sails whenever they dared to be disrespectful. Several times I was put into the position of having to transfer that person out of my unit with an admonishment.

With no room to fail, it was paramount to me to operate as a skilled leader, void of the stereotypical notion that by virtue of being Black you were not worthy or capable of an elevated role within the institution of policing. My approach to leadership was one of constructive diligence and not an unnecessary preoccupation with race. But . . . there is always a *but*. The organization constantly reminded me in subtle and not-so-subtle ways that I was in new territory, so be careful.

I had just been promoted to the rank of inspector and assigned to manage investigative services. The units under my command were Covert Operations, Technical Support, Integrated Crime Analysis, and Interception of Private Communications. This portfolio left no room for guesswork or fumbling. I inherited a major joint forces investigation led by my department that had been in operation for several months prior to my arrival. I started on a Monday and was immediately tasked with facilitating a presentation on Thursday detailing the project status to the executive command and several Greater Toronto Area commanders. Who made that decision and why? This was clearly a set-up. Space. The project was extremely large and complex. I had absolutely no knowledge of any part of it. There were other commanders who had been involved in the project from the outset who were more than capable of delivering the presentation competently, so why me? Understand a project of this magnitude requires knowledge of how and why the investigations were commenced, information on the groups under investigation, all of the involved players, how the groups and players are connected, all of the investigative steps that have been taken to date, what organizations are responsible for what parts of the projects, specialty teams, intelligence gathering, equipment, operational plans, projected outcomes, timelines, budgeting, accounting of expenditures, and so on. It's an exhaustive list, and an almost impossible task to absorb in two days. Whoever made that call had severely underestimated my determination and resolve not to fail. It was clear to me that my only option was to learn the project inside and out.

And that's exactly what I did.

I read every scrap of paper that had anything to do with the project. I enlisted the help of my team. I was very fortunate to have supervisors around me who knew their jobs and were willing to guide and direct me to competency. I had built up reputational currency throughout my time in the service that now paid dividends. There were so many moving parts that my head was spinning, but the bottom line was not to embarrass myself, to give them what they wanted, and to do it right.

At the presentation, there must have been a dozen or so commanders from around the GTA in attendance, along with representatives from other enforcement agencies. I kept reminding myself that, set-up or not, you're a winner, and losing is not an option. With my nerves completely frayed, I delivered the presentation professionally, deliberately, and with confidence. The tough questions came at me like bullets from a shotgun. I tackled each one of them by saying my piece, then referring to the subject matter experts for the finer details. It worked marvellously. It *had* to — there'd been no room to fail.

While completely aware that Black leadership was in its infancy and overscrutinized, I felt that one of the main tenets in my rise through organizational leadership was the need to be authentic by operating within the framework of the real me. To my core, I was a good person. I needed to maintain that perspective. I did not want to replicate the notion prevalent in many services that one needed to be an asshole or a prick to lead in senior management. I surely would have compounded my already compromised positional authority and have a completely different experience than my counterparts. As the person in charge, I felt that I possessed many of the qualities that a true leader might have, but if I didn't get the respect of my subordinates, I would not get the best out of my employees. It was incumbent upon me, as the one in authority, to demonstrate goodness and to operate in good faith that was not contrived but flowed with genuine care. I think we can agree that a good leader is a compassionate soul who uses the non-judgemental and empathetic aspects of their humanity. To avoid the potential corrosiveness often present in the work environment, I endeavoured to maintain an atmosphere of fairness and sound judgement. My doctrine was to be kind by operating with humility and grace, to treat people with respect. I gave people the room to make good judgements and provided them a degree of autonomy, allowing them to grow.

Ingrained in the service was an old prevailing modus operandi, which was to rule by instilling fear in the hearts of subordinates. This bullshit belongs in the classification of tyrannical behaviour, which serves no one, not even the perpetrator. No one respects a bully. Subordinates prefer to stay as far away from them as they can. It is not possible to get the best from employees when they are operating in the realm of fear. I did not rule by fear: to do so is destructive and ultimately leads to corrosive outcomes with very real negative ramifications. For whatever gains I might have achieved, had I used my authority in this manner there would have been a reckoning at some point.

Sergeant Thorpe, who I grew to admire, respect, and called a friend, was such a person. He drew the fear of officers under his supervision. Sergeant Thorpe held the persona of a mean, grumpy, vindictive sergeant. I came to realize that he was nothing of the sort, but he had created this character. Many officers did not like him and feared him. He had a habit of singling out a certain person and making it his personal project to disrupt and aggravate them as much as possible, then he'd move on to someone else. While working in 4 District as a uniform patrol officer, I reported off-duty to Sergeant Thorpe and was always intimidated by him and his ways. We all wanted to stay as far away as possible from this man. Sergeant Thorpe had a passion unknown to most of us. He was a practitioner of the martial art of judo and was a sensei (black belt instructor). I was also practising judo at the time and ran into him quite by accident when I visited a prominent dojo in Toronto. Sergeant Thorpe was one of the senior instructors. The instructor on the mat was not the same man I knew at work. He was kind, thoughtful, gentle, personable, and extremely likable. Could this really be the same man?

I was so impressed with him and the quality of his instruction that I made the effort to attend this dojo as often as possible. Back at work,

I tried to tell my workmates about the transformation, but they all, to a person, claimed that I must have been thrown on my head and was clearly in need of both medical and psychological treatment. Sergeant Thorpe and I eventually worked together in the Training and Education Unit as Use of Force and Academic Instructors, with him becoming my direct boss. This was where everyone came to believe my story. Sergeant Thorpe was exactly how I'd described him. Sadly, within a couple years of that transformation, Sergeant Thorpe passed away of cancer-related complications. He became a very special person to me and the organization, which posthumously created an academic award in his name. I miss the times we spent after class, at one bar or the other, having a pint and chatting. To me, the experience confirmed what I knew to be true. Sergeant Thorpe was able to accomplish more by becoming the better man. I respected his transformation and the authenticity of who he truly was. This experience validated and framed my conduct, as upward mobility was no longer as elusive as before.

Knowing that competency working alongside good decision-making is the hallmark of sound leadership — and that anything less would be judged harshly in my organization — my work to be consistently at the top of my game never stopped or slowed down. I felt I was not expected to know everything pertaining to my job or position, but I needed, in short order, to have a grasp on the macro workings and to be able to net out where I fit and what was required from me to make it work. Good leaders need to lead, and that involves providing direction, guidance, instruction, and mentorship along with producing results suitable to the organization.

Man, it was extremely difficult to follow someone who was not capable of performing at a respectable level, even if I liked that individual. I never wanted to be that guy. My followers depended on me to make decisions. They came to me with minor or major propositions that needed solutions. I did one of three things: made a decision; worked with them to come up with a solution; or, if above my pay grade, engaged my superiors. The beginning of the process was owning the power vested in me by virtue of my positional authority. I knew where the lines were and worked within them. Having the positional authority, I needed to be making decisions that clearly fell within my scope. Any deflecting, hesitating, or relying on my boss or others to make the decision would have been interpreted as ineptitude, diminishing my effectiveness as the officer-in-charge. Also, I might add, this would have been noticed by my superiors as a flaw in my overall skill set. Already operating from a position of disadvantage, this was something I could not afford.

Managing the Organized Crime Bureau required that I walk this line every day. There were three detective sergeants who ran the Guns and Gangs, Drugs and Vice, and Major Frauds units respectively and reported to me on current, past, or future investigations, which inevitably needed my authorization in some manner. Oddly enough, one of the constant decisions that I had to make, and call it right, was managing overtime. With these high-performing units, their investment in the work that they were doing required significant amounts of hours each day, often crossing the barriers of allotted work hours. Organizationally, it was my responsibility to authorize or decline overtime requests. Unofficially, I gave the supervisors the authority to make the call on reasonable overtime hours without coming to me, due to the fact that they were closer to the events than I was and had a better perspective.

One evening around 6:30 p.m., I was getting ready to leave the office when I received a call from the detective sergeant of the Guns and Gangs Unit. He told me that they were following a high-value target and were heading out of town. It had taken them months to acquire this person and he believed they were on to something big. He requested overtime hours for his officers to stay on target for several more hours. I authorized the request. Two hours later, I was contacted again, stating that the team believed the target was on his way to Montreal, some five hours away from our region.

Our organization was very particular about limiting overtime hours. My units were major consumers of additional hours, which was a constant headache in terms of balancing the budgets. I was now in the situation of allowing several of my officers to follow the target to Montreal or somewhere else. That meant that our service would have to provide food, accommodations, travel expenses, etc., for the officers, and there was no accounting for the outcome of this portion of the investigation. Also, we would need to gain authorization from the Quebec authorities to operate in their jurisdiction. I would need to provide justification to my boss on the cost relating to this one portion of the investigation and convince him that it was critical we stay with this target. This one decision turned into three days of continuous overtime for the team. I took a fair bit of heat on this one, but justified every step of the decisions made, demonstrating operational competency and organization awareness. And yes, the investigation was successful, garnering a substantial number of narcotics and firearms.

It was not lost on me that I needed to build up new trust and earn new respect while operating at higher levels within the organization. That meant there was an elevated pressure on me to let the officers under my direct command know I had their best interest at heart and was trustworthy. I found the perfect role model in the former president of the United States, Barack Obama. Here was a statesman who had defied all the odds. I felt the air of authenticity as I observed his approach in the delivery of information while comforting a nation. He was wrapped in a confidence in who he was, producing a refined ability to put one at ease, all the while guiding, directing, mentoring, or delivering tough messaging. That's what I wanted to emulate. I adopted that air of humility that spoke to the cohesiveness of the concept that "we are all in this together but play different roles." I became that leader who was out front day in and day out, not afraid to challenge norms if a better way was considered and in the best interest of the organization and the people who operated within it. I practised confidentiality with a demonstrated ability to confide small bits of information in a reciprocal agreement of trust. I practised risk management, not risk aversion. To me, risk management was an exercise in forecasting adverse outcomes and applying mitigating formulas to limit or eliminate the potential negative consequences. It was a bit of a gamble, but I owned my positional authority and used it to its maximum capacity. My guiding principle was to do no harm. Maximum effort was dedicated to the well-being, comfort, and safety of staff members. With that in mind, I had a working knowledge of the policies, procedures, and operational manuals that formulated the goals, objectives, and outcomes of the company. I was acutely aware of my tolerance in terms of the degree of accountability I was willing to absorb.

Understanding the inherent risk associated with the job, there were times I had little choice but to roll the dice and hope and pray that things worked out. Thank goodness those events were few and far between, but they did happen. Knowing that the spotlight was shining on me, I was always prepared to justify why I'd come to that conclusion and why it was the best option at the time. As a temporary member of the Joint Forces Provincial Weapons Enforcement Unit, I was responsible for managing assigned and self-generated investigations. I became the lead investigator in a case that was multi-jurisdictional, lasting four months. This was a particularly sensitive case, as the subject was a former police officer in possession of a number of illegal firearms believed to have been smuggled into Canada from the United States.

The degree of risk and the accountability placed on me was enormous. Gathering enough evidence to support a search warrant and arrest meant I had to manage the risks associated with public safety, officer safety, the organization's policies and procedures, human resources, the required equipment, surveillance teams, and the collection of physical evidence, including creative ways of obtaining that evidence, all the while dealing with a possibly armed individual. We eventually acquired a search warrant that granted us access to his home. There, we seized eleven guns, along with 290 rounds of ammunition. While we were in the process of executing the warrant, the suspect arrived home and was immediately arrested outside. Inside his vehicle was a loaded .45-calibre pistol. We did all that we could to mitigate the risk. Even so, this event could have unfolded differently, with dire consequences.

During my days in the service, it was a rare commodity to encounter Black folks in supervisory, managerial, or command positions. We were late arrivals, struggling to make up ground that had been denied us for so many years. When I gradually started to attain some authority, it often felt surreal and like more work than it should have been. There was a constant tug to validate my rise in the organization that should not have been premised on skin tone. The pressure was there from my first promotion. Commanding a group of primarily white men, who for many years held strong to the norm of being in charge, was at times problematic. This pressure, I suppose, was to a degree self-imposed, because I wanted to demonstrate that I was just as capable of positional leadership as the next person, who for the most part was white. That said, I believe the pressure enabled me to operate at an elevated level, producing good work and results. I did not see this specific type of pressure put on my white counterparts, because there was none. The pressures they felt would be considered normal, everyday business affairs.

For instance, due to some of the senior portfolios I held, I often attended meetings, seminars, or conferences with colleagues from a number of other services, sometimes from across the country. I was usually the only senior Black officer in the room. Often many of my colleagues had never encountered a Black senior officer, which meant that I was an anomaly, scrutinized to a degree that was not shared by other officers. I never felt that I had to convince them that I belonged, but I needed to represent myself and my service to the degree that they knew my command was earned. It was important to me that the seed was planted and would provide a chance for people of colour to get an opportunity to join their service or advance in it.

As time progressed, there was a sprinkling of Black senior officers — almost all of them men — representing some of the larger services, which was heartwarming to see. Having met some of them, I can attest that they were bright, intelligent, competent, and by all accounts deserving. They were now entrusted to do their part to carry the baton the required distance, bringing others with them in the hope of a successful handoff.

As a leader within my organization, I didn't have to change the world, so to speak, but I did need to contribute in some meaningful and significant way. I led within my sphere of influence. It wasn't majestic; it was about my personal values and walking that way in life, demonstrating those values that were true to me. By doing this, I led by example and influencing others through that demonstration of standards that I held so dear. As life unfolded for me, I soon recognized that up the road and around the corner was another hurdle that I needed to jump. The intuitive thing to do was to anticipate what I may encounter and to figure out a solution. At a certain point in my career, I realized that a holdback to a promotion could be that I did not have a university degree. So, I enrolled at the University of Guelph and ultimately graduated with a Bachelor of Arts degree in Justice Studies. My leadership commitment going forward was to set an example and expectation for others to follow suit with the goal of eliminating one of the potential barriers for upward mobility. Not earth-shattering, but significant.

The reality is, I was judged on a different level than my white counterparts. It did not come to pass that all was equal or balanced. Ascending into leadership roles required me to measure up and deliver. I knew that no room to fail meant having job familiarity, knowledge, courage, exposure, and organizational awareness. I knew that I needed to develop the ability to inspire and motivate my subordinates. My overall approach needed to include teaching, sharing, executing, directing, learning, coaching, and empowering others. The goal was to operate with positional and personal leadership strategies, with an emphasis on the personal aspects. Leading meant learning how to manage up, down, sideways, and in between. The notion of "as I learn, I teach; as I teach, I learn" (as often mentioned by a dear friend of mine) was foundational in terms of growth that was always applied to my upward mobility. It provided me with the consciousness of thought, durability, sustainability, and confidence that allowed me to feel good about the enormous effort that was necessary to achieve. My intentional efforts eventually created positive side effects that ultimately filtered throughout the organization, including the ranks of senior command, which I believed contributed to my upward mobility within the organization. All this and more from a Black leader . . . there was no room to fail!

DRIVING WITH A MAHOGANY HUE

Yes, "driving while Black" is a thing that I have experienced personally, alongside countless other people of colour. I have already recounted the story of my experience with the Toronto police officer who set upon me unjustifiably while I was parking my car at the Canadian National Exhibition. That incident happened many years ago, but still sits inside me; I'm sure it will never leave. So, I feel compelled to describe a few other incidents that happened to me while driving, when I was employed as a police officer.

During the early '90s, I had left the 2 District station in my work vehicle and was heading back to the Morality office. My role at the time was undercover, so I was in street clothes and driving a two-door Mazda Miata supplied by the service. In other words, there was no indication of who I was or what I was about. Heading north on a main two-lane artery, I passed a police cruiser coming in the opposite direction. Both vehicles were travelling at relatively low speeds, as the posted speed limit on the roadway was sixty kilometres per hour. As the vehicles passed one another, we both glanced at each other, making fleeting eye contact. Well, what happened next was no surprise. The cruiser made an immediate U-turn, sped up, and activated the cruiser roof lights behind me, indicating that I needed to pull over, which I did.

I waited in the vehicle for a few minutes before being approached by the officer. I knew why. It was because he was running a check on the vehicle and waiting for a backup unit to assist. The officer then ordered me out of the vehicle and told me to stand near the hood of my car. The second unit arrived very soon after. Once the first officer saw the second unit arriving, that's when he started to question me. He asked a quick round of questions relating to my name, who the vehicle belonged to, and what I was doing in this area. The paperwork for the car was in the vehicle at the time and was legit. The car was registered to a legitimate business, and my driver's licence and insurance were up to date.

When the second officer arrived, he recognized me right away. We had worked together on a project not long before and had spent many hours in each other's company. He met me with a huge smile while shaking my hand profusely. The first officer was shocked and, I presume, somewhat embarrassed. He was a staff sergeant working out of 1 District station. Even though I knew him, he had no idea who I was, but by his actions, he showed me who he was. And get this: when the second officer told him who I was, the first officer's comment to me was — get ready for this — the dreaded, "Nice place, this Canada, eh?" Fuck you, you racist bastard. There was absolutely no other reason for him to have pulled me over other than my mahogany hue. This obviously racist staff sergeant eventually left the York Regional Police to take on a chief of police position in a small Ontario town.

Another time, I was working in an undercover capacity on my way back to the Morality office. I was in street clothes driving a white five-litre Mustang coupe, a really nice, eye-catching car. This vehicle was on loan to the service from a local car dealership for my use. All the licensing and paperwork were in order, and the vehicle was in excellent working condition.

I had spent the better part of the day in Toronto, arranging a drug buy, and now it was time to head back to the station. The first stop occurred around 4:30 p.m., while I was heading northbound on Markham Road at a normal rate of speed, observing all the rules of the road. A Toronto police cruiser pulled up beside me on the left-hand side, looked at me, then fell back behind, and activated its roof lights. It was evident that the officer had some concerns about what he'd seen. I did the expected thing by indicating and pulling to the shoulder immediately. The officer requested my driver's licence and insurance documents along with the paperwork for the vehicle. His explanation for stopping me was the usual: *There has been criminal activity in the area, and the suspect description was male, Black, around your age and hairstyle blah blah blah*. All right, okay, sure. He checked me out through his system, and I came back clear. The officer politely gave me back my documents and sent me on my way.

Ten minutes later, I was pulled over again by another Toronto police cruiser that I didn't even see until the lights came on. Again, I was driving properly, observing the rules of the road, as I understood them to be, having passed my driving test some sixteen years earlier. Knowing the routine prior to the officer's arrival at the driver's door, I had my paperwork handy. I handed it over, and he informed me that I had crossed the lane lines several times, so he wanted to check to see if I'd had anything to drink. This was complete bullshit, and I understood that this was more about that dreaded mahogany hue than anything else, but I didn't get upset and simply let him continue. He advised me to stay put while he ran some checks on the vehicle and me. All was in order, and he advised that through his brief interaction he didn't detect any signs of impairment. I was free to go.

Just as I crossed the city boundary into York Region, at the intersection of Markham Road and Steeles Avenue, a York Regional officer who had followed me for a kilometre or so stopped me. Even I was surprised at this point. This was my third stop by the police within a forty-minute drive going in the same direction, all while observing the rules of the road. In my mind, there were three common denominators. First, the police: they all saw what they were doing as being part of their jobs. As they saw it, they were using the power and authority of the Highway Traffic Act as an investigative tool the way they saw fit. Secondly, the car. It was very nice and expensive, at the time. So according to their habitual profiling of drivers who looked like me, the presumption was that I should not have been able to afford such a vehicle. And lastly, my mahogany hue, which completed the trifecta. The York officer didn't know or recognize me. He claimed to be checking movements in this area, and the car had drawn his attention. I was again sent on my way. I ask you, the reader, what are the odds of this happening to the white everyday commuter going about their normal daily activities? This is just a rhetorical question, of course — the answer is obvious.

∞

There is one more incident that I would like to speak about, which makes one really contemplate the degree and depth that ordinary citizens, especially those of colour, feel about the imbalance of power that can be considered abusive at the hands of police. I will preface this with the caveat that most officers I have worked with did not take this approach.

This event occurred in 2005. I went to Pearson International Airport to pick up my daughter, who was returning from university in the United States. After a happy and excited reunion with me, she jumped in the car, and we made our way onto the highway, heading home. At one point in the drive, I was in the express lane, keeping up with traffic, which was slightly above the speed limit. On the Greater Toronto highways, it is common practice for vehicles to travel in the range of 120 kilometres per hour in a posted 100-kilometre zone. So, from my perspective, I was doing what everyone else was doing; keeping up. The traffic was moderate and moving well.

At one point, glancing at my rear-view mirror, I noticed that a number of vehicles were abruptly moving from the passing lane to the middle lane. The more I looked, the more noticeable it became. Then I saw the reason why. It was due to a police cruiser close behind them. The cruiser was not displaying emergency lights, nor did it have the siren blazing; it was simply tailgating, and the cars were moving out of the way. Enough cars had moved out of the way that the cruiser was now directly behind me. I had several cars in front of me at the time, leaving me with only two options: keep going, or move to the middle lane as so many of the other cars had opted to do. Well, I saw no reason to move over. There was clearly no emergency, traffic was moving well, and we all were travelling slightly over the speed limit, so I didn't change lanes. Apparently, that pissed off the officer to the point where they did a rapid lane change, pulling up alongside my vehicle, took a good look, then fell back behind and activated the roof lights for me to pull over. As soon as the lights were in play, I indicated and moved out of that lane. As I did so the cruiser moved with me, lane by lane, until I was on the shoulder of the road and stopped. What happened next was very disturbing.

The officer exited the cruiser and approached the driver's side of my vehicle. She started the conversation by asking me in a very angry belligerent tone if I hadn't seen a police cruiser behind me. I answered that I had. She then went on to lecture me, stating that when I see a police cruiser I should get out of the way and that I'd acted like an asshole! *What?* She then demanded my documents, which she snatched out of my hands and took back to her vehicle.

My daughter was aghast, asking me what was wrong with her. "Tell her that you're a cop!" she pleaded. I said no; I needed to know how this would end if I were deemed a private citizen. A few minutes later, she returned with my documents and tossed them into my lap with the comment, "You need to respect the police," and walked off. Both my daughter and I were stunned and repulsed at the demonstrated callousness, along with the sense of entitlement this officer afforded herself. She immediately drove off, leaving us on the side of the highway.

At the time, I was a uniformed staff sergeant working out of 4 District but on a day off. I was driving on a provincial highway patrolled by the Ontario Provincial Police. The offending officer was a York Regional Police officer working on the same police service out of the same division that I worked. When she stopped me, she was out of her jurisdiction and out of her patrol area. When she approached me, I recognized her immediately. She was a rookie officer with a couple of years' experience under her belt. She obviously didn't recognize me at all. A week prior to this event, this same officer had brought in a prisoner to be booked at the station. Guess who the booking officer was? We had, up to that point, crossed paths many times. But along the side of the highway, she'd had no clue. On the day of the incident, having pulled me over for no valid reason, what she saw was just another Black man in a new metallic silver-grey BMW who she felt was disrespecting her authority and status as a police officer. This is a bit of an assumption on my part, but it's informed by her actions.

I continued on my way, ultimately dropping my daughter at home. I then called the district and spoke to the staff sergeant managing the station. I advised him that I would be coming to see him about an incident relating to one of his officers. On arrival, I had a conversation with the staff sergeant and I asked that he call the officer off the road but not tell her why.

When she came into his office, I was sitting at his desk in the same civilian clothes that I'd had on during the stop. When she saw me, she lowered her head, fighting back the tears and the shame. Her world was about to get messy. She'd made the instant connection and folded like a deck of cards. The comeuppance was savoury and sweet. She was not getting off this hook. No way. Being deliberately provocative, I asked, "Do you recognize me?" She responded sheepishly that she did. "Why should anyone be treated the way you treated me a few hours ago?" With her eyes to the floor, tears welling, she whispered that she was sorry. Then came the lecture about abuse of power and compromising the integrity of the service. She clearly understood that her behaviour had been abhorrent and certainly would not be tolerated by internal agents or the citizenry we are sworn to serve. The other staff sergeant was disgusted as well and voiced his zero tolerance for anyone under his command to operate in this manner. The result was a written admonishment and verbal caution as to future behaviour. Several months after this event, this same officer was involved in a motor vehicle collision where she was driving at a high rate of speed and ended up in a bad accident. She was very seriously injured and never returned to duty.

These related incidents are more than an inconvenience. They are a testament to how people of colour are viewed and treated by some police officers. These are first-hand accounts —I did not have to rely on what I've heard or read about. If they happened to me, it is probable that other people of colour are dealing with the same issues. Although these interactions may be considered minor, being that they did not result in arrest or bodily harm, there is always the potential of something going sideways, with unintended consequences. The remedy is simple: do your job properly, fairly, and justly, and remove that biased lens.

· PART THREE ·

FIGHTING THE
POWER FROM WITHIN

RECRUITING WITH A VISION

It was solely due to a comment that I had made during a meeting that I became the officer-in-charge of the Professional Development Bureau, which included the recruiting unit. I had been invited to participate in, and become a member of, the Chief's Community Council Committee, chaired at the time by Inspector Ricky Veerappan. At one of these meetings, the topic of recruiting came up, causing me to have a great deal to say about the functionality of the unit that wasn't very flattering.

My issue was that over the many years of this service operation, the numbers of visible minorities one would expect to be hired — and were required, in my view — had not been. I expressed two main concerns: First, I personally had sent to our recruiters many diverse candidates who had the requisite qualities to be successful, but for one reason or another, not one of them had been hired. Yet many of these same candidates were eventually hired by other police services and were doing well. Why? My complaint was echoed by a number of other officers whom I had spoken to throughout my years of service. Second, what barriers in our recruiting process were preventing the visible minorities from being successful? I spoke to what I felt were some of those barriers: "We need to drill down into where and why our diverse candidates are falling off. On the surface,

I see a troubling area that in my mind should be looked into, and that is in the area of the background investigators."

Let me explain what I meant. As part of the recruiting process, a potential candidate was subjected to an investigation into their history. This phase was conducted by retired police officers who were retained by the service to perform this function. So here is the comment that I made that got me in trouble: "We as an organization should scrutinize a little more when it comes to hiring these retirees, because some of those former officers, I know personally, were bigots when they were on the job. Why should we trust that they have had a change of heart while doing this function?"

Well, *that* hit a nerve. The inspector overseeing the Recruiting Unit was in the room and took offence to my statement. I was not alone in challenging the performance of the unit, but clearly that comment had cut too close to the bone.

The next day, I was contacted by the chief and told to report to his office. He advised that he had been contacted by the Police Association with a complaint against me. The allegation was that I had called the Recruiting Unit racist. I assured the chief that was not the case. I reiterated what I did say, that some members of the background investigators acted like bigots when I had worked with and/or for them. He was satisfied with my response but still concerned by the association's involvement. I left his office pissed that someone had made a complaint against me based on a clear misrepresentation of what I had said. Clearly, the complainant did not have the fortitude to confront me directly. My next step was to contact the association directly and deal with this matter. Since Larry Woods was the association's representative dealing with this complaint, I contacted him directly. He was a true professional. He first described the issue as it had been relayed to him, then provided me with the opportunity to present my point of view. At the conclusion of our conversation, he was satisfied that what he had been told was clearly not what was said, and assured me that he would manage the resolution as best he could.

The following day, Deputy Chief André Crawford came to my office, inquiring what had happened in that meeting. I recounted the dialogue and concluded with my take on the whole incident — that it was a bull-shit claim. He instructed me to reconvene a meeting with all who were present to sort out what had happened — he would be at the meeting as an observer. This meeting did take place with a positive conclusion: that what I said had not been racist in any manner; rather, it was a statement of truth and discovery worth looking into.

The deputy and I met shortly after that, and he asked me quite bluntly if I thought that I could do a better job running the Recruiting Unit. Without hesitation, I said, "Yes, I could." All I meant was that I believed that with some specific and necessary changes to the unit, the diversity count would surely rise. By this time, I had been the inspector in charge of the Organized Crime Bureau, with Guns and Gangs, Major Frauds and Drug and Vice Units under my command, for the past five years. I really enjoyed what I did and hoped to continue serving in that capacity. But from the moment I said I felt that I could do a better job, the balls were in the air. It just so happened that the current inspector was looking to move on, so there was a potential vacancy available, and in some round-about way, I was now slated to fill that position. And that's how I ended up in recruiting. By the way, Larry Woods from the association called me one day, inviting me out for lunch on his dime. It was a really pleasant time spent chatting. He apologized profusely — which he certainly didn't have to do, but the fact that he made this gesture of taking me out was extremely appreciated.

The first order of business was to get the lay of the land, to understand the macro and micro functionality of the Professional Development port-folio. This bureau consisted of the Professional Development Unit and the Recruiting Unit. The Professional Development Unit, in essence, ensured that members of the organization were provided with the requisite training and education that enabled them to perform their jobs at the level required with competence and professionalism. The unit was also responsible for creating, sustaining, upgrading, and facilitating all levels of the police officers' promotional process. And of course, the Recruiting Unit was responsible for managing the hiring of candidates for uniformed positions within the organization. The unit also processed the hiring of members of our Court Officers Bureau and York Regional Transit officers. For now, I will concentrate on the Uniform Recruiting aspects of the bureau.

When I arrived, there was a bit of tension about the inner workings of the unit. Several members were not in agreement with the staff sergeant as to how it should operate. The staff sergeant, a recent addition, had made several changes that rubbed some the wrong way. I needed to sort that out as soon as possible, and I did. I was fortunate because the staff sergeant got an opportunity to move into another spot in the organization where he was more suited and certainly capable. This opened up a position that several other officers throughout the service requested to fill. I brought in Detective Sergeant Peter Casey, who had worked with me in the Organized Crime Bureau as the detective sergeant running the Drugs and Vice Units.

I had another prominent position to fill, that of a sergeant. It just so happened that a few weeks into my placement, I was visited by a former colleague within the 5 District Criminal Investigative Bureau, Detective Greg Connolly. He told me he was looking for a change from his current assignment, and I asked him if he would be interested in taking the position as a sergeant in the Uniform Recruiting Unit. This was not a position he had contemplated before, but he trusted me and knew that if I was asking him, it was for a good reason. Greg came onboard a few weeks later, for which I was truly appreciative.

Both Peter and Greg turned out to be the right people for the task. Those two officers complemented each other and enhanced my competency in managing the unit. Through a series of meetings, I laid out my vision of how I wanted the unit to run and the desired outcomes I expected. Both of them made it their duty to carry out my wishes, and did so in extraordinary fashion. The unit itself was in a sort of transitional flux, with the advent of four civilian human resources personnel recently joining six uniformed police officers in managing the hiring of uniformed officers. This had never been done before in our organization. The civilians were true professionals who brought a refreshing and needed lens to the hiring process.

It didn't take long for me to figure out what was needed to enhance the proficiency of the unit and create a methodology for increasing the diversity hiring. A big part of what I had to do was pointed out to me by an officer who had been assigned to work the front desk due to a placement issue at another unit. His position here was temporary. I knew him fairly well, so he felt comfortable confiding his observations to me.

One morning, I was sitting in my office when this officer asked if he could speak with me in private for a moment. He entered, closed the door, then presented me with an application. He went on to explain his concern about what had just happened. A candidate had come into the office to drop off his application, and the officer had had a brief conversation with him. The officer then called for a recruiter to receive the application. An hour later, that application was placed in the rejection file. The officer retrieved the file, scanned through it, and came to the conclusion that there was no valid reason for that application to be rejected at this time. The officer was Black, the candidate was Black, the recruiter was white. The officer asked me to take a look at the application objectively and determine for myself if what he just witnessed was concerning.

Judging by what was contained in the application, I concluded that there was a serious problem. The file had been rejected on the grounds that the applicant had received three traffic tickets in one year. That was it — three traffic tickets. Everything else I read was stellar, including a university degree. I looked into what those tickets were issued for. Ready for this? One was issued for speeding, not excessively, I believe it was around fifteen kilometres over the posted speed limit. One was issued for failing to come to a complete stop at a stop line marked on the roadway . . . no, *really*. The third one was for driving a vehicle without a valid renewal sticker. Needless to say, the application was subsequently transferred to the receiving pile and moved forward. It turned out that this applicant drove to school and work every day, meaning he was on the road more than three hundred days of the year. By the way, his driving a vehicle without a valid renewal sticker turned out to be a result of borrowing his mother's car while his was being repaired. She had failed to renew her vehicle sticker.

So there was a huge red flag in front of me. Where was the accountability on behalf of the recruiters? Was there a limit to their authority with respect to the files they were managing? Turned out that each recruiter had no accountability whatsoever. They were allowed to make those types of decisions according to their whims throughout the process. They would make or find a justification for disqualifying a candidate as they pleased. I can't say that personal biases played a part in the selection process, but to me it was suspect.

My first major decree was that no recruiting officer shall be able to reject a candidate's file without consultation with, and the approval of, the unit sergeant. Also, at any stage of the recruiting process where a candidate is eliminated, the supervisor must be consulted and approve that elimination. Any potentially good candidates with concerns in their files need to be brought to my attention for determination. This was a radical departure from the normal operation of business but, to me, very necessary.

Let me tell you about an unintended consequence of this major shift in the way we now do business. It was brought to my attention by members of the community, friends, and acquaintances that candidates had been complaining about being treated rudely by recruiters at various stages of the process. I validated these complaints by locating several letters that had been filed by my predecessors. I addressed this with the line staff and new supervisors. I reminded them of the changing of the guard, the new reporting accountability structure, along with the decree that there will be no compromise in our professionalism with anyone, including candidates. This behaviour ceased immediately.

Another issue that cropped up early in my tenure was the disproportionate, almost exclusive number of Black candidates who were disqualified from moving through the recruiting process due to carding (or otherwise referred to as street checks, a distinction without a difference). Carding was a process used by police services throughout the province of Ontario where police would make contact with citizens by means of stopping, questioning, and documenting them for intelligence-gathering when no particular offence was being investigated. The extracted personal information was submitted into police systems to be used if required at a later date.

The original intent of this exercise was to provide police with an investigative tool that was retroactive by way of access to prior information. For instance, an officer on patrol at 1 a.m. comes across a parked vehicle containing two individuals, in the back lot of a business that stores electronic equipment and has been closed for several hours. Police make inquiries as to why they are parked in the lot. The parties have no legitimate reason for being there, but they have committed no crime. Police would then obtain personal information in the form of a street check, and file that information in the Service Records Management System, which is retrievable at some point in the future if required. One reason for collecting this information, they argued then, could be that there had been a rash of break-and-enters in electronic stores in that area, and investigators wanted to know about any suspicious activity past or present. The same could be said if police came across one or several people hanging out in an area of town where they did not reside that was rife with drug activity. Police would inquire and "card" those individuals. Sounds legitimate, right?

But this practice morphed into something quite different. More sinister. The practice became abusive, long surpassing the original intent of being an investigative tool. The police targeted young Black men primarily, to the point that this practice was ultimately deemed racist. Citizens are now imbued with the power, by way of provincial mandate, not to speak with police if they feel it is not in their best interest to do so. The police now must abide by certain procedures when operating in this manner. But prior to this change, I was dealing with this major issue.

Again, sitting in my office, I received a phone call from a colleague who had worked in one of the units that I had supervised. It reminded me of the importance of achieving a comfort level with folks who deal with you, building up trust and confidentiality. This member advised me that his brother had applied to this service several times and had been rejected. He told me that his brother was a good person who had all the qualities and requisite skills to be an asset to this service. The question was, why was he being rejected? Now, it was a policy of the York Regional Police that we would not provide a reason for declining a candidate's application at any point of the recruiting process. I was never quite sure why this was the case, but it seemed to be a policy adopted throughout the province. Anyway, I said that I would investigate his request. I asked the unit sergeant to bring me the file on this individual for me to review. The candidate was a visible minority who was at that time employed as a schoolteacher. He held two degrees and presented as an outstanding potential candidate. Just one blemish though: a police check into his name revealed that he had been carded many years ago by the Toronto Police Service. This information told a story of him being in a vehicle that was stopped by the police in which several known gang members had been identified. The candidate was now associated with these members. In the candidate's file was a note disqualifying him due to this event.

I felt the need to look into this further, so I detailed the sergeant to investigate this carding incident and report back to me. In a few days, the sergeant was in my office with new updates that caused me to recoil in my seat. The sergeant had tracked down the officer who had submitted the report. That officer located the notes that he had taken that evening and on review stated that the incident was not nearly as serious and it would appear: he believed the candidate had never been in the vehicle. He believed that one of the individuals in the vehicle had given a false name, that of the candidate. This information had never been included in that report. I asked the sergeant to bring the candidate in for an informal chat to find out what he knew about the incident. Well, lo and behold, the candidate stated he had never been in the vehicle, and the people who were had played basketball in the same league as he had. He was never associated with them in any way other than playing basketball. The upside to this story was that this individual went through our recruiting process, was eventually hired, and became the valedictorian at the Ontario Police College cohort, out of more than three hundred other recruits.

One more story regarding this blight known as carding. It was brought to my attention that a young man of colour was having no success with his applications to several police services, including York Region, and that this individual was worthy of at least moving forward. When I looked into his file, it came down to a matter of having been carded. Taking a deeper dive, I discovered that he had been playing basketball in a town-house complex with a number of individuals who were approached by the police. Information was extracted from the boys, and a number of them had police interactions on their records. The candidate had no such record but was now classed as an associate to the boys who did. It turns out that the candidate lived in the complex and played pick-up ball with whoever was available on any given day. This carding incident from so many years ago was now affecting his life. A simple check on the part of the recruiters could have exposed this seemingly innocuous police prac-tice. Unfortunately, so many potential candidates throughout the various police services in the province were similarly excluded. That has led to a disproportionate number of people of colour being ineligible to compete. Many never knew that they were turned down erroneously, due to the policy of not being told why one was disqualified.

The chief of police would ultimately determine the number of new members brought into the organization each year, which was directly related to many considerations — the number of retirements expected, resignations, increase in service demands, budget allotments and other such concerns. As for uniformed officers' replacements, our unit at that time was operating on three recruit classes per year consisting of an average of thirty to thirty-five hires in each class. Typically, the makeup of the classes would look like this: one or two diversity members, four to five females, and the rest white males. I was assigned to this portfolio to change that equation, but how? To me, it came down to numbers. It should be a priority to deal an even hand to new or potential recruits. What typically occurs, however, is that discrimination begins at the recruiting level, whereby potential hires are not recruited with that kind of deliberate attention to fairness and equality.

Another way to look at it: if two people are sitting around a poker table and the dealer deals the first person five cards and the second person forty cards (not part of the rules, mind you) to construct a hand, the person with the forty cards should be able to construct the better hand almost every time, statistically. This can be repeated over and over with the same results, whereas if each player is dealt the same number of cards, then the probabilities change, resulting in balance and fairness.

When we were attempting to fill a class of 30 new recruits from a pool of approximately 150 applicants, typically the overwhelming majority of applications received were from white male candidates. To demonstrate the point, in that group of 150 applications we would see about 10 visible minorities and 20 female applicants. The breakdown would become 120 white males, 20 females, and 10 visible minorities. We would then vet the applicants and root out the ones who were the weakest or not at all suitable for the job. So let's cut the groups in half. This would result in 60 white males, 10 females, and 5 visible minority candidates remaining. Our new working number is now 75 applicants. Remember, our goal is to hire 30 new recruits. Continuing the process, we expect to lose another 45 people. Let's cut the groups in half again. Now we have 30 white males, 5 females and 2.5 visible minorities. Even if we erred on the side of the visible minority candidates and allowed the 2.5 to become 3 and we subtract 8 more white males, we still see that the overwhelming class structure will remain a predominantly white intake of new recruits. Just by sheer numbers alone, visible minorities and women were at a significant disadvantage in each class.

Now I'm making the claim that the females are white in this example. There will be times where a candidate will be female and a member of the visible minority groups, but I believe you get the point. What we needed was a balanced protocol, whereby the intake matched the demographic ratio of the population. Over the course of several months, the recruiting unit would receive hundreds of applications. Over time, we were in possession of literally thousands of applications that were not looked into until neces-sary. The answer was in front of us within the applications already on file. What I decided to do was to filter through those files and remove the female and visible minority candidates who self-identified as such. I then added them to the ongoing or current process. The result was the number ratio of the two underserved groups (women and diverse candidates) increased, making it more balanced as the process unfolded. The results were aston-ishing. Providing these two groups the opportunity to compete within a more equitable process allowed them to succeed at a higher rate, making the classes more diverse, as they should have been all along. And here is the beauty of what happened; we did not touch, alter, or change anything to do with the standards of the recruiting process. All the testing protocols and requirements remained the same. The interviews were the same, the back-ground investigations were the same. All I did was balance out the numbers.

If we had a process where 50 percent of the candidates were white males and the other 50 percent were diverse candidates, then may the best people win. At that point, we would have nothing to complain about. But when the odds are five to one, you're not going to get the balance that you intend — or maybe that was the intention all along. Remember, there was a time when visible minority officers were not hired at all, so in terms of numbers, we were already at a disadvantage. Anything that can be legitimately done to change or assist with that issue should be welcomed and advanced.

The results were immediate and impressive. By the third class, we had achieved a 30 percent improvement in the makeup of the classes. By the following year, we had achieved a 50 percent diversity ratio in our hiring. For this percentage, we include females and diverse candidates. So any given class of thirty officers going forward would contain fifteen racially diverse and female recruits and fifteen white male recruits.

This monumental achievement provides me with a proud sense of accomplishment as I revisit my past employment with the organization. Now, I must say the members of that unit worked extremely hard each day to facilitate the organization's goals. They were unwavering in the ideals attached to producing a balanced group of new officers and proud of the results of their efforts in that regard.

Another initiative was to increase the diversity within the unit itself. On my arrival, there were no Black members in the unit. To be fair, that had not always been the case throughout its lifespan. However, it was the case when I took over. The difficulty was that the unit was operating at maximum authorized strength, which meant that any new addition would have to come by way of someone leaving. My only option was to provide opportunities to visible minority officers by bringing them in temporally for three to six months of training opportunities. This move proved to be very advantageous for the seconded officers and the unit overall. It provided a way to supplement our manpower, allowing more candidates to be processed while providing training along with assessment of individual officers for future placements or advancements. This brought a diversity of thought and optics that I felt advanced the organization.

We delved deeply into the world of recruiting with a vision. Our service spent an exorbitant amount of money making sure that we were visible at the many events that would provide us with an opportunity to connect with racialized communities to showcase and recruit for the service. We delivered seminars espousing the virtues of policing in York Region and called for folks to join our team. We poured money and resources into outreach and cultural recruiting. We went to them. YRP was everywhere, recruiting in universities, shopping malls, cultural fairs, and ethnic events. We were in churches, mosques, synagogues, and temples. We held job fairs, information sessions, station tours, and ride-alongs. We attended conferences, seminars, backyard BBQs, and sporting events. We advertised in local newspapers, ethnic programming, radio, television, and every platform of social media that we could access. All in the pursuit of keeping a sustainable pool of viable candidates with the goal of creating a more diverse workplace. This was an investment in our organizational future.

There was no question that we were a great organization within the world of policing, both sworn and civilian. The results spoke for themselves. We were truly an organization favoured by many and emulated by others.

COMMUNITY EXPECTATIONS

In general, in North America, the public has come to regard the police, symbolically, as the keeper of their safety and security. What is paramount to any community is that they are safe and feel safe. The fear of crime, in a great many instances, interferes with their standard of living, thus reducing quality of life. The community looks for the police to provide service that adequately focuses on crime prevention and victimization reduction. They demand that criminals be caught, prosecuted, and eventually incarcerated. They want to know that their police service is properly equipped, trained, and capable of performing the required tasks that will address their fear-reduction needs. The public is also looking for fiscal responsibility on behalf of the service, along with some input and accountability in police matters.

Of course, one might ask, who do I mean by *public* when I refer to those who trust the police to keep them safe? I'd like to think I'm including all people, but there is an underlying truth that Black, brown, and Indigenous people of colour have a different take. To some, the police have come to symbolize tyranny and are not the keepers of their safety and security. They don't feel safe even when the police are nearby because the police are often the problem. This affects their quality of life, innately messaging that the quality of service they receive is that of an underserved group of people in real jeopardy. Yes, they want the police to be properly trained, equipped, and capable of performing their required tasks, but to do it without stereotypical views, bigotry, racial profiling, and all the trappings that go with inferior policing. When BIPOC parents are considered derelict for not giving their teenage children "the talk" about how they should deal with police interactions, we definitely have a problem. But all is not lost. During my time in the service, organizationally we worked deliberately towards credible solutions, one of which was incorporating community engagement into our police work strategy.

With the blessing of former chiefs Armand La Barge and Eric Jolliffe, our organization put an emphasis on working with the community through a Diversity, Equity, and Inclusion Bureau. The role of this bureau was to build and promote stronger partnerships within the community — getting to know each other. This bureau trained officers in the areas of human rights, diversity, hate crime investigation, and community relations. As a result, officers would gain sensitivity, and an understanding of the traditions, customs, and mindsets of those whom they served. We recognized the importance of being informed as to the spiritual and religious diversity within our communities. Many large communities within cities can be considered a microcosm of the world, and as such are susceptible to events overseas that evoke political discourse, passions, anger, revenge, elation, and many other real emotions that affect our communities. There is value in having a working knowledge of the cultural discourse of others. So a creative solution was to create and implement a mandatory place-of-worship tour for all new recruits, connecting them with religious leaders in an effort to gain a deeper understanding of, and appreciation for, the various religious faiths and practices within these communities and cultures. Most officers who have experienced this tour believed that it formulated a new-found understanding of, and a better tolerance for, these diverse cultures.

My definition of community engagement involves the commitment of not only law enforcement officials, but also citizens working together to utilize their knowledge and skills by first understanding the needs of both parties. It rests on the belief that solutions for today's disconnect can free people and the police to explore creative new ways to address persistent concerns beyond a narrow focus on individual crime incidents. The idea is to take a broad, futuristic view of how we should be interacting and work towards those goals.

During my time in the York Regional Police, forming alliances, especially with BIPOC community organizations, allowed staff members the opportunity to operate as ambassadors within these alliances. This approach assisted with achieving goals, increased the service's sensitivity to citizens' expectations, allowed emerging issues to surface, generated a deeper understanding of cultural norms of the various populations, and garnered support for public outreach. It forced officers to work in unfamiliar subject areas, form coalitions with new types of knowledge experts, devise and measure pertinent key performance indicators, and perpetuate a culture of learning. This type of engagement is the here and now in policing and offers the public solutions to their concerns about their perceived victimization at the hands of law enforcement. Community engagement emphasizes the police and the wider community working together to create innovative problem-solving initiatives — the right way of doing business, I might add — in their communities. In my assessment, when an organization is answerable to the public, there is an obligation on their part to find out what is expected along with how and when that expectation is delivered. When the police are recognized as part of the community as opposed to the overseers, attitudes change on both sides for the better.

In the Greater Toronto Area, several community organizations germinated and flourished as people searched for collective bodies to add to the weight of their complaints against systems that did not have a balanced formula upon application. Groups such as The Black Action Defense Committee, Tropicana, Markham African Caribbean Association, The Black Business Association, The Association of Black Law Enforcers, The Jamaican Canadian Association, and others made significant contributions to tabling concerns and working towards acceptable results. More specifically, they articulated what the Black community expects from the police. In every initial meeting that I have been involved with, there was a palpable excitement in meeting a Black police officer. That officer signified several things. There was a feeling that the group now had a chance to move their agenda forward. It is no secret that officers of colour are few and far between. Seeing one denoted that some of us are squeezing through the door that was shut so tightly for years. It's a rebuke of the notion, perpetrated through the various media outlets, that Black men amount to drug dealers and absent fathers. It denotes that some among us are talented and capable of becoming police officers, despite the job requirements and general opposition in our way. It's a statement that some of us are on the inside with a lived experience that is advantageous to the cause. It means that there is now a true, reliable connection between the community and the police service.

For the most part, the communities' expectations could be classified as enhancement, acceleration, engagement, and cooperation. Enhancement in the form of more officers of colour, representing the mosaic of the province. Acceleration in the placement of Black officers in positions within the service that were traditionally elusive, such as specialty units and higher ranks. Engagement by demonstrating commitment to working with the various community groups to understand their perspective on how their community is being policed. Cooperation in that each part needs the other. It's about working together and understanding the premise of shared experiences and exchange of knowledge.

I was often the conduit in this respect. My community was regularly surprised and extremely pleased by the magnitude of what our service was willing to do in order to enhance relationships. Several impactful examples are: partnering with the Association of Black Law Enforcers in several of their Annual Scholarship & Awards Balls; delivering police and civilian enhancement training to community members; sponsoring various organizations in putting on multicultural events; providing police resources such as Identification Bureau members to assist with documenting community functions, making police officers available to not only be present but to actively participate in events, as well as providing police vehicles and the use of police facilities as part of community support.

Some of the most productive results in terms of building credit in the community happened as a direct around-the-table conversation with community members. I was part of a number of committees where engagement was the key to unlocking our past entrenched positions. Because of our philosophy of community inclusion in all aspects of policing, we were very successful in building another arm of the service operated by the citizens we serve.

To whom much is given, much is required. Throughout my rise within the service, I noticed added expectations from the Black community on me. It was well known in the community that I was engaged and provided my contact information liberally. This was an intentional act on my part, because I honestly felt that I was able to help young people, as I had the knowledge, skills, and ability to advise and direct them. I was on the inside with a voice and intestinal fortitude to use my influence. They expected me to put their concerns on the table and use my placement to advance change. They expected me to show up at events and support their efforts culturally using my police connections. I made the time and effort to build bridges between the community and the police in hopes that we could find common ground to ease the distrust that was evident between these two entities.

My phone never stopped ringing. They wanted me to be an example for their children and to support their efforts to be successful in career endeavours. It was not uncommon for voices on the other end of the phone to let me know that a son, daughter, or relative was considering a career in law enforcement and would I consider providing guidance, mentorship, and utilizing my connections to support the cause? Community members would call me with a range of questions from wanting to know how to handle a traffic ticket to the best way to handle a domestic situation. Many calls were from Black mothers concerned about their teenage sons and police contact. Most of them were paralyzed with fear that their sons would be incarcerated or killed by being at the wrong place, at the wrong time, due to gang-related activities or at the hands of police. I spent hundreds of hours lending my inside perspective on many of these matters. What they wanted most was the mentorship, guidance, and coaching of these young men, either from me or someone from our community that I could recommend. They had little trust in white police officers based on past experiences. I took on many of these young men in a mentorship role with a good number of successes. Some did not work out so well. Let me tell you about a young man who will always stay with me. He is with me because my efforts to help him fell far short of what eventually happened.

My daughter Brianna was around fifteen years of age when she snuck several of her friends into the house for a party while my wife and I were away. It turned out that one of her friends went into our bedroom and stole money and jewellery. He was quickly pointed out by other attendees at the party as the one who had taken the items. Brianna told me the next day what had happened. I knew this young man's mother fairly well due to our common acquaintances and meeting her at several community events. Her son was approximately sixteen at the time. She arranged for me to meet with her son to retrieve the items and money that he had stolen. She further pleaded with me to mentor him as she could see the direction he was heading in and was terrified of the possibilities. I did exactly that. We spent dozens of hours together getting to know each other.

Early in our mentoring sessions, I asked him what he wanted to do with his life in terms of a profession in a few years from now. He did not hesitate and replied that he wanted to be a gangster. I asked him to explain. He told me he wanted the lifestyle, with the bling (diamonds and gold), cars, girls, drugs, and badass attitude of a gangster.

"Damn! That's what you want?"

"Yep, that's what I want."

With this revelation, I knew I needed to invest heavily in this young man, which I did. Together we explored what it means to be a gangster with all of the negative consequences that are connected to that lifestyle. We hung out, and I exposed him to as many positive environments as I could. About eight months later I received a phone call from his mother that her son had been arrested for a homicide relating to a drive-by gang-related shooting in Toronto. My heart was broken. I had come to really like this young man, who had all the possibilities in the world not to have ended up this way. He did what he said he would do. He was in the process of becoming a gang member. My understanding is he went on a ride-along with some gangbangers, and as part of the initiation process he was told to shoot the victim, which he did.

Fortunately for him, he was charged as a young offender and reaped the benefits of that status. He spent several years in a secure youth facility and is now back in the community. I seriously contemplated visiting him while he was in custody but couldn't find the strength. So much work, expectation, and hope had gone up in a puff of gunsmoke. I spent many days and nights revisiting our bond, trying to make sense of this madness. To this day, the right answers have eluded me.

What the community sees is another lost young man with potential. What I saw was a young man who slipped out of my hands and exhibited what was expected by others, influenced by stereotyping. I am at a loss to explain exactly what went wrong. This should not have happened. Yes, he was wrapped in the envelope of a single mother struggling to make ends meet and many of the societal trappings from that scenario, but from my vantage point, things weren't so far off the rails that this had to be the result. When he was released, I received a call from his mother. Another mother with perpetual tears in her eyes worried to death about the future of her children. We spoke a few times after that but eventually lost contact. As for the young man, I have never laid eyes on him or spoke to him since our mentorship days. I have often thought of reaching out, but I think I'm terrified of hearing the rest of the story, just in case it's worse than the one I've just related to you.

I must add that, overall, my encounters with community members have been invaluable. I have met some of the brightest, most uplifting future leaders on this planet. One day, out of the blue, I received a phone call from a young woman who'd attended a workshop that had been facilitated by members of our recruiting branch. She'd heard me speak at that event, keying in on my invitation to be accessible to any who would like more information, and took me up on it. At the other end of the call was an absolutely brilliant individual who, a minute or two into our conversation, had me committing to help her start a career with the York Regional Police. She was working with troubled youth and felt that she needed to expand her reach beyond this one specific calling. My strategy was straightforward mentorship, coaching, and guiding. This young woman never missed a step and really held me to account. She worked tirelessly, homing in on her shortcomings and resolving to make herself a better candidate. After several attempts, she finally received the phone call stating she would be hired as a police constable.

This story is important to me, as this young woman knew what she wanted to accomplish, and nothing was going to stop her in her quest towards that goal. She is a testament to the value of connectivity meeting willingness to help, equalling success.

I remember one evening, while I was chairing a campaign meeting for the candidate of record for the Jane and Finch community federal elections, one young man put up his hand and asked a question. I don't believe any of us at this particular meeting had ever seen him before. He surprised everyone in the room with his point and delivery, including me. My memory fails me as to the exact question, but that is not the salient point; his presence was. He approached me after the meeting and asked if he could join the campaign. The candidate and I welcomed him with open arms. This was the beginning of a truly great friendship that has endured to this day. This young man had heard about the meeting and made the effort to attend primarily to get a read on the leaders. Although accomplished in his own right, he knew that in order for him to grow personally and professionally, he needed to elevate his game. He often would say to me, "You have to walk among the leaders to be a leader." I took that as both a compliment and a challenge. I sensed his determination, which spoke to his commitment. I told him, "Put the work in, and I'll make you a leader." He did, and it worked. He evolved into one of my invaluable go-to guys during the campaign. Outside the election, I involved him in almost every program, event, task, engagement, networking opportunity, and assignment that I was part of. He relished the opportunities and committed to not disappointing me. He was by my side for a number of years. I'm pleased to say that this young man is now the owner of two companies and leads his own teams quite successfully. He is but one example of the quality within our community that, given a chance, will blossom and contribute in meaningful ways.

∞

As a member of the Black community by virtue of birth, I have known and felt the struggles that are inherent when your skin colour is exposed to the world in specific geographical areas that are controlled by non-Black people. Right or wrong, I have always felt an expectation from the Black community to work collectively in unison to fight back, with the goal of equal rights at the core of our opposition. The Black community in general is not a monolithic group in appearance nor in consciousness. We differ in perspectives and processes as much as the next group. What we do have in common is a judgement by some who see our skin colour as offensive and have the wherewithal to impact our lives negatively. When collectively we did have a meeting of the minds, it felt euphoric when the momentum was in full swing, usually after some horrendous tragic event involving a Black subject suffering injustice. For the most part, we would band together with a single voice, demanding and expecting something be done.

The Rodney King beating in 1991 at the hands of the Los Angeles police — captured on video in all its violent, dehumanizing technicolour for all the world to see — was one such event. Four officers were put on trial for savagely beating Rodney. Three of them were acquitted, and the jury failed to reach a verdict on the fourth. The ensuing riot lasted six days, killing 63 people with 2,383 injured. Having viewed the indisputable evidence in their living rooms, it was unfathomable to most citizens that the system could allow those officers to get away with the crime of unjustly beating a Black man almost to death. I, of course, like the rest of the community, was in lockstep with protesting; however, I did not condone the rioting. But the community did come together to demand justice and change. On the other hand, I have been supremely disappointed when there are causes that should be addressed by Black people with one voice but there are dissenters who for one reason or another work against their self-interest and the Black communities.

Closer to home, there was unity in our community when a young Black man by the name of Raymond Constantine Lawrence was shot and killed by the Toronto Police. This happened just three days after the acquittal of the officers charged in the Rodney King beating. A protest was organized by members of the Black Action Defense Committee, advancing the fact that Raymond, twenty-two years of age at the time, was the fourteenth Black man shot by the Toronto police since 1978. People took to the streets, converging in the downtown core of the city. The crowd was angry and had had enough of what was perceived as anti-Black racism resulting in the abuse, even murder, of primarily Black men at the hands of police. Tempers flared, glass windows shattered, and bricks rained down on the police, who were attempting to keep the peace. The Yonge Street Riot, as we have come to know it, had the Black community along with other diverse groups speaking with a collective voice. While I am not in any way condoning the violence or property damage, it was uplifting to see so many people come together to demand change for the better.

As a whole, our community is very much pro-police. It's the overreach in the form of racial profiling, the unnecessary use of force, and the extra-judicial application of the law that create resentment, along with the outward appearance of the makeup of many police services, denoting the oppressor that people rebel against. In my view, most of the complaints are warranted. As a young man trying to find my place in the world, I was bombarded with examples of this collective unfairness. On more than one occasion when I was hanging out with my group of friends, we were approached by police who treated us with suspicion and scorn. Knowing that we were not up to anything destructive or criminal, all we wanted was for the police to try to make us feel like we belonged and were safe. Unfortunately, the opposite was true. On the odd occasion that we ran into a good police officer, we were all smiles, cherishing the interaction. We view police as a special class of people who are necessary. We want policing and have no tolerance for the criminal element among us. A victim is a victim regardless of the colour of the perpetrator. Our community will continue to espouse this common theme until we are heard and believed. We are truly working towards solutions that allow police to perform their necessary duties in a manner that is detached from abuse. The police are, for the most part, working passionately towards the formation of a cohesiveness between the citizens they serve and the members they employ. If this ever comes to pass, quoting the great "Satchmo," Louis Daniel Armstrong, "what a wonderful world" this would be.

There are some activists among us who have committed a lifetime of work to the pursuit of what is right and just. Some have carried the slack of those who talk but lack the action or engagement to support the cause. They have invested thousands of hours of time for "us," encouraging all of us to unify as we know we are capable of doing, and moving the notion of unity forward. Equity is a right that should be enjoyed by all. Some have stepped into the ring and never left. I recognize some as champions among champions. Their contributions have changed the landscape of this country for the better, so another round of applause is not only necessary, it is well deserved.

ORGANIZATION FOR THE ENCOURAGEMENT OF CANADIAN CITIZENSHIP

The Organization for the Encouragement of Canadian Citizenship, formally known as the Citizenship Initiative Group, was created out of a perceived need to encourage, aid, and assist permanent residents who are in good standing to take the next steps towards Canadian citizenship. In 2009, I was contacted by Audrey Walters, former president of the Black Business and Professional Association, asking me if I would join her team, as she was now a candidate of record for York West riding, vying for the position of Member of Parliament in the upcoming 2011 federal election. Knowing very little about the inner workings of elections and believing that engagement at this level was indeed necessary, it didn't take me long to agree to participate.

Initially, my participation was peripheral — attending meetings, taking on assigned tasks, gathering material. I found that my organizational skills, gained from years of structure inherent in the very nature of my profession, were a valued commodity, making me one of the go-to foundational members of the team. My role increased, as did my immersion into the world of politics.

One of the critical necessary tasks of most campaigns was the concept of door-knocking, meaning getting out in the community, literally knocking on doors and meeting the constituents. York West riding consisted of an eclectic group of residents, with a large Black and brown contingent. The team contributed hundreds of hours meeting and speaking with community members and listening to their concerns and how and if they intended to vote.

What was absolutely shocking was that a fair number of the Black residents were excited at the realization of a Black female candidate and would vote for her if they could, but unfortunately they were ineligible to by virtue of status. Many of them were considered landed immigrants but had never applied for Canadian citizenship. To vote in a federal election in this country, one must be a Canadian citizen.

There are several ways to obtain citizenship: be born in Canada, be born abroad to Canadian citizens, be adopted abroad by a Canadian citizen, or by naturalization (meeting certain criteria and successfully completing tests for citizenship). Many of the folks we spoke to had been in the country for many years, even decades, but had never taken the next steps to become citizens. The reasons why were vast and varied, but suffice it to say missing out on this tremendous opportunity, in my mind, was truly unfortunate.

What are the benefits of Canadian citizenship? Well, let's start off with the right to vote in federal elections. Then there's the right to the cherished Canadian passport, which is valued and respected all over the world. You have the right to apply for certain government jobs that are exclusive to citizens. You have the benefit of visa-free travel to over 150 countries, including the United States. You also have the right to consular services while abroad. You have the opportunity to sit on some boards and commissions that are restricted. Also, children born to Canadian citizens abroad have the right to Canadian citizenship.

It was felt collectively by the team that we had stumbled into a problematic state of affairs that set the Black community further away from inclusivity. Readily at hand, politicians have information on who is actively engaged in the political process as it pertains to their voting patterns and their eligibility to vote. If you are not eligible to vote, the politicians will not waste their time or effort to make you relevant, because to them, you are not. They want voters . . . *period.*

It was a treasured experience having participated in that political campaign at an elevated level, with all its intricacies and machinations related to electoral politics. But there was still the dogged problem of so many folks not availing themselves of the right to citizenship, therefore disqualifying themselves as potential voters in a federal election. During one of the team's after-action reviews of our performance during the election cycle, it was clear that full participation of a large portion of the residents in that community could have made the difference to the election results.

Audrey and I agreed to hold further discussions on what could be done to rectify what was clearly a deficit in that community. In subsequent meetings, we founded the Citizenship Initiative Group with the express goal of informing and encouraging permanent residents, who were in good standing, to apply for and obtain Canadian citizenship. We felt that landed immigrants needed to understand the importance of civic engagement, and we wanted to empower these residents to take control of their future as equal members of the society in which they live. This would be achieved by showing them the benefits of Canadian citizenship, civic responsibilities, duties, and obligations, and teaching them how to prepare and apply for the process.

Our goal was simple and direct. We created a program that was, and still is, meaningful, tangible, measurable, and sustainable. We achieved this by using a three-pronged approach, the first of which is an educational presentation on the benefits of obtaining Canadian citizenship. We would follow this up with another session in which we assisted qualified persons in completing the required application forms, verify that they had all the necessary documents to prove their eligibility for citizenship completed, and provide resource information if required. The last portion of this initiative was to help facilitate citizenship ceremonies.

What was now required was a volunteer team ready and willing to make a long-term commitment for the extremely demanding task of delivering this messaging. Audrey and I hand-picked five of the most amazing individuals we have ever had the privilege of knowing. The founding members were: Rahel Appiagyei-David, executive administrator; Paulette Johnson, subject matter expert; Kay-Dean Lazarus, community outreach director; and Maureen and Cecil Emanuel, a wife and husband who took on the roles of hands-on steering committee. It is with profound sadness that I tell you that both Maureen and Cecil are now deceased. Our team collectively mourns each day that passes, knowing how wonderful they both were, and we certainly cherished the time that we were able to be in their presence — we are blessed by having known them.

In our presentations, we talk about the benefits of Canadian citizenship, qualification and disqualifiers, the application process, dual citizenship, the Canadian passport, and the recent changes to the law, and we stress the importance of voting. We discuss at length the collective value of each person's individual contribution. We affirm that they have the power to change the course of history in this country and that they have the right to choose government representation. We inform them that they have the right to the full protection of this country while travelling abroad.

In 2006, as a result of the Israel-Lebanon conflict, where loss of life was imminent, fifteen thousand Canadian citizens who were in Lebanon and in harm's way were returned to Canada at the government's expense — how powerful is that! We stress that it is incumbent on all of us to be civically engaged, because that is what is required to adequately represent our people. Be a part of the solution. We know knowledge is power — we need to pass along that information through "Each One Teach One." We know that there is solidarity in numbers through collective representation. We have to position ourselves to effect change by exercising our right to choose who represents us in the nation's capital, provincially, and at our city halls via local governments and municipalities. We stress the need to position ourselves so that we have access to certain government positions, understanding that not all federal jobs are open to non-citizens.

The support that the Organization for the Encouragement of Canadian Citizenship has received from various organizations, such as the Caribbean Consular Corps, the college of bishops, and the community at large, has been invaluable. Big thanks to Omar Dingwall, who dedicated countless hours to ensure we would prevail. We are truly grateful, and as we move towards the future, we endeavour to maintain those relationships and create new partnerships in pursuit of the best possible outcomes.

There is an urgency in the Black community to take control of our future as equal members of the society in which we live. Canadian citizenship allows you a simple and tangible way to have your voice heard. Canada is considered one of the best countries in the world in which to live and raise a family. It is a safe country, offering political freedom, a thriving economy, multiculturalism, employment opportunities, education, and social programs. Canadian citizenship means participating in our democratic lifestyle, utilizing the enormous economic potential, and enjoying the rich cultural traditions of this country. Citizens have an opportunity to participate in the governing of this nation in fundamental ways. By becoming Canadian citizens, you are now part of the solution, working towards creating a fairer and more just society. As new Canadians, you have a duty and responsibility to work towards making this nation a better place than when you arrived.

BLACK HISTORY MONTH

One of my most cherished times while working for the police service was the month of February, Black History Month (BHM). To me, it was our time to showcase who we are and what we're about. It was a time when officers of all stripes and colours were actively engaged in exposing and elevating the Black experience in all its iterations. Black History Month fed my soul.

As I advanced in prominence in the organization, I was called upon not only by the service but also by the community to organize events and take on the role of keynote speaker. In the latter part of my career, it was a rewarding chore to sort out, make the time for, and commit to the many events that crossed my path. In particular, York Regional Police hosted a grand celebration each year at one of their facilities that attracted hundreds of community folks. I must say that the organization's commitment to this cause was second to none. We were the envy of police services across the country. There was not a single BHM event held by York Regional Police that I was not part of, either as a member of the organizing committee or as a participant. I was proud to wear the uniform, standing in front of so many with the opportunity to speak to my passion *with* passion. These events gave me the opportunity to infuse my story into the greater narrative of what was possible.

I have some thoughts around BHM that formed the cornerstone of many of the speeches that I presented, but first, a brief history of how Black History Month evolved in Canada. Founded in 1978, the Ontario Black History Society is the organization in Canada that successfully initiated the formal celebration of February as Black History Month within the city of Toronto. In December 1995, after a motion introduced by the first Black woman elected as a Canadian Member of Parliament, the Hon. Jean Augustine, the Canadian House of Commons unanimously voted in favour of officially recognizing the month of February of each year to be Black History Month.

So, one might ask, what are we as a people trying to achieve with such a distinct recognition and appreciation of our history? It's sad to even have to utter that question in the first place, but quite necessary to answer. I viewed Black History Month as an opportunity to display the rich heritage, significant contributions, and outstanding achievements of Black Canadians in building our great nation of Canada. The essence of Black History Month events is not so much the singing and dancing, nor is it the show and spectacle. It's about remembering the past, dealing with the present, and working towards a better future. It's because we care. It's because we owe it to our past to keep a promise to build a better future. It's because we shall never forget the legacy of injustice, slavery, inhumane treatment, the stench of being violated, and the separation and despair. It's to ensure that human deprivation is addressed, challenged, and ultimately eradicated. It's to forgive and not forget; it's to repair, not to acquiesce; it's to provide hope and not hopelessness; it's about building self-worth; it's about standing proud and holding to your principles. It's about knowing who you are and knowing your value. It's about our history and our future. We need to be engaged at all levels within agencies, organizations, boards, commissions, as well as governmental bureaus and the like. To effect change, you — we — need to be at the table where decisions are made. Our future and that of our offspring depends on it. Sitting on the sidelines complaining is not acceptable. Banging at the door from the outside is not as effective as being inside with the ability to unlock the door.

It was not unusual to have politicians of all levels of government representing various governmental agencies in attendance at Black History Month events. It was important for me to state that our governments need to have a covenant to operate with openness, trust, and honesty with their community partners to share values, objectives, and goals. The community must also do the same. This is what we call unity, and that is why we celebrate together. Together we have the knowledge base, required skills, and proven ability to achieve. We must continue to work together as a unified group equipped with our wisdom, experience, sense of justice, education, and fair play. Time has taught us that together we can achieve. Progress depends on the choices we make today for tomorrow.

As we recognize the tumultuous journey that Black people all over the globe have travelled for these many years, we must also speak to the resilience and progression demonstrated from the first steps, and to the founding principles and guidance that enable us to advance in our spiritual and life-sustaining values. This recognition also speaks to the invaluable mentorships and partnerships that have enabled thousands of individuals to enhance their lives. Yes, we have been on a journey; let's talk about that journey for a moment.

To a person of colour, the road to justice and equity is not always straight and is always under construction. There are curbs called unfair work practices. Roundabouts called systemic racism. Speed bumps called human rights violations. Red lights called Canadian Charter of Rights breaches. Caution signs called intolerance. Flat tires called bigotry and hatred. But if you have a spare called determination; an engine called perseverance; insurance called Martin Luther King, Malcolm X, Barack Obama, Lincoln Alexander, Jean Augustine, Rosa Parks, Viola Desmond, Denham Jolly, Violet Williams, Bromley Armstrong, and too many others to mention here; and a little faith along with the drive to make it, you will reach justice and success.

Proud members of our Black community who happen to be officers and civilians serving in law enforcement, are part of the rich legacy that encompasses this country. We are ambassadors espousing the virtues of this union and are uniquely positioned to provide testimony in the first person. I bring your attention to Staff Sergeant Tony Browne, who up until his retirement was the longest-serving Black York Regional Police officer, having dedicated more than thirty-three years to that organization. There was a time when Tony was the only Black officer on the service. Staff Sergeant Browne in many ways laid the foundation for the brothers and sisters who eventually joined him on this epic journey.

I would be remiss if I didn't mention two others who forged the way, carrying the load, determined to make this organization one of the foremost leaders in terms of the diversification of its members and enhancing the dialogue and partnerships within our diverse community. Deputy Chief André Crawford and Superintendent Rick Veerappan were instrumental in leading meaningful, lasting relationships deep within our complex communities.

Understanding the profound concept of unity, several brave and astute Black officers, led by now retired provincial assistant deputy minister of children's services, David Mitchell, working in the criminal justice system, formed a collective body to address a number of inequalities and injustices that were pervasive in the system in the 1990s and beyond. This led to the formation of the Association of Black Law Enforcers (ABLE) in 1992, with an aim to improve the image of law enforcement within the Black community.

Since its inception, ABLE has provided support and advocacy to Black and other racial minority law enforcement professionals and members of the visible minority communities. They engage in social issues relating to race, discrimination in the workplace, and general encounters and experiences of unfairness. ABLE's determination to improve the lives and the day-to-day experiences of members remains at the forefront of their efforts. In 2011, I became president of this organization, serving two terms. I did so believing that our work in promoting racial harmony, cultural pride, equal rights, and justice improves the working relationship and image of law enforcement within the province of Ontario and the nation of Canada. My mandate was to challenge assumptions, shift attitudes, and redefine change as this accurately denotes our function throughout our existence. Challenging assumptions in the early days was a risky business. The formulation of organizations such as ABLE was initially viewed as racially divisive and unnecessary. The work of shifting attitudes is evident in the respect and inclusion that this association has received from many of the organizations that make up our criminal justice system and various communities. During ABLE's inaugural ball, held on April 20, 1993, the chief justice of the Federal Court, Julius Isaac, said the following: "The formation of the association marks a new level of maturity in the Black community in Ontario and in my view will contribute greatly to the promotion of the public good."

Through the spirit of collaborative partnerships, ABLE engages other agencies to work collectively on justice-related issues that affect communities. ABLE provides mentorship, counselling, coaching, and guidance to those interested in law-enforcement-related careers. Additionally, ABLE provides annual scholarships to students pursuing post-secondary studies in areas relating to criminal justice. To this end, to date, it has provided around $262,000 in scholarship funding to 148 recipients. I know that we have contributed to building the leaders of tomorrow who will advance our cause. The secret to success was following the time-tested and proven methods of community involvement, community engagement, powerful mentorship, coaching, and support. Understanding that there were specific issues that we were not equipped to manage on our own, I would then reach out to established groups already engaged in doing those very things.

During my tenure, I had the opportunity to facilitate an annual career fair that successfully provided unique opportunities for Black and other racialized applicants. My aim was to cause a positive generational shift in thinking as it pertains to the representation, fairness, and elevation of Black and other racialized individuals working within the criminal justice system.

One of the major issues of the day was dealing with the matter of racial profiling, which landed squarely at my feet. Our organization defined it as "investigative or enforcement activity initiated by an individual officer based on their stereotypical, prejudicial, or racist perceptions of who is likely to be involved in wrongdoing or criminal activity." It was a matter that needed to be confronted head-on with no agenda other than to call it out for what it was and provide practical, responsible solutions. I had the responsibility to stay laser-focused on the position taken by the association that racial profiling is real, not a perception in the mind of some. We organized community meetings, agency workshops, and public town hall gatherings and facilitated conferences offering solutions from our point of view. We collected statistics for documentation and monitoring purposes, and with this information we were able to pinpoint and specifically address the problem. Just as important was giving our colleagues a *Reader's Digest* guide of who we, as Black people, collectively, are. Using a quote from David McFarlane, national coordinator of the National Black Police Association United Kingdom: "If they don't know anything about the people they're policing or their culture, they're necessarily going to treat them differently."

As the association evolved, institutions big and small that were engaged in the business of justice reached out to ABLE for advice or requested our point of view on evolving matters. It was important to me that ABLE lead by example by providing the knowledge base, required skills, and proven ability to achieve. On Saturday, June 24, 2018, I represented ABLE as a panellist on the Policing People: Society and the Justice System panel held at the Harbourfront Centre Theatre in Toronto. This session was part of the Luminato arts and culture festival.

The session commenced after viewing the play *Out the Window*, written and directed by Liza Balkan, which focused on the death of Otto Vass, who had a mental crisis episode in 2000 that resulted in police engaging Vass physically. At the end of the contact, Vass died. The officers were charged with manslaughter and were eventually acquitted. The play also focused on the inquest and public sentiments.

I was on a panel with John Sewell (former mayor of Toronto) and Mike Federico (retired deputy chief of Toronto Police), speaking to issues of police interactions with people in crisis, moderated by Idil Abdillahi. The overall theme and line of questioning centred on police training. John

Sewell spoke to the issues he'd had over the years, calling upon the Police Services Board to make changes to the way police operate, in particular the application of force. Mike Federico spoke to the policies, procedures, and training his members received. I spoke on the evolution of police training and what I felt was a deficiency in the current training. Although police receive very good training on how to manage a variety of situations, which is evident in the number of events that end appropriately, there are some that clearly are not handled properly. My point was that the clear gap in the current training is the lack of responsibility and accountability of on-scene officers in managing each other. It is incumbent on each officer, upon seeing other officers out of control, to indicate as such, to stop the behaviour, and to take over the interaction. This is but one example of the intricate role ABLE has played that directly contributed to the creation of a more informed community.

We have been blessed with leaders such as Jay Hope, Lynell Nolan, D.J. Marks, Karl Davis, Keith Forde, Peter Sloly, David McLeod, Sonia Thomas, Kenton Chance, Ingrid Berkeley-Brown, and Dave Mitchell, each of whom has redefined change and made us see and aspire to new heights and elevated dreams. We draw on their accomplishments to inspire the new collection of members that are keen to do the same.

So I'm going to drift a little bit and speak to the converted, which is probably most of the readers of this book. The issue is our children and the genocide that is being perpetrated by them on each other. The statistics are staggering, especially involving our young Black men. The reasons are varied and often complicated.

How do we reach our youth, disenfranchised and depressed, angry at themselves, their immediate family, and the world? The ones who are doing poorly in school? The ones who are right now taking that hit of crack cocaine or crystal meth? The ones who are at this very moment planning a drive-by or home invasion? What about them? How do we reach them? How do we get them to a point where they realize that thieving and gang life is not the way? That this world needs them, and that they deserve to be safe?

Dropping out of school and preying on others is not the way. The quest for bling, the Bimmer, and the Bentley by any means necessary is not the way. I don't have all the answers, and neither does ABLE. But the answers are within the realm of the reader. Right here, right now, are chiefs of police and members of various police organizations. Right here, right now are senior officials of corrections, members of social services, community organizers, lawyers, teachers, and professors. Operating among us are people we refer to as Your Worship, Your Honour, Minister, and Right Honourable. To your right and to your left are doctors, dentists, nurses, lab technicians, business owners, moms and dads, brothers and sisters, aunts and uncles, and clergy and faith healers. We have the ingredients that can formulate the answers, but we need to work collectively to put into action what we already know. We need the power of partnerships. The opportunity presented to us is to network. Tap into the resources in our sphere of positive influence. Make the connections, get past mere words, and put into action what we already know. Do something tangible. This is what the Association of Black Law Enforcers has done and is doing right now.

I believe that knowledge and creativity are the driving forces in our organization. However, the collaboration between the wisdom of the elders and the insightfulness of youth will ultimately generate new thinking, new ideas that will be essential to elevate us to new heights, as the issues facing our diverse society grow in their complexity.

My continued message to our youth is if you are willing, we will honour your commitment to making a difference and effecting positive change in your communities. To you, I say the future is going to happen whether you are ready for it or not. This is an indisputable truism. It is evident to us all that most of you are preparing for that future. Don't lose track of your dreams. When you dream, include others. Build a commitment to service and be your brother's keeper. Don't be afraid to go outside your comfort zone, for the bigger your hopes and dreams are, the higher your pain threshold and resilience becomes. Open up to the experience and don't forget to ask as many questions as possible. If you haven't already done so, find a purpose and define yourself before someone else defines you. Create your own future or someone else will hire you to create theirs. To define yourself, you must have courage. You must have strength of character and be bold. You have a reason for being born and a reason for being at this place at this time. There needs to be no apology for your existence, so do not fear your greatness. Realize your full potential and accomplish your goals. As you move forward, always remember that one of your life's tasks is to take complicated things and make them simple to enrich others, as opposed to taking simple things and making them complicated in order to serve yourself. As writer Vivian Greene once said, "Life is not about waiting for the storm to pass, it's about learning to dance in the rain."

DEFUNDING, REFORM, OR BOTH

S ir Robert Peel, founder of the Metropolitan Police, London, in 1829, states in his second principle of policing: "To recognize always that the power of the police to fulfill their functions and duties is dependent on public approval of their existence, actions and behaviour, and on their ability to secure and maintain public respect."

North America is again in crisis mode with respect to current policing contacts and tactics used against its citizens, primarily those of Black and brown descent. We are at a crossroads where drastic and immediate measures need to be endorsed by the public and governmental bodies, and implemented by police services in order to head off the cataclysmic collision that looms. There are now calls, by a number of citizen coalitions, for the defunding of police organizations across nations. What does that even mean? Well, some groups are calling for the complete abolishment of police services. As drastic as that sounds, their rationale is that the current way of policing is broken to the point of no redemption. They see demolishment as the only way racialized groups will be safe from the targeted injustices at the hands of the police.

My question is, what do you replace them with? In my experience, the concept of general policing works. If police operate the way most citizens want to see them operate, there is no argument that they are a valued commodity that we don't want to be without. Some groups have voiced their revulsion at the amount of funding granted to police organizations, making the accusation that the more money they receive, the more lethal weapons they purchase to unleash on the diverse population they are sworn to serve and protect. The term "occupying army" has been thrown around.

I have trouble wrapping my head around the argument of defunding the police, which sounds capricious and not well thought out — though taking a drastic stand and demanding meaningful change is often necessary to jolt the oppressor into some type of reform. I don't believe that "defunding" is the answer, but I would certainly advocate for reallocating portions of the police budget in order to reform the manner in which some police are currently operating. In some cases, I will petition for more funding for an increased number of officers and better overall training. The truth is that police reform is absolutely necessary. The notions of cause and effect are necessary when any concept of reform is considered. What we know for sure is that spending more on harsh policing protocols, without considering the cause and effect of bringing the police into negative interactions with the citizenry, is not the right step. So why the resistance? Why not try other ways of getting the job done with perhaps better, more satisfying results for everyone? I have some ideas that are not new but are certainly novel in terms of their potential application. These thoughts are on fiscal responsibility on the part of the service, utilizing true professionals in designated areas, and changing the way enforcement is done, with the goal of changing officers' attitudes when dealing with the public.

We need to address the call for reform from those who have stated that they are antagonized, victimized, and traumatized by the kind of police conduct that is once again at the forefront of North American–wide protest. I don't know what apparatus would replace the police if the organization were completely abolished, and I don't believe that is the answer. We don't need to defund the police; we need to utilize police budgets or reallocate monies to be more effective at what we are doing and how we are doing it.

Understanding that policing sectors countrywide are working towards keeping budget lines flat and in some cases decreasing them, the prudent thing to do is to seek efficiencies within the service without diminishing the core responsibilities and eroding public confidence. Here is where cost-effectiveness through productivity efficiencies is required. *Effectiveness* and *efficiency* are terms typically synonymous with "do more with less." However, maximizing effectiveness and efficiency is a continuous process not based solely on the number of resources.

Police services should seek efficiencies by creating and committing resources to an independent task force with experienced team members. This task force should work with external consultants to perform a detailed analysis on the business of policing across all divisional levels and identify suboptimal areas.

Changes such as combining or realigning units garner efficiencies that directly translate into productivity gains. The impact on the operating budget demonstrates fiscal responsibility and will, no doubt, have a positive influence on the external image of police services as a well-managed organization, while internally setting a mandate for efficiency and effectiveness.

Even with all its positive attributes, policing is not the panacea to solve the ails of society. In their professional capacity, officers are peacekeepers, law keepers, obligated to serve the community. But they are not psychologists, psychiatrists, social workers, nurse practitioners, or mental health experts. They are not trained professionals in these areas. Since many of the interactions police have on a daily basis are with people who require expertise in a number of these areas, the police approach should be a multi-tiered one. Police need to be teamed up with professionals who can assist or even lead on interactions crying out for the right person. In some situations, police are necessary but may lack the nuance and specific knowledge required to deal in that instance. So, in my mind, defunding (the better term would be "reallocation of funds") would mean that, along with finding efficiencies within the services, a portion of monies would be allocated to a shared service system. Having directly dealt with many people in mental health crises, for the most part, I believe that the situation could have been handled better if there had been crisis workers in the mix.

I would like to cite one example that happened recently in Mississauga. In June 2020, the daughter of Ejaz Choudry called para-medics requesting assistance with her sixty-two-year-old father, who was having a mental health episode and had armed himself with a knife. The mention of the knife prompted the dispatcher to involve the police, which makes sense. Ejaz suffered from schizophrenia and was on medication for it but had stopped taking it. The result left him confused and in need of help. Ejaz was said to speak very little English and was infirm, meaning he was frail and had difficulty walking. On arrival, two officers accompanied his daughter into the apartment. At that time, Ejaz became more agitated and pulled out a larger knife from under his prayer mat. The police and daughter retreated from the area, leaving Ejaz as the lone occupant in the apartment. This interaction prompted the officers to call for their tactical unit. What we now have in technical terms is "an armed barricaded person." Remember, this is a call for help from a daughter for her father who is in crisis. Family members were making attempts to speak with Ejaz through the door. Once the tactical team arrived, they directed family members to leave the scene and to stop trying to talk to Ejaz. According to police, when Ejaz stopped responding to them, they decided to force their way into the apartment to check on his well-being. Officers entered through the balcony door, and when Ejaz moved towards them, he was shot and killed.

Responding to this incident, the chief of Peel Regional Police, Nishan Duraiappah, stated, "We recognize that more has to be done to support those in crisis, and police should not be the primary responders called upon to manage mental health calls. While we are addressing the growing needs for mental health support, we know that gaps still exist."

In the correctional system, a number of trained officers form part of what are known as extraction teams. That is exactly what they specialize in: removing violent armed inmates from confined locations. They do this very well, with little injury to staff or inmate. What if teams of police offi-cers were trained in extraction techniques or were able to use correctional teams if the situation required their expertise? In the real world, outside an institution, these events are extremely rare, but they do occur. And, as in the Ejaz Choudry case, they can have dire consequences.

Many of us live with the challenges associated with mental illness. So how do we survive interactions with the police when the situation becomes extreme? Are there better ways of dealing with these interactions? What are the novel approaches when dealing with those in crisis? Racialized citizens feel that mental illness is another excuse for the police to formulate the justification for killing them. Let's now address police contacts that often put them at odds with the general public.

The Ontario Human Rights Commission's 2020 report *A Disparate Impact*, based on information gathered from the Toronto Police Service, is quite disturbing but validates what Black people have been saying for many years. The executive summary begins:

> Black people are more likely to be arrested by the Toronto police.
>
> Black people are more likely to be charged and over-charged by the Toronto Police.
>
> Black people are more likely to be struck, shot, or killed by the Toronto police.
>
> Toronto Police Service data, obtained by the Ontario Human Rights Commission (OHRC) as part of its inquiry into racial profiling and racial discrimination of Black persons by the Toronto Police Service (TPS), confirms what Black communities have told us — that they are subjected to a disproportionate burden of law enforcement in a way that is consistent with systemic racism and anti-Black racial bias.
>
> TPS data ranging from 2013 to 2017, collected and analyzed by a team of experts, reflects the many ways Black communities are over-charged and over-policed, ranging from laying low-quality discretionary charges to police use

of force, with all of its negative and detrimental physical and emotional consequences.

Black people are grossly over-represented in discretionary, lower-level charges and are more likely than white people to face low-quality charges with a low probability of conviction.

- The charge rate for Black people was 3.9 times greater than for white people and 7.1 times greater than the rate for people from other racialized groups.
- Although they represented only 8.8% of Toronto's population in 2016 Census data, Black people represented 42.5% of people involved in obstruct justice charges and were 4.8 times more likely to be charged with obstruct of justice offences than their representation in the general population would predict. By contrast, white people and people from other racialized groups were under-represented.
- Black people represented 35.2% of people involved in "out-of-sight" driving charges (such as driving without valid insurance), which are charges that only arise after a stop has already taken place, suggesting other motives for the stop.

We have been exposed to a great many horrible outcomes when police operate outside their professionalism and equitable treatment that is expected for all. The numbers in study after study say the same thing, striking the same tone, that this injustice is real. Individual members in police services are emboldened to continue this reprehensible behaviour, misusing the legitimate and discretionary authority bestowed upon them. Drastic reform is necessary now.

I would like to draw your attention to the following quote: "For this, as chief of police, and on behalf of the service, I am sorry and I apologize unreservedly. The release of this data will cause pain for many. Your concerns have deep roots that go beyond the release of today's report. We must improve; we will do better." These are the words of the Toronto interim police chief, James Ramer, at a press conference held on June 15, 2022, after the release of race-based data concerning his organization. In 2020, the police service was required to collect race-based data by adding "perception of race" to the use of force reports required after certain interactions with the public, including the pointing of firearms. And guess what the data showed? What was already known: Black people were subjected to almost 40 percent of all use of force incidents in 2020, despite only making up 24.4 percent of enforcement action. Closer to home, a 2023 report conducted by Dr. Lorne Foster of Foster and Associates titled *Enhanced Community Engagement and Community Policing: A Review of the York Regional Police Service Anti-Racism Practice* outlined "significant concern of anti-Black racial bias in York Regional Police activities" and revealed a significant equity and inclusion gap within the organization. York police data reveals that Black individuals were subject to 21 percent of all use-of-force incidents when they make up just 2.5 percent of the region's population. Is anyone surprised? I can tell you, no one in the Black community was. As a Black man, I have known this most of my life, and it didn't require a multitude of studies to tell me that.

∞

So what does reform look like? Based on my overall experience in policing and having the unique perspective of a Black citizen, I will provide a list of twenty-one recommendations that should form the basis of reform. This is in no way, shape, or form a comprehensive list, but I am convinced that if these thoughtful recommendations were implemented immediately, there would be a rapid causal effect that would be beneficial for all citizens, especially the BIPOC community.

For starters, I would suggest a deeper dive into:

How we recruit members into the police service. My experience in recruiting has left me with a positive outlook as to how most Ontario police services are exercising a standard process that has been producing good officers; however, there is certainly room for improvement. Who comes in the door will be a reflection of the organization in the future, so extreme care and attention is necessary to be sure of the right candidates and calibre of recruits. Reform in this area would be in the psychological profile of potential recruits. This is not my area of expertise, so I will defer to others as to how best to improve in this assessment. One other thought: we need a continued emphasis on recruiting of Black, brown, and Indigenous persons. Think outside the box when it comes to attracting, engaging, informing, and including them in the recruitment process.

Increase the diversity within the service ranks. This is long overdue but is a must when we are speaking about reform. The service must reflect, at all ranks, the makeup of the community. In fairness, some services are working diligently to move the needle when it comes to getting diverse members into elevated positions, but in my experience, they fail miserably in maintaining that cause by not grooming replacement officers to fill the gap when those current folks move on. This ostensibly creates what is referred to as a rank gap. Filling the rank gap will take a forward approach to promotions and courage on the part of the executive command, but whatever it takes, get it done.

Every recruit must be exposed to training that is accountability-based. Their personal responsibility in duty of care (the proper treatment of the people they are sworn to serve) must be enshrined in them; they must be made to understand what that is and how to properly manage situations that run contrary to that basic premise. We need duty of care directives across the board. Any officer at the scene of an incident where one or more officers are not performing their duties as required and are causing harm or the continuation of harm has a duty to intervene on behalf of the subject in order to safeguard that individual's rights, safety, and liberty. Failing to do so would result in their being fully accountable and liable for the misdeeds.

My point is that the clear gap in the current training is the lack of responsibility and accountability of on-scene officers to manage each other. It is the responsibility of attending officers to create, as best they can, the best outcome for all involved. An example of this is de-escalation, sometimes exemplified by creating time, distance, and projecting calm in the face of a dynamic situation. I see this as critical decision-making. Dynamic simulation training (as real as you can make it) should have scenarios that include dealing with out-of-control officers. Based on my personal and professional experience, police officers presented with an immediate critical situation involving force will revert to their training. I contend that the implementation and effectiveness of that training will, to some degree, correlate with the amount of time attributed to practising physically and role-playing mentally within the framework of the scenario. What I've seen over and over, both on and off the job, are the many "in the moment" situations where police create their own confusion. How many times have you, the reader, seen news footage of half a dozen police officers confronting a perpetrator with guns drawn, all of them screaming instructions at the top of their lungs: "Don't move, put your hands up, take your hands out of your pocket, turn off the car, get on the ground, drop the weapon, on your knees, stop resisting, do it now, turn around, back up, stay where I can see you." Confusing? Of course it is.

As part of their progression, recruits should participate in a place-of-worship tour. The worship tour should include the major established religions and be hosted by the religious leaders. It is important that police meet these groups, extending a hand of cooperation and understanding as best they can. Insight into various religions often translates into better communication and tolerance, which we know improves relations at both ends. If there is an opportunity to demystify actions and behaviours in a religious context, then we all are better off.

Change the promotional process. If your promotional process does not provide your service with the inclusivity that is warranted, revamp the process. Or better yet, suspend the process and have the executive command promote diversity within the ranks until the proper representation has been achieved, then reinstate an updated program that ensures equity across the board. This will take immense courage and intestinal fortitude but is necessary to balance out years of deliberate exclusion experienced by officers of colour. There is a challenging headwind that is known as the police association that will fight voraciously to not make this happen. They have a duty and an obligation to fight for all members, which I respect, but drastic measures are required now, not later, to address the significant imbalance.

Create the environment that you seek. There must be a willingness for the police to immediately call out mistakes, poor performance, and criminal behaviour on the part of officers. Add to that the willingness to immediately make the necessary changes in rules, regulation, and procedures in performance of duty to correct the problem. The messaging must be clear, unequivocal, and constant. It should be woven into policies, procedures, and command directives, and promoted by supervisors, managers, and command staff. There should be zero tolerance when it comes to workplace harassment, bigotry, discrimination, and biases, and there are no bystanders as far as this is concerned. There is a duty on each and every one to do what they can to create a fair, equitable, safe environment for all employees.

Purge bad officers from the service. Get rid of them! I'm all for due process, but when an officer has a history of bad behaviour that has been appropriately documented and addressed, and the behaviour continues, it's time to move them out. This is where our labour laws need adjustment. Police associations are intricately involved in discipline matters and have evolved into a force to be reckoned with. I agree that officers need representation, but why defend rogue officers who are bad and dangerous for business? Some of these defended officers have caused irreparable damage between police and the folks they are sworn to serve. We had an officer with a propensity for violence, especially against people of colour, whom the organization suspected operated this way. We, front-line officers, knew this was the case. This officer and I crossed paths several times, and each time his aura was not good. Our Professional Standards Bureau was closing in on him, so he simply relocated to another police service, effectively circumventing the York investigation. I still don't know how he was able to pull it off, but he did. Word was that his father was a high-ranking officer on that service and made it happen. I have it on good authority that this officer has been a blight on that service and a disgrace to the profession. Oversight bodies should immediately institute a registry of bad or violent officers who have been released from other services and make it accessible to every other policing agency across the nation. Services should be required to incorporate and review that list as part of their hiring process, ensuring that these officers are not employed by other departments.

Make it mandatory for all police services across North America to subject each working officer to a psychological evaluation every three to five years. There needs to be an enormous amount of design, effort, and funding to accompany and facilitate this programming, but it is achievable. The health of our policing system is held up by the human beings we have commissioned to operate on our behalf. We must ensure that they are healthy in order to keep us safe.

Stop slow-walking change. Police agencies and governmental bodies charged with oversite and implementation of positive changes must act expeditiously to implement agreed-upon recommendations. Case in point: In a 2016 report, Ontario ombudsman Paul Dubé recommended a standardized, mandatory de-escalation training for police across the province of Ontario as part of several other recommendations issued in the wake of the death of teenager Sammy Yatim, who had been shot and killed by police three years earlier while having a mental health episode. As of writing this book, there has been little to no action in this direction. There is no reason, after more than six years, to have this unsatisfactory result. Where is the accountability for this non-action and many others? Another death in similar circumstances is only a matter of time.

Police leaders need to grant community leaders access to speak directly with them about their specific issues. There needs to be greater emphasis on the lived experiences of over-policed victims of police abuse. Don't just hear them from afar — listen to them around the table and have dialogue.

We need to train officers on professional first contact, critical decision-making, de-escalation, and disengagement techniques. Proper first contact is a major strategy for how well engagement between police and citizens progresses. By first contact, I mean the professional approach that officers take when dealing with initial engagements. Most police contacts are of non-violent, low-risk situations, such as traffic stops for road violations or responding to general calls for service. As a uniformed supervisor, most of the complaints that I received from citizens about my officers surrounded civility, the officer's behaviour, and the escalation that they felt could have been avoided if they had been spoken to and treated respectfully.

Change the mindset of officers from arrest-first to problem-solving. What I mean is that officers are trained in the powers of arrest, which is absolutely necessary and certainly has merit. Placing a person under arrest may be reasonable but not always necessary. I found that in my case it was not my primary go-to decision; I preferred to use my discretion. Early in my career as a uniformed patrol officer, I was approached by a seasoned detective at the station who advised me to make more arrests. I asked why. His response was that it demonstrated that I was working, and it would give me more experience in processing paperwork, making me more viable for promotions. He was giving me advice, and he wasn't wrong. I just couldn't get past the fact that there were real consequences on the back end of that advice. We were dealing with people's lives. We were public servants and should be looking for the best outcomes when managing situations. Young and somewhat naïve, I started to make arrests. My numbers went up, and I was praised by my supervisors. But it didn't feel right. I knew that some of these arrests could have been handled differently. Problem-solving would have been the best course of action. There was this insipid culture within the service of "let's go make some arrests." No, let's go and problem-solve as best we can. To me that is every bit as important as the arrest numbers attached to your badge number. As I see it, our role as law enforcement officers is to serve and protect. We carry the notion that "Deeds Speak" — our actions matter. Without executing the principal notion of service, the culture that embraces the self-serving practice of arresting as a primary function of policing is wrong. Police organizations need to create incentives for officers to do better in this realm, perhaps by way of documenting details of successful problem-solving for each situation and officers recognized for not making arrests, if other, more compelling options are present or available.

Have a rigorous process to select your coach officers. Services should seek the very best members to train and influence officers-in-training. The newbies are sponges that absorb what you put in front of them. You get out what you put in. Also, the assignment of coach officer should not be linked to the promotional process. That just encourages some to seek it as a platform for advancement. Provide other incentives if feasible. During my time in the service, I did not see the encouragement from senior management to diversify their coach officer pool. To me, it is exceedingly important that officers of colour be intricately engaged as part of the solution by participating in the educational and emotional growth of newer officers in the area of race relations. Otherwise so many beneficial opportunities are missed.

Every officer should have immediate access to less-lethal tools that do not require the deployment of specialized teams or the presence of supervisors with this equipment. Often critical situations are emergent. They materialize in an instant. It is essential that all officers are prepared with the tools to properly and effectively deal with these circumstances. It is not good enough to reflect back on a situation and note that assistance was on the way . . . but then it's too late.

Every service should be equipped with both body-worn cameras and vehicle-mounted cameras. The policies surrounding their use should be unambiguous and rigid, meaning no disabling or tampering with the equipment. Numerous examples show the effectiveness of these devices, not only to advance the truth, but also to protect the officer from malicious false allegations.

No officer should be promoted to a supervisory level if they have not served a minimum term of one year in a community-based unit or function. Departments need to emphasize that policing is a service-oriented business. We are there for people, not the other way around. This philosophy needs to be reinforced at every level.

Stay focused on the matter at hand. I was on a call once where a woman contacted the police for assistance because her husband was being abusive. While dealing with the matter, officers questioned her on her immigration status, which had no relevance at all to the call for service. The purpose of the police is law enforcement. The intention of such an interaction should remain law enforcement and the duty of care, not citizenship and immigration monitoring. They now, in a sense, were re-victimizing her, making her a target of an investigation about her status. Why would any woman under those circumstances call the police for help, when there's a chance she might end up deported? A better solution would be for the police to sort out the domestic call and move on. Let the governmental agencies that deal with those matters do their job. It's the lack of empathetic policing that leaves a sour taste in the mouths of the people. Police need to do a better job of commiserating with the people they serve and to stay in their own lane.

Use real-life situations of racist police behaviour in training to show officers what *not* to do. Now that we have thousands of hours of videos depicting poor judgement, poor behaviour, racial profiling, biased policing, favouritism, overreactions, misbehaviour, lying, and the unjust outright killings of Black and brown folks at the hands of police, we need to use them as training aids to reinforce the never-ending narration that policing in North America is not fair and has not been fair to people of colour since the incorporation of the policing industry. There are very few things that resonate with officers as much as viewing fellow officers engaged in misconduct while the behaviour is dissected by police trainers. I have experienced the reactions in the classroom and participated in after-action reviews that I know have changed outlooks. Some saw themselves in what they viewed and instantly knew they needed to change.

The police must do a better job of messaging the public on how they do their job, along with how they can do it better. Perspectives on both sides is a powerful thing. The task at hand is to merge both points of view until they are indistinguishable — probably not possible, I know, but we should be working towards that goal. This is being done to some degree in Canadian policing, but more times than not, it is as a result of some event going sideways and the police sounding defensive. Let the police explain why it takes four officers to restrain one violent individual or why it's not realistic to shoot a knife-wielding suspect in the arm or leg. Explain to the public the inherent dangers in certain situations and how officers need to react. While in the training unit, we often invited the press into our facility and allowed them to participate in actual training, including use of force. We had them act out scenarios and use firearms on the range. The thought process was, the press has the reach to provide sobering information to the masses on the realities of policing, including the instantaneous decisions officers make and how they are trained to manage them. I must say, there were times that I was very surprised by veteran reporters' limited understanding of police training. I suggest citizens workshops inviting the public to educational forums that present the police side of the story. These must be frequent and ongoing.

Allocate portions of the ever-expanding police budget to prevention strategies such as investing in mental health centres, health services, violence prevention education, housing in general, and homelessness specifically. Calls for service involving non-violent mental health and substance issues do not need to include a police response except under extreme circumstances (which should be defined). This policy change will save valuable police resources and shift responsibility to trained health care professionals, who are capable of providing better outcomes. Also, many current police duties could be reassigned to civilians, significantly reducing costs. Implementation would need to be examined in detail and the expected resistance by officers and police associations met head-on, but it is absolutely the right course of action and very achievable.

And here's a big one that will no doubt be extremely controversial: we need non-police alternatives to traffic enforcement. I have ambivalent feelings about this proposal, but I'll put it up for consideration. I personally have done traffic stops that resulted in solid arrests. An example would be a seat belt violation that resulted in the arrest of an individual wanted on a first-degree Canada-wide warrant for robbery and aggravated assault. I have had situations where occupants were arrested for breaching their release conditions, usually by possessing illegal weapons or substances. These events happen all the time to the point of being somewhat routine. But no matter how good this may be operationally, it doesn't balance out a single death at the hands of police after an unjust escalation.

Data from the U.S. Department of Justice shows that over twenty-four million people in America encounter police during traffic stops, which can be especially dangerous and discriminatory for people of colour. According to the Stanford Open Policing Project, based on research into more than one hundred million traffic stops, Black drivers are 20 percent more likely to be stopped than white drivers, and as much as twice as likely to be searched. The *Washington Post* database of police killings states that 11 percent of all fatal shootings by police in 2015 occurred during traffic stops. And the Bureau of Justice Statistics' 2018 table of contacts between police and the public shows that traffic stops are the most common way people in America come into contact with police, and those encounters can often turn deadly. Extreme examples are the cases of Philando Castile, stopped over a broken taillight, and Daunte Wright, stopped over an air freshener dangling from his rear-view mirror. Both stops resulted in their deaths at the hands of police.

If the end goal is to enforce traffic violations, then why can we not try something different? There is a movement calling for the disengagement of armed police officers from traffic enforcement. I believe that should be considered. Why not try something different, bearing in mind the statistics that emphasize the current way of doing business is not being applied equally.

The proposal is to limit the powers of officers as it relates to traffic stops. Officers would no longer be able to stop vehicles for minor traffic offences, such as broken taillights, failure to signal, failure to indicate left or right turn, tinted windows, expired validation sticker, etc. This would all be in the jurisdiction of traffic monitors (in the case of Canada, special constables). These monitors would be a separate entity from the police, unarmed and without the powers of arrest, detention, investigative detention, or search.

Their function would be strictly to enforce traffic violations and handle minor non-injury vehicle collisions, with the authority to issue citations for infractions under the Highway Traffic Act. Their duties and responsibilities would not preclude them from calling the police for assistance when more serious infractions are detected, such as impairment, failure to stop, or assaultive behaviour. Police would not be prohibited from traffic stops if they were investigating serious traffic matters or situations where apprehension is required, such as a stolen vehicle.

In a way, some policing agencies have already tested the waters by utilizing parking officers, whose sole job is to enforce the municipality's parking codes, including tag-and-tow if required. Very few things piss people off as much as receiving a parking ticket, especially when they're about to leave.

I would suggest that there would have to be a massive public education on the changes in order for people to understand that this independent body's interaction is not a prelude to a fishing expedition but rather a matter of dealing solely with the traffic offence(s) and moving on. An important distinction in uniforms and vehicles would be necessary.

This would free up police officers to apply their time to more serious tasks, including crime prevention, detection, and enforcement, roles that I'm sure most people would agree are more suitable for police. It would also detangle police from the dreaded ticket-quota system that does exist and is inextricably attached to their performance evaluations.

So, there you have it — some of my ideas for reform. As stated earlier, this is by no means a complete or comprehensive list of what is required, but it does provide some real solutions. My hope is that police leaders will find the courage to challenge the establishment and implement changes to transform policing culture and build the bridges with the community that most of us so desperately want.

▪ PART FOUR ▪

POLICING:
THIS IS WHAT WE DO

THE EIGHTY PERCENT THAT I LOVED

I have chosen over the years to concentrate on the important parts of my day. The day starts with an internal conversation about what I really need to achieve and what I want to do. As the day evolves, I revisit that dialogue, applying the principle of what really matters and needs to be done to ensure a successful day. In its simplest form, it worked like this: 80 percent of the day, week, month, or year, I need to operate in the zone of ordinary; 20 percent of the time is reserved for outstanding performance. Ordinary is a state that one must practise everyday. It's about you being you all the time. It's about fitting in at home or work and operating as expected but just a little bit better. When your performance moves to extraordinary, you break away from the herd. If you want to stand out and deliver better outcomes, then you must perform at this level when required. The reason for the 20 percent is that it would be nearly impossible to maintain this hyper-level all the time. That's truly not necessary, and the energy output required would be too great for most of us. To put it succinctly, it is about going above and beyond. It requires an extra infusion of effort, energy, patience, empathy, generosity of time, nobility, understanding, engagement, commitment, endurance, perseverance, and determination. I honed many of these qualities during my years of athletic endeavours, culminating with competing and teaching the art of judo. There is a correlation between the output and the results.

Now, let me tell you about the 80 percent of policing that I loved that would compel me to provide the reader with a resounding YES if asked if I would do it all over again. I loved the symbolism of the uniform. For me it meant many things, but first and foremost it represented service. Police are the first to be called in on the majority of emergencies in which the public requires assistance. I absolutely loved arriving on scene, making the initial assessment, creating a plan of action, and executing it. Of paramount importance was to deliver the right type of service bearing in mind the best interests of the people I served. Every time, the challenge invigorated me, especially when the envisioned outcomes were met. I loved meeting people who immigrated to this country and now call Canada their home. I loved meeting the visitors, whether vacationers or business folks, and demonstrating the wholesomeness of police officers in this country.

I loved the time when I met an old Italian man who had been in a moderate motor vehicle accident. There were no injuries, only some damage to the front end of his car. This gentleman lived half a block away and wanted to drive the vehicle home. The vehicle was drivable. Because I was the second officer attending, it was not my accident scene to control. The determination by the lead officer was that his vehicle must be towed. The man pleaded and pleaded, to no avail. When the lead officer left the scene to continue his paperwork, I told the gentleman to get in his car and I would follow him in my cruiser to his house. We took our time, and I escorted him home. This man thanked me profusely, asking me to wait while he went inside. He emerged shortly afterward and presented me with a bottle of wine. He said to me, in that sweet majestic broken English, that this bottle was his best homemade wine and he wanted me to have it. I gently and politely declined the offer but thanked him nevertheless. I saw tears well up in his eyes as he continued to beseech me to take it as an appreciation of his gratitude. I felt I had no choice but to finally accept. His smile was effervescent. I don't remember his name, but I will always remember how he made me feel. By the way, I brought the wine home and told my wife that amazing story. I found a lovely place in the house to put that bottle of wine, with the intention of keeping it for a few more years to keep the memory alive with the extra benefit of aging it. A week later, the wine disappeared. What happened to it? Let's just say, at that time there were only two people in the house and one of us (the person who brought it home) never got to taste it. But I digress! Moving on.

I loved the excitement of those critical emergent situations when immediate and, at times, life-saving decisions had to be made. We dealt with bar fights, domestic assaults, bank robberies, high-speed pursuits, armed barricaded suspects, mental health engagements, criminal code search warrants, firearms search warrants, break-and-enters in progress, downed power lines, personal injury accidents, gas leaks involving evacuations, critical weather-related events, unknown trouble calls, homicides, industrial accidents, missing persons, emergency hospital runs, fires both residential and industrial, VIP security . . . the list is endless.

I loved the investigative aspects of the work, from the immediate preservation of a crime scene to the assigned caseload of files that needed attention. From the processing of an impaired driver to the detention of a domestic assault perpetrator. From the gathering of information on organized crime groups to the execution of search warrants for child exploitation online. From the tracking of firearms used in crime to identifying persons of interest involved in drug distribution. From working with other surrounding police services to aligning with international policing agencies around the globe. From building a case from scratch to presenting evidence in court during the prosecution. From interviewing witnesses to interrogating suspects. From working with a Crime Stoppers tip to arresting con artists bilking people out of their life savings. I enjoyed it all.

I loved doing paid duties (extra paid work sanctioned by the service). Each officer, if so inclined, had the choice to pick which paid duties they would like to work. The hours varied, but our organizational policy was that the party requesting this service had to provide a minimum of four paid hours. A particular duty that I enjoyed was the eight-hour assignment at Canada's Wonderland, an amusement park just northwest of Toronto. Most of the time, I would choose the park security detail, which afforded me the opportunity to roam the facility and meet hundreds of happy people in a safe, secure environment full of smiles, joy, and laughter. By virtue of the uniform, you became a feature of the park, with many folks requesting photos with you or introducing you to the children as an interesting person one should meet. And let's not forget that I got paid handsomely for this enjoyable work.

I loved the training that the service provided. I have had the opportunity to work in many different areas within the organization, and each area required some training to become proficient, not to mention the risk management aspects of certain critical assignments. As I progressed through the ranks, the courses and training elements grew more intense, giving legitimacy to the portfolios that I occupied. It felt good participating at the table as a senior officer with the requisite knowledge, skills, and ability to hold my own. I enjoyed representing my department at joint forces operations and seeing the reactions from my counterparts when we initially met, as I was usually the only Black officer around the table. I enjoyed being sent to all-expenses-paid out-of-town or country conferences courtesy of the York Regional Police. It felt really nice being able to build up a comprehensive résumé that would accompany me the rest of my life.

I loved being an ambassador for the service specifically and policing in general. To me, policing is still a noble profession, illustrated by the great work many officers do day in and day out — often with little notice of their efforts and the level and degree of their commitment. There was a time when, on average, I would be out at one community event or another representing the organization a minimum of three times per week. For the most part, I would put on my number one dress uniform (formal uniform) with all its brass buttons and stately appearance, which commanded attention while signifying strength and authority. There was an air of professionalism inherent in that dress uniform that made me stand a bit taller, shoulders back, with my chest expanded, making people take a second look. In those moments, I felt proud of my accomplishments, starting with having the opportunity to be seen as a police officer and culminating in the addition of higher-rank insignias and portfolios that I eventually occupied. Meeting people under these circumstances was pure joy, especially when I would make a concerted effort to work the room, approaching people randomly and engaging them in conversation. For the most part, they were receptive to the contact and appreciated being noticed. The organizers almost always acknowledged the presence of the police and thanked us for our service. That gesture alone was positive reinforcement for my belief that I had chosen the right profession. I was always on the hunt for potential recruits. When provided with an opportunity to address an audience, there was always a built-in acknowledgement of the commitment to service by the police and the tried and proven positive engagement of policing working with the community and vice versa. People are the public and the public are the police. Many of these events proved to be rich environments for prospects. It felt good to be able to assist directly in the process by way of providing valuable information or introductions that mattered.

I loved the times when I had the option of exercising my discretion, especially when it came to dealing with youth interactions. I remember those occasions when there was an option to charge someone with a criminal offence, which seemed somewhat drastic for the circumstances when a better, simpler option was available. I am reminded of a young person who was grabbed by mall security for shoplifting some candy. On my arrival, the young man was shaking, certain that he was in serious trouble. Oddly enough, he was willing to go through the process of arrest and charge but did not want his parents to be contacted. Well, I had a different idea. No arrest, no charge, but he was getting driven home and delivered to his parents. And that's what happened. He begged me not to tell his folks. He didn't want to be driven home in a police car. His father answered the ringing doorbell. I explained the circumstances and handed his son over to him. The final lasting word from Daddy to me was, "No worries, officer, I'll look after this." I did follow up some time later and was pleased with the apparent outcomes according to both Dad and son.

∞

Now to some aspects of the job that were not so nice. I don't intend to spend a great deal of time in this area, because many aspects came with the territory and often it was what it was. In policing, one gets to see and deal with the tragic aspects of the human condition — the hurt, pain, and damage inflicted upon victims. You get to witness first-hand some of the inhumane treatment one person perpetrates against another. Often, the viciousness did not match the gratification sought at the onset. Child predators, for example, are a scourge on the earth. Not much more needs to be said about them. There is a real cost to your psyche having to deal with traumatic events throughout a career. There will be residual effects whether seen or subconscious.

I didn't like dealing with the real devastation that often occurs as a result of scams. It was extremely disturbing to know that many of these victims would be forever out of their life savings as a result of being conned. I didn't like coming across poor outcomes having to do with mental illness or drug addiction. So many people continuously fall through the cracks and are not caught by the system. The price they pay is often incalculable. Then there are the ordinary folks that go to work and don't make it back home by virtue of misadventure — accidents of one sort or another. There is no fun in arresting bandits who are locked up that evening, attend court the next day, and are released back into the community, when you know in your heart that they are a menace to society and dangerous. Our court system is in dire need of revamping.

Some more stuff that wasn't so nice: the paperwork was horrendous. Some days it was almost overwhelming. For instance, processing an impaired driver. By the time that person was brought to the station, it would take you around four to five hours per arrest. Making an arrest at the end of a twelve-hour shift when you have commitments at home is not good for the family dynamics. Death notifications — where I had to go to family and tell them their loved one has died — were particularly troubling, and the reactions were most times heartbreaking, other times perplexing and unexpected. I had a call one time where a gentleman was playing cards with some friends in a back room of a banquet hall. He suddenly keeled over and died on the spot. He was subsequently transported to the hospital, pronounced dead, then moved to a side room, awaiting removal to the morgue. I ended up in the room with him; just the two of us spending time together, awaiting positive identification from his wife, who was supposedly on her way. During that time, I imagined all kinds of things about this man's life — his kids, his family interaction, his work, how others would miss him, and so on. Eventually, his wife entered the room. I immediately started with my condolences, talking about how hard this part of the investigation is. The lady showed a laissez-faire, nonchalant attitude, walked past me, pulled the sheet from over his face, looked him dead in the eyes, and said to me, "Yeah that's him." She flung the sheet back over his head with reckless abandon and walked out of the room. Clearly there'd been no love lost there.

I didn't like when the administration played politics with its members. An example of this would be overreacting to one lobby group or another that directly interfered with how we did our jobs, with no real benefit, just more headaches. For example, the service implemented a no-idling cruiser policy after a complaint from an environmental group. Have you ever parked for any reasonable amount of time in the middle of winter on a freezing cold night without the car running due to idling-time restrictions? Let me tell you, when the car is not running, there is no heat pumping. It doesn't take long for the tingling of hypothermia to set in. If you don't believe me, try it sometime. Not sure what happened to that policy, but it disappeared pretty quickly.

Suicides are devastating to everyone involved. My take was "just one more day could have made the difference," but who knows. That brings me to a radio call of a suicide that I attended so many years ago. It turned out to be a young man who was attending university and had failed to qualify for medical school. The pressure brought down by his parents, whose cultural expectations demanded him to be a doctor, was too much for him. I went into the victim's bedroom and saw him on the floor beside his bed, with one hand extended on the bed as if reaching for something.

He had consumed poison. Would one more day have made a difference? I don't know.

.I didn't like being assigned radar details. Yes, there is a quota. You are expected to bring in a certain number of tickets based on averages across the service. I saw this as a source of revenue for the province off the backs of officers and the citizenry we serve. The pressure came down from on high to the Police Services Board, who were provided with a monthly review of tickets statistics at board meetings. Police command had all the numbers and did a monthly review of how your platoon compared with other platoons. Your platoon had better not be last or low in numbers, or the district superintendent would get an earful, then the inspector, then the staff sergeant, and that means you would too. There was value to running radar, but it was often difficult to set up in some of the really concerning traffic areas where speeding was a dangerous proposition. Many of these areas would not produce the numbers that would demonstrate you had spent the day doing your job productively. That's why you see officers in what are commonly known as speed traps. Find a nice speed trap and the numbers flow: it's no problem bringing in twenty or thirty tickets for the shift parked alongside a stretch of roadway with a low speed limit, as opposed to eleven or twelve tickets operating at a congested intersection where you are visible and you end up impeding traffic. These tickets count as part of your evaluation, purportedly to demonstrate your work efforts, so the more the better, as they say.

In this job, I found the purpose that I longed for, the honour and respect I sought. The profound enlightenment I desired, the dedication to service that should be a part of every person who wears the uniform — the ability to see the majority who are the ordinary, everyday people who make the world go round, and the few who change the norms and make them quite extraordinary. I see no other vocation that could have fulfilled all that I required and more. It warms my heart to have had the opportunity to contribute to the betterment of the masses who deserved my help and, in return, provided me with the blanket of comfort and confidence that we are in good shape as a people, in the overall scheme of things, to prosper in the future. There is no pessimism in me as I ponder what is to come for my children and yours. In my view, 80 percent of us will do the right things, make the right moves, and invoke the right edicts to maintain the collective good. The other 20 percent will need convincing.

THE SILENT BUT DEADLY
STRESSORS OF PATROL

I count my blessings each day, having had the opportunity to live and work in the unique Regional Municipality of York. Founded in 1971 upon the amalgamation of nine cities, towns, and townships, York Region encompasses more than 1,760 square kilometres (680 square miles) bordering the City of Toronto to the south and expanding to the shores of Lake Simcoe to the north. The region has a composite mixture of urban and rural existing quite comfortably with each other as "cottage country" invites the city folks north with a promise of relaxation, leisure time, and vacation spots, while the city suggests a place of work and play and most certainly provides all the amenities of urban life. The uniqueness of the region is also based on diversity: it boasts residents who identify with more than two hundred ethnic origins in a population of more than a million inhabitants. It's the fastest-growing region in Canada. It also contains an Indigenous reserve where the Chippewas of Georgina Island First Nation reside.

For a region of this size, it is a relatively safe place to raise a family and live one's life to the fullest. I was indeed very fortunate to have started and finished my career policing the citizens of York Region, which I considered an honour (after some hard, dogged determination and persistence in the pursuit of the job, mind you). York Regional Police, as of this day, consists of around sixteen hundred sworn officers and just over six hundred civilian members. It comprises five districts, which serve the various cities and towns within the region. The service is flush with new, up-to-date equipment for its members, with a slight edge in technology compared to other surrounding and comparable services in the country. We even have a helicopter, which is a scarcity in the Canadian policing world.

Law enforcement is a noble profession, and one that I embraced with enthusiasm and a sense of civic duty. I vividly recall the day I received the phone call congratulating me on my successful acceptance to the ranks of the York Regional Police. Deep in my core, there was a feeling of elation — my single-minded goal of becoming a police officer, ready and willing to make a difference, had just become a reality. In 1990, I was transferred from the Morality Bureau to uniformed patrol duty. This was my first opportunity to interact with the citizens of York Region in a public way. It was what I had joined the police service to do. I remember looking at myself in the mirror and being proud to wear the uniform of the York Regional Police; it filled me with a deep sense of accomplishment. I was proud, I had made my parents proud, and I was ready and willing to serve a community of people who were satisfied with the tasks and duties of the policing profession.

Uniform duties were truly a blast, answering radio calls of all shapes and sizes. Several months of working on the same platoon created a comfort level and trust between officers, which increased mutual bonding. I was then approached to work the 3 p.m. to 3 a.m. shift. This meant that I would be covering a patrol zone for several hours until my regular shift started that night, at 6 p.m. I was to work this shift alongside members of another platoon with whom I was not familiar. I found this somewhat strange but not uncomfortable.

On the first day of the 3 p.m. to 3 a.m. shift, several primary response officers were dispatched to a residential alarm call. On arrival, one of the officers located a side door that was insecure, which had presumably set off the alarm. Along with two other officers, I entered the residence and did a walk-through, ensuring that the premise had not been entered. Having satisfied ourselves that the door had in fact triggered the alarm, we then attempted to contact the owners of the house. During this, I noticed one of the officers pick up three Game Boy–type video game cartridges. He showed them to his partner, and they both laughed. The officer then placed the cartridges in his pocket. These items obviously belonged to a young child who had some connection to the house. It was apparent to me that the officer was intent on stealing them. I did not personally know these two officers and was frankly shocked that any police officer, detailed to assist the very citizens that they swore to serve and protect, would take the opportunity to steal from them.

My dilemma now began. I was relatively new on the job — just transferred from a specialized unit into a uniformed position — and I had just answered a radio call with two other officers whom I did not know, both of whom were senior to me . . . and one of the officers had just stolen several items in front of me. It has never nor would ever occur to me to take any items from that or any other house, because that would be stealing. If one has developed a habit of integrity, taking advantage of the situation is not part of the program. My moral path would not and could not justify this action.

Being well aware of the code of silence, what was my loyalty to these officers? How do I correct this wrongdoing and not be considered an informer? How do I maintain trust among my other colleagues? Should I consider this act a minor transgression, or do I treat it as what I perceive it to be: an inexcusable breach of our oath of office, and a criminal offence? How committed was I to seeing both officers face justice and possibly lose their jobs? These questions formed part of my reasoning for doing what I did.

At the time of this event, I viewed egoism (self-preservation) as the best theory to adopt. I considered my available options. It came down to what would be in my best interest, and that was keeping my mouth shut. Was this right? Absolutely not. It was ingrained in me that the "code of silence" was the rule to be adhered to in that moment, and given my naïveté and lack of seniority, I chose self-preservation.

One of the compelling arguments for doing the right thing is that by not reporting the wrongdoing, I would be complicit in the act and allow bad cops to continue on their path of misdeeds. In the end, this would not serve the greater good. This argument is tempered by the deontological theory that discretion and secrecy are obligations one assumes by joining a police force. The truth was, I wanted to save my skin and put this behind me: absolute egoism.

This incident haunted me at the time and has continued to do so throughout my career. The action of those two officers and my response to the situation defied the values that I held dearly and the sense of duty that I had sworn to uphold. On the scale of right and wrong events that I have witnessed over the years, this one is minor, but is the one that tested me, and I failed.

Where am I now? With many years under my belt and a perspective that is not comparable with that young officer who was strong in his convictions but weak in his courage, I would certainly approach a similar situation differently. I say with little hesitation that the offending officer would be told to return the items, and the incident would be reported to a senior officer. If this officer refused, then I would invoke my public duty and arrest him. The consequence would no doubt be condemnation by some officers who truly believe that the code of silence and overlooking "minor" transgressions must be maintained at all costs. I would be labelled as untrustworthy and unsuitable to work with. The undercurrent of this rebuke would have lasting negative effects on how I would be treated going forward. It would have been a heavy price to pay for doing the right thing. Today I would do it anyway; at the start of my career, the personal stakes seemed too high.

Living according to one's convictions is an enormous commitment that at some point or another will challenge one's strength of character. In the case of the two officers, morality and ethics appeared to be situational. The very fabric of oath-based duty and care-based thinking (ask before you act: What would it feel like if you were the recipient?) were diametrically opposed in this one incident. The officers, acting in the capacity of law enforcers, presumably attended this call with the intention of investigating whether a crime had been committed and, if so, arresting the perpetrator. This in essence is good. What did happen was the very same officer(s) committed the crime of theft.

According to philosopher Alasdair MacIntyre, author of *After Virtue* (1981), virtues are described as "those dispositions that will sustain us in the relevant quest for the good, by enabling us to overcome the harms, dangers, temptations, and distractions which we encounter, and which will furnish us with increasing self-knowledge and increasing knowledge of the good." It is my belief that the two officers were void of many dispositions of virtue, leaving me wondering how they have conducted themselves over the years.

I looked towards individual conscience to guide me through life in general and policing specifically. I have a solid foundation in the pillars of right and wrong along with what I would consider a semi-religious-based ethical system — if I feel uncomfortable with a certain action, it is most likely wrong. I refused to be put in a situation again where I had failed to act and had to live with the consequences. Looking back at the incident, I am upset that I did not stick to my convictions; however, I understand why it played out the way it did. A valuable lesson was learned that day, and in many ways I am thankful for it.

∞

One of my really rough days as a uniformed patrol officer affected my psyche for years, and I'm not really sure why it did for so long. I was dispatched to block off a section of roadway due to a major vehicle collision. There had been a fatal head-on car crash. A southbound vehicle had veered into oncoming northbound traffic, causing a catastrophic accident that claimed the life of a young child. I was informed that the little girl had been sitting on the lap of her mother, riding in the passenger seat, and was crushed against the dashboard upon impact. The young girl was two years old. My daughter was two at the time. I never saw the accident, but the death of that child resonated with me because of my daughter. Prior to this event, I had seen and experienced all manner of calls for service, some with extreme visuals, but this one bothered me for years.

I have two more motor vehicle accidents to tell you about that occurred a few years after, while I was working uniformed patrol in 5 District.

On one particular evening, I was patrolling the southernmost area of Markham, which borders the City of Toronto on the east end. I was dispatched to what was called a personal injury accident — a person struck by a vehicle. Upon my arrival, several fire trucks and an ambulance were already on the scene. There were no frantic movements, just sombre looks and slow walks by the responding caregivers. A very large tractor-trailer was on the roadway, clearly involved in the accident. Underneath the rear section of the tractor portion of the truck was a sheet covering the body of an eight-year-old child. On the sidewalk, opposite the truck, was the mother of that young boy, comforting another younger child. The emergency responders were struggling to keep their composure; their heads were bowed in quiet solitude. The scene was heartbreaking. I had the gut-wrenching task of speaking with the mother to piece together the sequence of events that had led to this tragic incident. As she spoke, tears welled up in my eyes, causing me several times to turn slightly away, pretending that something had caught my attention, while I dabbed the tears away. Through her sobs and heaves of unimaginable pain, she told me that she had been out for a walk with her two sons and for some unknown reason her eldest had broken away from her hand and ran onto the roadway. The truck struck him, and he had died instantly. I have carried the pain of that distraught mother in my heart for years.

On the scene of another accident, I discovered that it is possible to feel immense joy and relief after attending what was initially deemed as a disastrous accident. I arrived at a call for service, a single motor vehicle accident. The scene was straight out of an epic action movie. A Chevy Corvette convertible had been travelling at a high speed. The driver lost control, and the car rolled several times, coming to rest upside-down. The car was fully engulfed in flames and smoke was rising high into the air, but neither the fire department nor the ambulance were on scene yet, just myself and Constable Ralph Jackson. We both grabbed fire extinguishers from our cruisers and began fighting the fire, making frantic attempts to locate the driver through the flames and smoke but that was not possible due to the immense heat and flames. We were concerned that the vehicle would explode, yet we had to try, as there was someone burning up in that car. Very soon afterward, the fire department arrived and quickly extinguished the flames. They were able to examine the interior of the wreck and told us that there was no one inside — we had all been expecting charred human remains, but the vehicle was indeed empty. Where the heck was the driver? It turned out that the single occupant of the vehicle had been ejected onto the sidewalk, became disoriented, and wandered off into an adjacent field. It was another ten minutes or so before we located him, but finding this man shaken up but not seriously injured was an incredible relief.

∞

The heart and soul of any police organization is the contact that the first responders make with the general public in any capacity. In my experience, I would always try to seek the best outcome, understanding that what we did was fluid, and sometimes it was impossible to put the genie back into the bottle. My responsibility was providing a service, which I trained for and was expected by the public to do. On the other hand, there are times that members of the public will not allow you to do the job the way it should be done. Underlining all of this is the sobering reality of the job itself. You are one call away from experiencing a human condition that can and often does change you or affect your working shifts and off hours in not so nice ways. Encountering some of the worst situations, such as sudden infant deaths, suicides, industrial accidents, death by misadventure, or jumpers, has a residual effect.

Intimate involvement in many tragic occurrences comes with a price. The currency is pieces of you. It's a price that some officers don't realize that they are paying. Officers are exposed to unbelievable events that are traumatic and severely harmful, both physically and psychologically. Unknown events requiring immediate action at all hours of the day or night inflict a shock on your body. Shift work can be a destructive force to your circadian rhythm (the twenty-four-hour internal clock that controls your body's sleep-wake cycle). Other job-related functions consist of consoling a grieving family that has lost a loved one in a motor vehicle accident or sitting with a family that has just been notified of the death of someone close to them. This is gut-wrenching.

Fear is a constant factor that can be viewed as part of the complexity of the job. Most of my career did not involve fear, but when it did, the stark reality of what I might be called upon to do was thrust upon me with a jolt of "this is really happening." I can recall several situations that were sobering, taking me and others from a zero state of calm to the red zone of anxiety-induced adrenaline within the span of a few minutes. Most patrol days consisted of low-risk, high-frequency calls that were contained within the acceptable realm of the day-to-day. But you were always one radio call away from entering the unnatural zone of the high-risk, low-frequency demand for service. A call of a bank robbery in progress, or shots fired with suspect(s) still in the area, or an armed and barricaded person with a hostage will set your heart racing, adrenaline flowing, and provoke a reactionary motor response that prepares you for what is to come. As the initial responder, you know that your response matters in a way that most other professions cannot attest to. In some rare cases, the call for service can quickly degrade into a matter of life and death.

So, the question is, what are the coping mechanisms or skill sets employed by officers in order to deal effectively with stress and trauma experienced on the job? Imagine for a moment that you are an officer who has had a particularly bad day (*insert incident here*). You have spent hours intimately immersed in that event and have contributed all that you can in terms of your job requirements and your innate humanity. Now your shift has ended, and it's time to be home, engaging with family or friends, doing what would be considered normal. But it is not normal.

The events of that day and other days are still with you. The bad days seep into your everyday in a thousand different ways. I endured countless sleepless nights, a preoccupation with reliving the events, many silent days when I didn't want to talk policing to anyone, and numerous days when I wanted to engage anyone who would listen about what I had experienced on the job. I demonstrated an irritability in situations where it wasn't warranted. Sometimes I could be overly argumentative at home when I knew better but persisted anyway. Many evenings I did not want to come home straight after a shift due to the little-understood need to shed some of the toxins that were in me, manifestations of the trauma I had experienced. The compulsion was the overalignment with people who shared a common experience and truly understood the reality of what we have been exposed to. I never developed a dependency on alcohol or medications but was more than willing to spend more time than I should have engaging with those that did, in safe spaces such as our Police Association building.

All of what I have mentioned is the familiar experience of an urban police officer over the span of their career. Officers are people who make up part of society and are susceptible to the fragile and fractional emotional and psychological composition that being human can impose.

The saving grace in my case was my wife, Cheryl, and daughters, Jasmine and Brianna. There was nothing more important to me than being home with them, spending quality time, and actively participating in their lives as a proud husband and father. My promise to my girls was that I would be the best father anyone has ever had, no matter what the personal cost. Those girls put everything into perspective for me. With them, my purpose in life was redefined, from my personal success to enhancing their lives and preparing them to thrive in any environment that they may encounter. I relished that prospect in addition to basking in the love bond that we share to this very day.

I have often said and truly believe that it is important that we self-check as often as possible by asking ourselves questions such as, "What has changed in my view of the world since I first started policing?" Ask loved ones if they have noticed a difference in you as the years on the job passed by. In this exercise, you will need to listen, absorb, reflect, and monitor. The next part is to put into action the necessary changes that hopefully will make for a healthier and more functional you. I did exactly that, which helped realign me year after year. Any highly stressful, dangerous occupation should require a yearly psychological assessment by professionals to help root out and deal with the early onset of post-traumatic stress disorder (PTSD), which affects so many of us. This is only a suggestion, as I am clearly out of my lane, but it's an important one.

During my early days in policing, we weren't taught coping skills for this invisible killer. We carried around with us, in silence, the malignancy now known as PTSD, not ever daring to share in a professional way that we were in fact injured. We internalized the stress and carried on, which outwardly projected a degree of toughness. We had to. The police culture demanded it. Wrong! Wrong! Wrong! I know of far too many law enforcement suicides that have a direct link to work-related events. If you are in a profession that can produce this type of injury, please, please seek professional help.

ORGANIZED CRIME — INVESTIGATIVE SERVICES

V aughan is a rapidly growing urban setting that comes not only with escalating crime, but also with the expanding variations of the types of crimes. It is an interesting setting by virtue of its large Italian population, which, for many years, has defined and shaped the city. Their positive contributions to the development and environment of the area are immeasurable. Policing the city for several years as a uniformed officer, with every passing day I loved the city more and more. The pride that emanated from the hearts of the people made many of my interactions pleasurable. Culturally, the motherland was ever present, blended with the Canadian identity, a combination that worked so well. Collectively, those folks loved the meaningful aspects of life, with an enduring priority of family first, a deep respect for community, and an adherence to an order that made their balanced existence work.

However, there was a dark side: a plague brought over from the old country, known as La Cosa Nostra, Italian mafia, or specifically 'Ndrangheta (thought to mean "society of men of honour"). 'Ndrangheta was the mafia that originated out of Calabria, Italy. The Siderno crime group, known as such due to many of its members coming from the town of Siderno in Italy, formed part of the conglomerate that operated throughout Canada, Australia, Europe, and the United States, and was composed of a group of families related by blood or marriage. Two such families, the Commisso and the Figliomeni clans, resided in Woodbridge, an area within Vaughan. A number of other notable organized families in the area brought a cloud of despair and caused irreparable damage to the cohesiveness of the folks living there. There were some notable names associated with the Greater Toronto Area (which included Vaughan): Mafia boss Paul Volpe, in 1983, was shot twice in the back of the head, dumped in the trunk of his wife's car and left in the parking lot of the nearby international airport. The Commisso brothers trafficked in narcotics over three continents; one of them, Cosimo Ernesto Commisso, was shot and killed on June 28, 2018. Mafia chief "Boss of Two Worlds" Alfonso Caruana helped run a multi-billion-dollar cocaine trafficking and money laundering empire. Angelo Figliomeni was part of the 'Ndrangheta organization that was invested in the world of gambling. Carmine Verduci was a GTA mobster killed in 2014 outside a Woodbridge café. Giovanni Costa, in 1991, was gunned down near his home in Vaughan. Francesco Loiero was shot to death in 1996 sitting in his car in a Vaughan parking lot. Mila Barberi, an innocent veterinary assistant, was gunned down on March 14, 2017, while seated in a parked car in Woodbridge. The intended target was her boyfriend, Saverio Serrano, also connected to organized crime, who was in the vehicle at the time. He was shot twice in the arm and survived. This botched hit has been connected to the killing of notorious Hamilton mobster Angelo Musitano.

There was, and still is, very little outward evidence of the vicious underworld lurking beneath all the beauty and normality experienced by most residents. As police, we are keenly aware of who some of the connected villains are, but they remain deeply insulated within the apparatus of the clans. When I was part of the Morality Bureau, I worked on many investigations involving mafia activities, giving me a unique perspective and intelligence on who some of the main players and associates were, along with the inner workings of the major groups. As a uniformed officer, I regularly visited a number of the so-called "social clubs" that were known hangouts for the mob. I met with many of the members and was on a first-name basis with some. They were unique in that they had no outward beef with the police, viewing our interactions as part of the deal. They were extremely polite and generous to a fault, always offering a cappuccino or pastry along with an ingratiating smile and simple conversation. To me, it felt like the catch me if you can routine playing out in real life. My one negative interaction with one of the bosses was during a traffic stop on Woodbridge Avenue, where I gave one of the mob bosses a ticket for a seat belt infraction. Well, he lost it, yelling that he intended to get his lawyer to fight this outrageous, egregious act. (I am paraphrasing — his words were a little more colourful than mine.) I probably caught him on the wrong day at the wrong time. By the way, he eventually paid the ticket. Many of these men ran legitimate businesses, from construction contracting to restaurants or bakeries. Their tentacles are everywhere, reaching major Canadian cities such as Toronto, Hamilton, Niagara, and Montreal. Vaughan has played an integral part in mob-related organized crime in this country.

One of my more interesting assignments as an undercover officer, and one it was an immense pleasure to participate in, had to do with investigating outlaw motorcycle gang members. York Region hosted a number of motorcycle clubs, including several well-known and dangerous organizations. We had Hells Angels, Satan's Choice, Para-Dice Riders, Bandidos, Black Diamond Riders, and Loners, to name but a few. During my time as an undercover officer, I not only encountered them in various establishments but also befriended several to the point of purchasing illicit drugs from them. This was always a tricky proposition due to the level of organization within these gangs and their propensity for violence at the slightest provocation, usually initiated by them. For the most part, if they control a certain territory and they see you enough times, they become very curious as to who you are. This curiosity allowed me to engage in conversation, which at times opened up enough space for me to ingratiate myself to whomever. There was never an opportunity to hang out with them other than a passing chat or a beer every now and then. It was their associates who would give me the time to nurture a relationship. In my days, the main nemesis was the Loners Motorcycle Club. They were very prevalent and controlled a number of very lucrative businesses. Francesco "Cisco" Lenti and Gennaro Raso founded the club in 1979. Gennaro went on to open chapters in Portugal, Italy, Spain, and the United States. A favourite hangout for both bikers was a strip club known as the Pro Café in Vaughan, a well-known establishment where Francesco Lenti would fatally gun down one Satan's Choice member and critically injure another, considered unwelcomed guests.

Later on in my career, I served the organization for eight years in the capacity of special services inspector and the organized crime and intelligence services inspector. Units under my command within Special Services included Integrated Crime Analysis, Surveillance, Interception of Private Communications, Technical Support and Covert Operation. As the officer-in-charge for the organized crime units, I was responsible for Guns and Gangs, Drugs and Vice, and Major Fraud units within the Organized Crime Bureau. My task was to fulfill the bureau's mandate of detection, disruption, and dismantling of organized criminal elements operating within York Region and surrounding areas.

I will have limited commentary about managing both these units because I was in a strictly administrative role, while the women and men who reported to me did real work. Collectively, that work resulted in some major detection, disruption, and dismantling of a number of individuals and organizations that were deep in the fabric of our everyday existence. Organized crime is pervasive. It exists everywhere and at every level in society, across ethno-racial and cultural groups. It crosses borders, whether locally, internationally, or globally, not sparing anyone or anything. If something has an intrinsic value, then it is open for corruption. Section 467.1(1) of the Canadian Criminal Code defines organized crime this way: "Criminal organization means a group, however organized, that (a) is composed of three or more persons in or outside Canada; and (b) has as one of its main purposes or main activities the facilitation or commission of one or more serious offences that, if committed, would likely result in the direct or indirect receipt of a material benefit, including a financial benefit, by the group or by any of the persons who constitute the group." It does not include a group of persons that forms randomly for the immediate commission of a single offence.

But despite the amazing results we achieved in this area, it was an exercise in futility. Police and other agencies that have organized crime enforcement as their mandate are capable only of maintaining a semblance of order but in no way have a decisive hold on the magnitude of the problem. The larger organized crime groups have been well established over many years, to their advantage. The newer groups have incorporated all the latest technologies, making detection and dismantling exceedingly difficult for police. Every once in a while, agencies are able to infiltrate these groups, causing a hiccup in the operation, but rest assured that these interruptions are quickly managed by way of reformation or other groups filling the void. Despite these realities, the work of investigating organized crime must continue with all the vigour, enthusiasm, dogged determination, technological prowess, and financial resources that we are able to apply, because the flip side is not something that society would want to even contemplate.

However, we must speak about the broad perspective of the drug world and combatting this notorious industry. Throughout the years, not much has changed in the drug world in terms of the people at the top of the food chain who make the most money. They are the brains behind the operation, and their goal is to flood the streets with as much product as possible to sell for the largest possible amount of profit. The further down the rung you happen to be, the greater the risk and lower the reward.

Even after decades of intense enforcement, we still have outlaw motorcycle gangs, traditional organized crime, Asian organized crime, Black organized crime, and many other groups that live extravagant lifestyles with little to no legitimate income. A large portion of their financial accruements has always been attributed to drug production and trafficking. There are a couple of distinctions in today's enforcement that compound the difficulty of disruption. These drug criminals have become educated because of continuous court disclosure requirements and requests. They have learned and made adaptations to the way police have traditionally employed their techniques, making it more difficult to investigate and prosecute for criminal offences.

The advent of technology has also allowed many of these groups to advance in their criminal enterprise. If we look back over the last ten years, changes in technology have fundamentally changed the way we think, interact, and deal with the matters of crime abatement. Technology such as encryption of electronic devices, ready availability of tracking devices, 3-D printing, creative and efficient ways of transporting goods, and the evolution of surveillance equipment that can be purchased online, along with the now-standard methods of communication such as Twitter, Instagram, Facebook, Snapchat, and iPhone or iPad messages, are just some such examples that have materialized. With these advancements come sophisticated, more efficient, less detectable ways to conduct illegal business, including identity theft, electronic money laundering, electronic funds transfers, GPS tracking, and better encryption of communication devices. Police are continually evolving our policing practices, including intelligence gathering and analytics, and keeping up with technology in the attempt to manage and get ahead of these crimes.

Agencies are constantly struggling for resources (staffing, equipment) and finances in order to keep up with the ever-changing creative minds of these criminals. An example of this can be demonstrated in clandestine lab investigations after we have investigated, arrested, and assisted in the prosecution. These organized groups make the adjustment by simply altering one chemical in the manufacturing process of the production, and now this new drug does not fall under the Controlled Drug and Substance Act (CDSA) schedule of controlled drugs and becomes harder to prosecute. For those who can't afford the primary drugs found in our region, such as cocaine, heroin, MDMA, methamphetamine, and marijuana, you always have prescription drugs, where lower-end users and dealers will profit while defrauding the health care system.

Part VI (interception of private communications) investigations are one of the most effective methods, in some cases the *only* feasible method, of investigating these criminals. Unfortunately, with these investigations comes a high price tag: the minimal cost for an independent Part VI investigation can be, on average, $150,000 in the initial stages. Due to the nature of serious investigations in all investigative services, funding was always an issue as the Drugs and Vice Unit, in particular, essentially had to compete for funding in order to progress an investigation. Even with this method, once disclosure was received, criminals upgraded to better ways to beat the system.

Another method (also coming with a hefty price tag) is paying Confidential Human Sources (CHS) for information. Law enforcement agencies often run major drug investigations primarily by paying their CHSs a substantive amount of money for their valued information. An even more effective use of people resources is the use of an agent. An agent differs from a CHS by being an active participant in the investigation, whereas the CHS provides information only. Both can be extremely problematic and can compromise the investigation, with the CHS crossing the line by actively participating or, conversely, the agent engaging in illegal activities pertaining to the case. Either way, it's a thin line that can potentially jeopardize good investigations.

During my on-the-street undercover days, I managed a career agent who earned a pretty good living working with the police in this capacity. I will refer to him as X. He was in his thirties, approximately five-foot-six, and stocky, with long, stringy black hair and a thinning beard, and he was covered with tattoos. X had worked for the Ontario Provincial Police, who eventually turned him over to us for the investigations that we were embarking on. X was a fantastic agent in some respects but a loose cannon in others. In terms of infiltration in the underworld, there were probably few better. He knew his way around organized crime groups and in no time at all was able to provide pertinent investigative information that we were able to use. On the other hand, he was hard to control. As this line of work was his career, he would often do it his way, which on occasion included crossing the line into criminal activity. In this investigation, he did exactly that. Through other investigative means, one of the project leads got wind of his wayward behaviour. X was suspected of inducing several people to commit crimes for his benefit that that person would have otherwise not committed. This was clearly entrapment. We immediately terminated his employment. We were in real danger of jeopardizing this large, very expensive, multi-service, cross-border investigation — it could have been catastrophic for the project if we hadn't caught on when we did.

During my tenure running the drugs and vice unit, there was an epidemic of marijuana grow operations across the country that had found fertile ground in urban areas, primarily residential homes. The usual modus operandi was for operators to rent homes, set up the grow ops, and have "farmers" tend to the crops, including harvesting. These grow ops required equipment in the way of lights, trays, wires, dangerous and volatile chemicals, fertilizers that aided in plant growth, fans, plastic pipes, lumber, growing pots, etc. Often, culprits would rework the heating and venting system in an effort to hide odours and disperse the heat they generated. The operation often required a significant amount of electricity, causing drastic increases in hydro bills. The common workaround was to set up a bypass into the home, avoiding the hydrometer. We quickly realized that this, for the most part, was part of a large-scale organized crime syndicate cashing in on a growth industry. Our drug teams did outstanding work locating, dismantling, arresting, and aiding in the prosecution of people involved.

We also experienced the rise of fentanyl overdoses and in the drug-related death rates as a result. Fentanyl is a synthetically produced opioid traditionally used as pain medication and is considered fifty to one hundred times more potent than morphine, but it has taken on sinister attributes as a street drug. It is often mixed with heroin, methamphetamine, or cocaine, producing a deadly cocktail. Organized crime is deeply involved in the manufacturing, smuggling, and distribution of said drug throughout North America and beyond. We worked extremely hard to slow down the various elements of this notorious drug by targeting the pharmacies and doctors who knowingly over-prescribed the narcotic. We worked with the pharmaceutical companies and other stakeholders to formulate solutions and made a continuous effort to pay attention to the importation of precursors used in the illegal production, which are imported into this country in staggering quantities.

Another resurgence from the old days was the renewed interest in crystal meth (methamphetamine). Illicit labs were turning up everywhere, including in high-density middle- to upper-class residences, creating a very dangerous and real potential for explosions, which have occurred from time to time. Meth, also known by its street name, "ICE," is highly addictive, producing a long-lasting euphoric effect. It can be manufactured by combining over-the-counter drugs with toxic substances. Profits gained through street sales are enormous. Again, organized groups such as outlaw motorcycle gangs were intricately involved in the manufacturing and distribution of this product.

The drug ketamine, known as Special K, found its place in the market, bringing along a whole host of problems in its wake. Ketamine was primarily used in the 1960s on the battlefields of Vietnam as an anesthetic. It worked to ease pain and acted as a sedative. Under medical supervision, it can be an effective medication for serious depression or bipolar disorder, but it has also become a dangerous club drug. It can produce an altered state, along with hallucinations, referred to as falling into a "K-hole." In 2015, I was the officer-in-charge (OIC) of a drug investigation called Project Ice Castle, involving several clandestine drug labs hidden in a wealthy area in Markham. At the height of the project, more than 150 officers were involved. The outcome was the largest ketamine drug bust in Canadian history. We seized $300,000 in cash, sixty kilograms of ketamine worth $2.5 million, and charged seven people. This was a very organized drug manufacturing and distribution operation put out of business for the time being.

For the OIC managing such high-profile units, the responsibility is enormous, considering the work that was conducted each day by high-performing officers, who for the most part are self-motivated, diligent, and resourceful, and are alpha personalities. Holding them back without causing lasting relationship damage was always a work in progress requiring a certain set of skills that one learns on the job. The trick is to know when to allow them to run full-tilt and when to apply the brakes, regroup, and proceed with caution. The supervisors were indispensable as far as the micro-investigations as the overall investigation evolved, whereas I oversaw the macro components, including resource management, budgets, dissemination of information, acquiring the proper authorizations, signing off on search warrants, operational plans, safety protocols, participating as a member of joint forces operations command structure, reporting up to the bureau commander, and executive command. This position requires you to either stand and take a bow when the investigation has produced the intended outcomes while giving the organization its five minutes of fame . . . or you can find the nearest coat closet and hide out for a few days when the shit hits the fan. I had a number of those days when things didn't go as anticipated after an enormous expenditure of money and equipment and human resources. Trust me, you don't want to ever be in that position. Or there's the epic mistake of acting on bad information or poor investigative leads and putting the organization into disrepute. I had a number of those bad days, including the time I received a call from one of my detective sergeants letting me know that the Emergency Response Unit had forcefully entered a home, flash-banged the house, and arrested at gunpoint a couple who were in bed asleep, only to find out that the team was at the wrong house. It took a considerable amount of personal apologies, both verbal and written, along with footing the cost of repairs incurred by the forced entry, to right the wrong in that incident. I couldn't even find a closet to hide in, as all of them were already filled by other team members who had got there before me.

∞

Finally, I would like to recount a story about my younger days as an undercover operator, infiltrating the underbelly of the drug world and organized crime. Part of that mandate included the world of sex work, which we had otherwise understood as prostitution. In the region, we had a number of establishments known as hives for pimps, prostitutes, and johns. The worst offenders were the Major Mac Hotel, the Black Hawk Hotel, the Pro Café, and Whiskey A Go-Go. The bureau acted as the moral authority, cleanser, and sanitizer of these dens of iniquities. My job was to get to know the players, build up a case against them, and ultimately gather enough evidence to validate a search warrant. This often resulted in what was referred to at the time as a "door knock," police jargon for a raid. We became very good at conducting these types of operations. We laid hundreds of charges relating to lewd behaviour, found-ins (clients caught on the premises at the time of the raid), solicitation, procuring (obtaining material benefits from the sexual services of another person), operating a brothel, drugs, etc. We treated everybody we met as part of the greater problem. We viewed the women as willing participants and the material principals in this scourge.

My awakening came many years later, as a recently promoted inspector. I was now the unit commander for the Organized Crime Bureau, which included the Drugs and Vice Unit. This unit is the evolution of the former Morality Bureau. Prior to my arrival, the Vice section had gone through a transformation in how it viewed and dealt with individuals involved in sex work. A young detective ran the unit, Thai Truong, who was as dedicated a public servant as they come. He was smart, committed, determined, proactive, caring — I could go on all day. Suffice it to say, he was the right person at this time for the right reasons.

On my arrival, Thai came into my office and spoke to me about what the unit was engaged in. He turned my entire perspective on vice upside-down. He viewed the women in the sex trade as victims — not willing participants, but real victims. He introduced me to the notion of human trafficking of these girls and that we, the police, should not be the persecutors but in fact the saviours and facilitators to a better and safer life. After that meeting, I was unsettled; my mind was not at ease. I kept going back to my days where we had arrested, charged, prosecuted, and imprisoned these girls. We'd formed biases and stereotypes in conjunction with the power and authority of the law. We'd acted as if we were working on behalf of the citizens, with very little consideration for the circumstances of these women. What and how much damage did we contribute to? That question will never be answered, but I know that I must take ownership of my biases that manifested into actions contrary to our empathic, caring, and supporting nature. I wish I could apologize to every trafficked person we harmed. My penance now is to educate.

I would like to commend the women and men who comprise the Vice teams. What an amazing group of officers, who literally save the lives of the women and minors with whom they come into contact. For the most part, their mission is to rescue those who are victims of human trafficking and incarcerate the individual predators and organized crime groups that cumulatively profit millions of dollars from the sexual exploitation of vulnerable young women and juveniles. These officers develop unique approaches, such as visiting group homes, transportation hubs, and even schools to establish rapport with the at-risk women, providing the opportunity to help them towards a better lifestyle. They work closely with social services to refer them to and ensure that they are provided with the right services that meet their needs. I witnessed first-hand the beyond-the-call-of-duty efforts exhibited by these officers, which I would classify as nothing short of heroic. They have my admiration and thanks.

TRAINING AND EDUCATION

After two years of 4 District uniform patrol, I was transferred to 5 District uniform patrol. As part of the Police Services Act (a provincially mandated part of legislated policy) it was required that every serving police officer in Ontario must receive specific annual training in a number of areas, adhering to the policy guidelines. This training was known as annual requalification. It was at one of these training sessions that I met Sergeant Kevin Smith. Kevin was known as the Use of Force subject matter expert. He was a traditionally trained martial artist, having received his black belt in the art of old-style jujitsu. I refer to it as such because this art has had a rapid infusion of mixed martial arts to the point where the old standard style of self-defence is somewhat obsolete and is not taught to the degree it once was. This distinction is relevant because, having attended several of these requalification Use of Force sessions, I quickly realized a huge gap in the training.

By this time, I had received my first-degree black belt in judo and had competed at a high level. Based on what I knew, it was easy for me to spot the deficiencies in the program and the potentially lethal consequences that might possibly arise. After one of these classes, I asked Kevin if I could demonstrate to him what I had noticed and suggest a possible remedy. He was more than willing to hear and see what I was talking about. My whole contention was that the standard training at the time did not contain a ground component. The training assumed that officers for the most part would be in control when dealing with a resisting individual. We were shown and taught standup techniques that gained compliance to the point where the individual was secured, either standing or on his/her back or stomach in a handcuffing position. What was missing was the fight.

To demonstrate this in a meaningful way, I lay down on my back, had Kevin straddle me, and told him to put me in a compliant position. I told him to choose any position that he wanted, and to take as much time as necessary. Kevin was no slouch, but try as he might, he was not able to put me into a compliant position. Just to solidify the point, I had him lie on his back, then I took the mounted position and told him to get me off him. He didn't stand a chance. Every move he made was anticipated by my years of ground fighting. To tell you the truth, I didn't even break a sweat. The point was made.

Most physical encounters end up on the ground. The reason police usually come out the victor in these situations is sheerly the overwhelming numbers of other officers present. My point was, what happens if an officer is alone and the fight ends up on the ground? Will they be capable of winning that match knowing that they are carrying a great deal of equipment, including lethal force, which can be turned against them? Why not incorporate training that addresses this very real scenario, which I'm sure has happened before and certainly will happen in the future? Kevin was very impressed, to the point that he asked me to consider transferring into the Training Bureau as his partner. Supported by Kevin's endorsement, in 1994 I entered into the world of police training.

Sergeant Smith absolutely loved what he did and was making a name for himself in the world of police Use of Force training. He was eventually deemed an expert in providing service interpretation relating to operational policies, command directives, and training associated with matters of applied force. He was also called upon to provide court testimony in a number of cases. We had the best of what would be considered a working relationship and became very close. He was my immediate supervisor, providing mentorship, coaching, and unwavering support. Kevin proved to be one of the best, most likable, and most respectable members that I encountered in my years of service.

For the first two years in the unit, my focus was primarily as a Use of Force instructor. This meant I was responsible for both new and refresher training for all police members of the organization, ensuring that they received both mandated and currently applied arrest procedures, suspect apprehension, and self-defence, along with academic instruction. To be more specific, I taught police defensive tactics, which included use of non-lethal force such as baton application, handcuffing techniques, using pepper spray, hand-to-hand combat, disengagement techniques, prisoner transport, the use of force continuum (a chart explaining escalation and de-escalation of force), and verbal judo (the art of communicating with non-compliant subjects).

I also taught the lethal aspects of the job, such as the use of deadly force, primarily the firearm. Firearm instruction included nomenclature, cleaning, servicing, handling, loading, unloading and making it safe, proper shot placement, when it is permissible to resort to your firearm, transporting, and storage, along with handgun retention. At that time, firearms training included the Remington Model 10 shotgun and the Smith & Wesson six-shot .38-calibre revolver. Within a year or so of my arrival, the department had decided to transition from the .38 revolver to the .40-calibre 96D Beretta semi-auto pistol. This move was sparked by several situations where criminals outgunned the police with better, more sophisticated weapons, resulting in the deaths of some officers. Eventually, I split my time between Use of Force instruction and academic instruction, where I facilitated classes in police powers of arrest, bylaws, common law, provincial offences, and criminal code offences, along with race relations and employment equity.

Kevin, completely believing in the identified gap in the use of force training, put me in charge of creating a teachable solution that would revolutionize the training delivered at York Regional Police. His mandate was for YRP to be the leader in this type of training in the province. I immediately set about creating a program that has stood the test of time. My creation was groundbreaking then, and to this day, I don't understand why I was one of the first to implement a comprehensive ground control component to defensive tactics police training.

Most police-oriented defensive tactics at the time included a number of striking techniques. There is little doubt that these techniques were very effective in controlling offenders who became resistive or assaultive. Even so, it was unrealistic to believe that most confrontations would end after the first few strikes or kicks. The majority of real confrontations and assaults occur within grappling range. This should have been a wake-up call to most trainers to realize and understand the very real possibility of their officers ending up on the ground. Think about it: whether there are five officers attempting to restrain one individual or one officer in a one-on-one confrontation, in the majority of resistive cases the situation ends up on the ground. Along with this, there were many variables to consider. For example, incomplete techniques, off balance, unsure footing, environmental conditions, wet grass, snow, mud, etc. The possibility of ending up on the ground is substantial.

What I created were some very simple survival techniques for individual officers to deal with when taken down to the ground; therefore, they would not feel lost or exposed and could gain control while on their backs. The first stage of implementation was to train the other instructors in this concept. We spent hours developing, refining, and getting comfortable in delivering this new component. The program was a huge success. The training was hands-on and intensive. It was also immensely fun for the participants, as they had a chance to roll around in a safe, structured environment that exposed them to a foreign discipline. This training struck at the core of reality for many of these officers, who previously would have been completely lost but now understood that being down was not being out. Having that knowledge made surviving that kind of encounter completely surmountable with only a few hours of training. For those who wanted more, we set up extra training during the days and evenings, where students would roll around with instructors.

My time spent in the Training and Education Bureau was probably the most enjoyable and rewarding part of my policing career. I enjoyed reporting to work every day. The long hours morphed into a feeling that there was not enough time as the days sped away. Preparing for classes and delivering the material — along with cleaning up and getting ready for the next day's facilitation — made long stretches feel like non-issues. Each session involved a new crop of officers, providing me with the opportunity to meet every officer in the department, including senior ones. Part of the reason I enjoyed this portfolio was that the training team were considered specialists in our field. We were extremely good and executed excellent programming each time. One of our claims to fame was not providing the same course every year. We would figure out how to deliver the required training and introduce new material differently and effectively. For the most part, the reviews were very positive.

∞

Two years after entering the unit, I was selected to participate in a unique experimental program involving an exchange between the York Regional Police and the York Region District School Board. With an intent to build long-term positive relationships, both organizations embarked on an ambitious program to assign a police officer to two local high schools, teaching law-related classes, while a member of the board was embedded within the Police Service to get direct exposure to police operations. This was a six-month assignment, split evenly between Newmarket High School and Milliken Mills High School. This had never been done before within our region.

I was assigned two hours per day to provide instruction to students in various grades within the school. There was no template for this. I decided the subject matter to deliver; prepared the course outlines, goals, and objectives; created the lesson plans; and put in place ways to measure performance. My delivered courses were Youth and Police Perspective, The Canadian Criminal Code, Application and Rights of Citizens, and Why and How Police Do What They Do. I ended up spending three absolutely special months at each school. This experience was one of the rich blessings I have received in my lifetime. What I encountered was a renewed sense of excitement for the future of this country, and I will even go as far as to say the future of the world. The young folks I met were truly amazing, full of curiosity, youthful energy, and a vibrancy of epic proportions. The innocence of youth, the zest for more, and the brilliance of play mixed with real-world issues. They were amazing. They were extremely inquisitive, having difficulty comprehending what a cop was doing in their classroom not lecturing or cautioning them about bad behaviour. This cop was actually teaching subjects! That mystification aided me in keeping their attention and led to some very interesting, dynamic conversations.

One of the recurring conversations usually began this way: "My friend was beat up by the cops for no reason." To me this was a lob over home plate that I could knock out of the park. Implied in that question was an opportunity for me to systematically and logically walk through that statement and arrive at the conclusion that I had already anticipated. The very first response was for the student to tell the class about the incident. As this unfolded, there was inevitably more information that came out that could be used to elicit a pattern that did not line up with "beating up" and "no reason." As part of the Q&A, I would ask probing questions such as, "Where was your friend when they interacted with the police? Why did the police need to be there? What was the interaction between your friend and the police? How many officers were there? Did all of them beat up your friend?" And so on . . . until the big clarification: How many cops does it take to take control of an individual who is not compliant and is in full resistive mode? If the answer is one, to me, that seems like a fight. If, however, the answer is more than one, then that suggests to me that an effort to control that individual is in order.

Almost always, when you have more than one officer trying to control an unwilling subject, the optics are not very good — onlookers often perceive that as numerous cops pile on top of a person, they are beating the crap out of them. However, there is a clearly denoted line as to where control ends and excessive force begins. We know that the line is crossed from time to time, but from my experience that is the exception among thousands of physical arrests happening every day across Canada and the United States. For the most part, these confrontations result in the intended outcomes of control, arrest, charges, and prosecution.

As far as I know, I was the first and only officer to have participated in this program. If memory serves, as successful as this initial program was, its author, Dr. Avis Glaze (a wonderful woman, I might add), was directed to other work-related matters, and no others revisited this program. It was an unfortunate conclusion — the benefits, in my mind, were on another level. The trust that was built up, along with the familiarity of now knowing a cop, clearly built bridges and restored some faith in policing while displacing deeply held distorted views caused by various influences.

∞

Another interesting assignment was to take over the Race Relations and Employment Equity program that was in place at that time. The facilitator was Sergeant Bisson Ramdewar, who has since retired and passed away in 2019. Bisson was of East Indian descent, making him one of a very few officers of colour in the service at that time. When I took over from him, he was still a constable. Bisson was a lovely man with a genuine smile that always greeted you at the door. He had a presence that warmed those who were near him. Sergeant Ramdewar deserves mention in this book as he was an influencer in my and other officers' stint within the service, and I truly miss his presence.

Race Relations was a separate entity from the Training Unit, and there was a recognized need to bring it under the umbrella of the bureau. Seeing that I was in the Training Unit and delivering programming along with my unique perspective as a Black police officer, I was asked to provide this component to the members. It was not an easy decision to make, because I completely understood the cold, blunt truth of where some officers stood, being told that they must attend an internal race relations program. The chatter was palpable, spinning into a quandary of resentment. They took the mandate as accusatory and insulting. Some felt that the invasion had started and predicted the end of policing as they knew it. Poor Bisson; he had been run over in the classes, and now it was my turn.

Understanding what had occurred previously, the service assigned a second instructor, Sergeant Denyse Ross, to work with me in the classroom. We worked really well together, and seeing that we both had no training in this area, we were privileged to create almost all of the content. Measured by the written reviews we received at the end of each session, it was clear that the calibre of our work had been excellent. Our approach was, "Here's how we can keep you out of trouble by doing and saying the right things, and oh, by the way, it's how you should be providing service anyway." By this time, I had built up a reputation of being a competent, good cop and a nice guy. This bought me valuable respect from other officers and spared me the wrath and affront felt by those officers who questioned the decisions made by the organization. The truth was that most of the officers, having heard from others who had completed the class, were willing to sit through it and even participate to a degree. I believe that because the classes were delivered in a non-accusatory, respectful, non-judgemental tone and directly addressed the truth about how we were policing, the messaging was received.

The only truly unfortunate incident was the one I described earlier in the book (see "Race Relations" chapter). In addition to those outright racist officers, there were some who no doubt attended because it was mandatory, with no purpose of gaining knowledge or changing their ways. In fact, it was very easy to spot them. They were the ones who sat with their arms folded and had no interest in participating in any aspect of training. For them, the best we were able to do was to mark them as attending the class. That was it. Some brave souls engaged us in stimulating debates on the current state of affairs as it related to race relations and policing. Some spoke about being accused of racist behaviour for treating the accused the same way they dealt with other folks. In many of these conversations, it was extremely difficult for them to comprehend how one might interpret police action as racist. What seemed to shine some light on the cause was providing a historical context between people of colour and the behaviour of law enforcement. That said, what started out as mandatory training proved to be worthwhile in the end, again based on the written reviews.

A special note of thanks goes out to Sergeant Mark Ruffolo, who assisted in the Race Relations training and conveyed the importance of the topic as only Mark could. He is a sincere, authentic, and decent person who I have an immense degree of respect for. Mark is now retired, and I wish him all the best in his future endeavours.

Over the four years that I spent in the training bureau, what we taught and how we delivered the training evolved tremendously, providing the service with first-class instruction to the point of emulation by other services. We had many visiting officers from surrounding agencies take part or sit in as observers. The Use of Force training moved quickly from static or closed exercises to more realistic, dynamic simulations. For example, in early classes, officers were told to strike a man dressed in a padded suit with hands, kicks, or baton strikes, and shoot at paper targets (static/closed). This training advanced to dynamic, active scenarios where, to the best of our efforts and abilities, we incorporated real-world situations, including the use of simunition (an equivalent to paint gun ammunition, used in replica handguns). Even back then, we had an emphasis on de-escalation and disengagement tactics that has served our officers well throughout the years.

∞

In 1994, while I was a member of the Training Bureau, I come across an information pamphlet advertising the International Law Enforcement Olympics being held in Birmingham, Alabama, with judo listed as one of the sports. I was immediately excited on two fronts: I had never been to Alabama, and I truly believed that I could be competitive at that level. I made up my mind right then and there that I would sign up to represent York Regional Police and Canada. Incredibly, there was no qualifier attached to the application other than you had to be in law enforcement.

Bureaucracy, of course, always steps in, so what should be simple turns into wading through bullshit first. I approached the Police Association with a request for sponsorship, as the cost of attending was quite expensive to manage on my own. My request was customary — this was the route that other members had taken when involved in representing the organization at competitions. I believe it was in the amount of $500. My request was denied. I was pretty pissed; the year before, the association had sponsored three members to fly to Australia to participate in the World Police and Fire Games to play darts. It was never disclosed to me how much was given to these officers, but rest assured it had to be more than $500. I went anyway, on my own dime.

My days off were booked, travel arrangements made, and confidence intact. Two other YRP members were slated to participate in the same competition in very different sports: Maxine Biros, a triathlete, and Dave Mackie, in the body building event. I don't believe that they were sponsored by the association either, but I was never sure.

Birmingham, Alabama, is the Deep South, known for its deeply racist and troubled past. My very first observation, upon landing at the airport, was the number of Black people and other people of colour who were working at various jobs throughout. They were behind the counters and serving in stores; they were porters, waiters, cleaners, baggage attendees, ramp guides. For the most part they were all pleasant and seemed content from the outside. My second observation was that in conversation with the general public they didn't make eye contact. There were several occasions when I needed to ask questions in order to orient myself. In those few interactions not one of the folks would look me in the eye; instead they'd cast their gaze slightly towards the floor. It was strange, for sure, but consistent throughout my stay in the South. I observed the same behaviour at the hotel where I stayed. It was evident that almost all the lower-level positions were filled by people of colour, primarily Black people who seemed to be conditioned to respond in this same fashion. I wondered if this behaviour was a leftover habit from programming during slavery and emancipation that still has a hold on many.

On the evening of my arrival, I was in the hotel gym, working out and preparing for my competition in a couple of days. That's where I met Marino Santini, a Canadian police officer from the Ottawa Police Service. We immediately became friends. Marino was to compete in the wrestling event along with another Ottawa police member whom I'll refer to as Mike. There was a third Ottawa police officer who would compete in the taekwondo competition; I'll refer to him as Ted. I would meet both Mike and Ted the next day.

The next morning was the opening ceremony. It was a grand affair, with athletes from literally all over the world. There were over three thousand competitors from every continent on the globe participating in thirty-five events. One of the more impressive spectacles was the large contingent of officers from the United Arab Emirates, who were all dressed in very expensive black suits, white shirts, and black ties. I was able to chat for a few minutes with a couple of members who told me they'd come to this event on a private plane chartered by the Emirates. It turned out that within that contingent were several world-class athletes who really made a mark on the games. Thank goodness the three York Region participants were given matching tracksuits prior to attending (courtesy of the department) so we didn't look quite so out of place. We also brought our YRP and Canadian flags, which we displayed proudly. After the ceremonies, Marino invited me back to his room at the hotel to hang out with the Ottawa crew. The four of us gelled as if we had been friends for many years. The beer flowed as freely as the conversation, putting us in a mood of confidence and invincibility for the next day's competition.

The day of my event unfolded in a smooth, transactional way. I was ready physically and mentally, and was eager to put my many years of dedication to this sport to the test once again. I arrived at the arena with plenty of time to get my thoughts together and take in the air and buzz of competition. No matter how well prepared, there is always a touch of nervousness that accompanies athletes, which is most intense right after the warmup session and the beginning of the tournament. For me that feeling was internalized and redirected into energy, a booster shot that would propel me onto the mat with the zeal necessary to perform at an optimum sustainable level. I will spare you the details of each fight, but I will say that at the end of the day, I was standing on the podium with a gold medal around my neck.

With my event out of the way, I had time to take in the other events that were unfolding. I was fortunate to be able to watch Marino and Mike in their wrestling matches. It was very exciting and nerve-racking — I had taken them on as team members and now felt like a coach watching his students perform. Ted was outstanding in his taekwondo competition, displaying several unique techniques that had the crowd in awe. The four of us hung out, drank beer, and formed a brotherhood that can best be described as a solid connection. My understanding is that in today's vernacular this would be considered a bromance of sorts. In any case, those guys made this particular event most memorable. The Law Enforcement Olympics lasted just under a week, giving us more than enough time to get in the latest police gossip, seasoned with opinions on a variety of global issues that of course we had the answers to. After the closing ceremonies, there was an exchange of contact information with promises of getting together in the not-so-distant future.

Several months later, Marino drove the four hours from Ottawa to York Region. We had spoken on the phone a few times, and this pleasant visit rekindled our friendship. Several months after that, Marino called me with some very disturbing news. He told me that Mike had passed away. Completely shocked, I asked him what had happened. The answer was so unexpected and haunting — Marino explained that Mike had committed suicide as a result of a domestic situation with his girlfriend. I felt like I had been punched in the gut as hard as humanly possible. The hurt, the pain, hit me very hard. Within a year of hearing that news, Marino called me to say that Ted had *also* committed suicide, also over a domestic situation with a girlfriend! Both of these young officers were now dead by their own hands and within a very short time of my having met them. Policing creates its own unique set of stresses and trauma. Compound this with what life in general can bring, and you often have a recipe for disaster. I don't know the specifics as to what these young men were going through, but the final condition of ending their life by their own hands is not uncommon to me or that of the policing world. Citing just one example, Colin Freeze and Molly Hayes, reporters for the *Globe and Mail*, published an article in March 2020 that speaks directly to this issue. They reported that during an eight-year period (2012–2020), the Ontario Provincial Police suffered seventeen suicides of their members. Other sources have been consistent in reporting only one death of an OPP officer on duty within that time span. Although there is real value in the statistics that show more officers die by their own hands than are killed in the line of duty, they don't adequately convey the tragedy that we are losing far too many officers by suicide, which verges on being an epidemic.

The value and importance of police training should never be understated. The one thing that we can be assured of is that the better trained your service is, the better the community is served as it relates to law and order. People are the commodity in which police agencies deal. In the end, it is all about the people. From a Canadian policing perspective, I can unequivocally state that the training provided is extremely good — certainly not perfect, but very respectable. In comparison to many other nations, we are fortunate by way of our investment in training practices. There is a special importance placed on education with an emphasis on critical thinking that forms a vital foundation. I was the beneficiary of receiving this training along with creating parts of it. It has served me well. The educators I served with were second to none. They were unsung heroes, the best of the best.

NOT JUST ANOTHER DAY

I n this chapter, I will detail some memorable days that fell outside of the expected, providing me with many hours of stories when asked about my job.

The answer to the first question I am always asked is a resounding *no* — I have never shot anyone. However, there have been a few occasions where I removed my gun purposefully from its holster and pointed it in the direction of persons who I thought at the time posed an imminent threat. I will tell you about two such occasions.

On the morning of Saturday, September 21, 1991, I was partnered up with Police Constable William Goetz. We were on patrol in uniform, assigned to the Woodbridge area of Vaughan. A busy Friday evening had turned into a slow Saturday morning, but we stayed vigilant, checking industrial properties and patrolling residential areas. At 3:41 a.m., we observed a vehicle turn right from a side street onto westbound Steeles Avenue, speeding. Constable Goetz caught up to the vehicle, which was now stopped at a red traffic light, preparing to make a left turn at the intersection. A quick check of the licence plate revealed that the vehicle was stolen. As the light turned green, the driver proceeded southbound, with us directly behind him. A few metres down the road, we activated the roof lights, accentuated by a short, growling blast of the siren. I guess the driver decided that the police wanting him to pull over could only mean one thing: his ass was in trouble. With the pedal to the metal and a bucketful of bad intentions, the driver decided to outrun the law. We were now engaged in a vehicle pursuit.

In an attempt to shake us off, the driver executed a series of dangerous manoeuvres, making sharp, sudden left turns into a residential area. He eventually lost control, mounting the curb and striking a van parked on a driveway. Parts of the vehicles were flying everywhere. He came back onto the road, striking another car parked curbside. We came to a sudden stop behind him. As I exited the cruiser, his car door opened, and he rolled out onto the roadway as if in a combat stance, facing us. The lighting was poor, a situation complicated by a massive dump of adrenaline, and I saw something in his hands. I didn't have a clear view, but it seemed as if he was in a combat semi-prone position, which immediately sent me into defensive mode. I drew my revolver, and I remember the feel of the trigger easing back. At the same time, out of my peripheral vision, I saw the figure of my partner run out in front of the cruiser towards the suspect. I immediately eased back on the trigger. Constable Goetz tackled him, more than likely saving his life. There'd been no gun in the suspect's hand after all — this fool had grabbed an ice scraper on his way out of the car. In the split second available to me, I interpreted that object as possibly a firearm of sorts. Thank goodness Constable Goetz stopped things from escalating too far.

When we initiated the pursuit, we were actually in the jurisdiction of the Toronto Police Service, so they eventually took control of the subject and the investigation. This was one of the events that evokes thankful memories for how it turned out. I didn't ever want to fire my gun in the line of duty, especially under questionable circumstances.

∞

In May 1988, I was a rookie assigned to the Morality Unit as an undercover officer. May 19 was a Thursday; I was working with Detective Constable Ezra (Tony) Browne in an unmarked car, popping in and out of targeted establishments and taking the temperature of drug activity in those bars and clubs. It should be noted that I was as green as they came in terms of actual police work. The only thing I knew comfortably was undercover work. Ezra was an experienced officer with the benefit of having worked in a number of different policing units.

Around 10:40 p.m., we pulled into an outdoor shopping plaza in the area of Kennedy Road and Denison Street in Markham. Our sole intention was to catch up on recording our activities in our notebooks. Ezra pulled the vehicle into a parking space with several other parked vehicles spread out around it. As we settled in to do our notes, Ezra said to me in a steady but firm voice that the person sitting in the car approximately one parking spot ahead of us has a gun.

"What gun, where?"

"Look at the driver, he has a gun."

Looking straight ahead, I saw one occupant in the driver's seat and a man standing outside of the vehicle on the passenger side. Holy shit! The driver had a gun in his hand that I could clearly see. Then the panic set in, and I started asking Ezra all kinds of stupid questions in rapid succession. Why would he have a gun? Are they gonna rob a store? What the hell do we do? Using his calm, confident, effective tone, Ezra gave me clear, sober instructions on what to do next. He instructed me to get on the radio, provide the dispatcher with our location and observations, and request backup. I bumbled my way through the call, trying my best not to sound alarmed and to give details as best I could. Thinking back now, I must have sounded "rookie-ish" — the dispatcher had to ask for a 10-2, a repeat of the information. Once that was done, my instructions were to cover the person on the outside and he, Ezra, would advance on the driver to effect an arrest. As we exited the vehicle, the driver passed the gun over to the suspect, who was now reaching in through the passenger side window. Both Ezra and I drew our service weapons. At that time, I had a Smith & Wesson six-shot snubnose revolver. The stubby, as we called them, had a two-inch barrel as opposed to the four-inch barrel of the regular pistols. As we advanced on the two unsuspecting bandits, my hands started to shake. That little snubnose revolver felt as if it weighed fifty pounds. My heart was pounding, resonating off the inside of my skull. The ambient noise around me was no more. I was singularly focused on the guy with the gun. I was terrified! I had no confidence that I would be able to handle this potentially dangerous real-life confrontation. I heard Ezra giving commands to both suspects, identifying us as police officers and telling them not to move. He told the party with the gun to slowly put it on the ground and back away, which was done without a hitch. We arrested both parties; they were cuffed, given rights to counsel, and cautioned (standard procedure upon arrest). It turned out that the gun was an imitation, which damn well looked real at the time. The driver was twenty-two years of age; the guy with the gun was only eighteen. The lingering question is and will always be: Would we have shot those boys if the situation hadn't unfolded as it did? It certainly was possible.

∞

Why some people react to certain situations in the manner that they do is a mystery to me. Take Richard Deschamp, for instance. When I first met Richard, he was in a curled-up heap on the ground with several people on top of him holding him down. I was responding to a break-and-enter-in-progress call that turned into anything but that. You see, several neighbours were holding Richard. He lived in the immediate area but was not known to them. By all accounts, he was someone who kept mostly to himself and was not considered a menace in any way. However, he was about to spend this particular night away from his home at the courtesy of the York Regional Police. Richard was eventually arrested, handcuffed, searched, given his rights to counsel, and placed in my cruiser for transport to the station. Other officers were detailed to take statements from witnesses and those involved.

We arrived at 5 District station around 12:55 a.m., at which time Richard was presented in front of Staff Sergeant Scarlett to be booked and shown his new overnight accommodations, replete with a concrete bed and steel toilet, and oh, a McDonald's breakfast sandwich included at no extra cost. We also provided Richard our premium package by relieving him of his property, which would be stored by us, compliments of the house of course: it included a Crossman 357–style .177-calibre pellet pistol, two cylinders containing six pellets each, one spent CO_2 cartridge, one full CO_2 cartridge, one axe handle, one flashlight, one roll of electrical tape, and four photographs of a lizard. That last item is what this was all about.

Now, this wasn't just any lizard; it was a big-ass iguana that the accused claimed belonged to him.

Let's rewind a bit and get some perspective on this arrest. Richard Deschamp lived in a middle-class, well-to-do area in Markham where the lawns were manicured and folks walked their dogs while waving hello to their neighbours. It would be considered a lovely place to raise your children. Richard had a pet lizard that he'd raised to a healthy size through tender loving care and an assortment of plants required for a healthy balanced diet. Did you know that iguanas are herbivorous? They eat plants, leaves, flowers, and some fruits. News to me, but to each his own.

Anyway, one day in mid-August 1992, the iguana orchestrated and successfully executed an escape that would have put Papillon's efforts to shame. However, he was not as accomplished as he thought and was soon caught by a neighbour, who I will refer to as "PR." Not knowing where the lizard came from, PR decided to keep it, and within a few days had the lizard up for sale. Richard saw the ad and reached out to PR, explaining that the lizard belonged to him and he wanted it back. PR declined and was intent on selling his newly found gain at a hefty price. Well, the rest is history. Richard showed up at PR's house at about 12:20 a.m. and rang the doorbell. When PR answered, Richard demanded his iguana and started to remove the pistol from behind his back. PR reacted immediately and an epic struggle ensued. PR's wife called the police while neighbours, upon hearing the commotion, came and assisted PR in securing Richard on the front lawn. That's where I met all involved. Now, to this day, I can't understand what Richard's intentions were that evening, having in his possession the items that he did. I assume he was planning something sinister, but who knows. Unfortunately, I have never followed up with this case as detectives were assigned the investigation and I moved on to the next radio call. I don't even know how it was finally resolved. The moral of the story should be when someone kidnaps your loved one (in this case a lizard), call the police and don't turn into Rambo!

∞

It was one of those extraordinary evenings where the temperature is twenty degrees Celsius and the sky is clear and bright. This particular late evening, I was on patrol in Markham. For all intents and purposes, it started out as a typical shift. The district was moderately busy during the earlier hours but settled down to not much happening towards 11 p.m. A few hours earlier, our district had been monitoring a high-speed pursuit in the neighbouring 2 District, where police were engaged, for the second time that day, with the Supra Bandits. This name had come about due to prior investigations involving a small group of men whose modus operandi was breaking into stores and businesses then making their escape using Toyota Supras. These particular vehicles, when modified, were extremely fast and very controllable at high speeds. This group was operating throughout the Greater Toronto Area, engaging police in pursuits, presumably on purpose. On both occasions that evening, police were easily outrun to the point where chasing the suspects was extremely dangerous and not worth the risk to officer safety and of collateral damage if a crash were to happen.

I had parked my cruiser just off the roadway on Highway 7 east of Woodbine Avenue. I had both the driver's side and passenger side windows down, enjoying the cool cross-breeze and the solitude of the evening. There was little to no traffic on the road. The police radio was unusually silent. Then, suddenly, a call came through for all available units to respond to a break and enter in progress at the variety store located in the area of Highway 7 and Warden Avenue. I picked up the microphone and advised dispatch that I was a minute or two away. I pulled onto the roadway and headed eastbound on Highway 7 with no traffic on the road.

As I reached the intersection, I heard another unit on the radio calling out that the suspect had jumped into a Toyota Supra and the officer was directly behind him. How the heck that other unit beat me to the call I'll never know, but what I saw was the cruiser with the emergency lights flashing, chasing the suspect vehicle through the plaza parking lot, both vehicles making their way to the exit on Warden Avenue. I immediately blocked off the southbound lanes of Warden Avenue at Highway 7. The Supra came out of the plaza, made a left turn, and headed straight towards me. I still remember the sound of the vehicle accelerating as it barrelled towards me. I was watching this transpire as if in slow motion. This bastard was not slowing down or trying to evade the blockade. Rather, he was speeding up! This dude was on a suicide mission. I literally had a split second to decide what to do. What saved me that night was that I had not put the cruiser into park; rather I was on the brake pedal. I stomped on the accelerator, pushing it to the floor and jetting the cruiser forward in the split second before the Supra would have hit me. It was so close that I still get a visceral reaction when I tell the story. He must have missed me by inches. I felt as if I had just escaped death. If we had connected, he would have hit me on the driver's side door, giving me little chance of not being seriously injured or killed. By the time I got myself together, both the Supra and the pursuing cruiser were long gone. A supervisor called off the pursuit a short time later, as the speeds exceeded any acceptable measure. That evening the bad guy won. He successfully evaded police, but as is the case with so many criminals, he didn't stop. This continuing behaviour ultimately led to arrests, charges, convictions, and the dismantling of the Supra Bandits.

∞

It looked like a war zone. It could best be described as the aftermath of a World War II blitzkrieg. The destruction was on an order of magnitude that shocked everyone, including veteran police officers, emergency medical services, firefighters, municipal managers, and ordinary everyday folks. I saw roofs of houses completely gone, crumpled vehicles slammed up against structures. I saw huge trees uprooted and tossed into buildings. I looked right through brick homes that were stripped wide open, exposing each room, with contents strewn everywhere. There were no lights, no water, and downed hydro poles were causing multiple power outages. Debris of every description littered the streets. People were out of their homes and huddled in groups, comforting each other. I heard whimpering, crying, people yelling, some just talking loudly, others with their arms wrapped securely around children and loved ones. There were police, fire department, and emergency medical services vehicles by the dozens. Ambulance buses lined the roadways. Every single York Regional Police officer that could be spared was at the scene.

No, this wasn't a scene out of an epic feature film; it was for real. This was the aftermath of the August 2009 tornadoes in Vaughan. The weather system that caused so much destruction and devastation was the largest single-day tornado event in Ontario's recorded history.

My ride to work proved to be an exercise in the love of duty and questioning how brave you really are. My vehicle was assaulted by torrential downpours causing visibility to be near zero at some points. With the car wipers at maximum capacity and an average speed of barely twenty kilometres per hour, I plodded on. When the rain let up slightly, I could see that those massive, thunderous, ominous clouds were certainly up to no good. On a typical day, my journey to central headquarters was almost a straight fifteen-minute drive north. However, on this day, having seen the potential for problems, I left my home very early, and thank goodness I did. I took an hour and ten minutes to actually reach the station.

My portfolio at the time was that of duty inspector, and my overnight shift went from 6 p.m. to 4 a.m. The duty inspector's responsibilities included the overall management of the service operation in the absence of other senior officers (command and control, as it were). The inspector would be provided real-time information on what was unfolding operationally and ensure that it was managed satisfactorily. On arrival, I met with Inspector Doug Connolly, who was signing off, having worked the day shift. I had not yet changed into my uniform when all hell broke loose. The phones were ringing off the hook. One call after another from dispatch, divisions, and senior and junior officers — at one point I swear I heard from one of the canines, but no doubt fatigue had set in by that point. Anyway, every call was about several tornados touching down, causing massive damage.

Understanding the enormity of this event, Inspector Connolly volunteered to stay on and manage the situation on the ground while I coordinated the logistics and mobilization of resources. Before I forget, I would like to give a big shout-out to Inspector Connolly, who did a magnificent job in managing several scenes during the worst of times.

This is where the word *multitasking* truly means what it is supposed to mean. Working several landline phones augmented by my department-issued cellphone — all at the same time — was truly taxing. Executive commanders wanted a minute-by-minute status update, which meant I needed information immediately. Operational decisions had to be made on the spot. We were in the process of shift changes throughout the service. One of the big decisions was who in the organization would be held back from leaving and who did I need to call in. I ordered both 2, 4, and 5 District officers to remain on shift. I ordered the communication staff to stay in place. I sent out a call for all available communication staff to try to make it to work for added support. I called in all available auxiliary police officers, court officers, special services officers — pretty well anybody I could think of who would be helpful at this time. Then there was the media, who were relentless in calling for the police perspective on this major catastrophe. And in the middle of all of this, I was trying to change into my uniform. Believe it or not, that one exercise took almost two hours to complete.

That day marked the most tornadoes ever seen in one region in Canadian history. At least eighteen tornadoes were recorded across Ontario. Many were classified as F2 tornadoes, producing wind speeds up to 225 kilometres per hour and resulting in over 650 homes damaged in Vaughan alone. Property damages throughout the Greater Toronto Area were estimated to be well north of $100 million. A state of emergency was declared by Mayor Linda Jackson, giving the municipality immediate access to agencies that would be able to provide assistance. Mass evacuation orders were implemented and enforced by officers. Emergency shelters were opened, providing safe haven for those in need. Tragically, this unfortunate event resulted in the death of an eleven-year-old boy in the neighbouring region of Durham.

Eventually, I had the opportunity to leave the office and take over managing the scene. A Mobile Joint Operation Command Centre was in place. This provided an area for a coordinated approach from the various organizations that were assisting. As you well can imagine, there were structural engineers, hydro workers, hospital workers, tow trucks, City of Vaughan employees, heavy machinery clearing roadways and debris, rescue teams, food and water trucks, buses to transport people to shelters, and friends and family coming into the area in support of loved ones. The scenes were unbelievable.

A quick mention to all those members of the combined emergency services, joint command operation, and neighbouring police services, and to the ordinary citizens who came to the assistance of those in need: I extend a heartfelt gratitude. To the members of the York Regional Police, who truly demonstrated our motto of "Deeds Speak," you are to be commended for how well you all performed in the face of adversity. Our communications staff, call takers, 911 operators, dispatchers, and supervisors were all outstanding. And a note of thanks to Sergeant John Lockery, who did a magnificent job on the ground managing all the moving components in real time. This was certainly not just another day.

∞

Being an undercover operator engenders a wee bit of arrogance, which I'm sure I possessed in my third year in this capacity. I remember I was working an afternoon shift with no specific game plan as to what was to unfold for that day. When time permitted, the team would venture out to tie up loose ends by checking target locations, serving notices, gathering licence plate numbers, and seeing who was out and about. Those were the only agenda items I had in mind. The building that housed the Morality Bureau was a nondescript two-level affair, with offices on the top floor and occupying about a third of the bottom level, which also provided a large vehicle bay. At that time, we shared the building with members of the tactical unit, the traffic unit, and the quartermaster stores providing equipment for members.

On that particular day, my undercover car was out for servicing, so I needed to use one of the secondary vehicles parked in the garage. When I went to look at what was available, there it was: a brand-new, straight-out-of-the-box Dodge 500, silver, complete with the new car smell. The car called me over and lured me inside. The allure was too much to resist, seeing that I was without transportation or a real destination that would necessitate another type of vehicle. So the deal was solidified. This would be the vehicle of choice for the evening. The keys were in the vehicle with a tag indicating that the assigned designation was D642. My partner at the time, Constable David Jazwinski, wanted to serve some notices (documents indicating police action that the accused needed to be informed about). We drove separate vehicles so that he could serve the notices and I could attend as a backup officer, observing him from a distance, ready to provide assistance if required. So that's what we did for several hours.

I felt pretty special rolling around in a brand-new ride, kicking back some tunes, absorbing my status as a free-roaming, getting-paid agent of the province. On this day, life was good. We served the final notice around 10:45 p.m. in the area of Fenton Plaza, Markham. We decided that we would head over to the Cotton Club so I could make an appearance and see what targets were at that establishment. Constable Jazwinski was just ahead of me, driving eastbound on Steeles Avenue. He pulled into the left-turn lane and stopped for the red light. I was directly behind him but decided to pull up on his right side in order to talk to him through my driver's-side window. Yelling through the window, I told Dave that I would meet him in a few minutes, that I had to find a spot to remove my service revolver prior to entering the club. As soon as he acknowledged me, for some unexplainable reason I proceeded into the intersection, completely forgetting that the traffic light in front of me was still red. That's when it all happened in slow motion. I saw a vehicle coming towards me rapidly. Instantly, I realized that my ass was in trouble.

The impact was jarring. The gut-wrenching sounds of crumpling metal, breaking glass, and folding plastic were deafening. The world as I knew it faded to black. My body was at the mercy of the centrifugal energy and G-force. The Dodge was hit on the front passenger door, causing it to whip around and face north. It was a furrowed mess of scrap metal. The other car sustained major damage to the front end. I am thankful there were no major injuries. By the magnitude of the damage all around, there should have been. Other than a sprained wrist and slight bruising of my lower back, I was fine, and there were no injuries to the other driver. The following several hours were somewhat blurry, but suffice it to say all motor vehicle protocols were observed. Eventually, I was driven back to the office by Dave to complete my reports and sign off.

The following day I was summoned to headquarters to meet with Deputy Chief Robert Wilson, and he informed me that the vehicle I'd taken out for a romp was his brand-new car that he had ordered, and it had arrived yesterday. Oh, snap! Out of all the available cars in the bay that evening, I'd chosen the deputy's! He was not impressed, to say the least. He informed me that there would be an accident review commencing immediately and he would set the date for me to attend. A few days later, I was again summoned to headquarters to be adjudicated. I sat in the deputy's office as he looked up from his desk over his glasses and proceeded to step through the sequence of events leading up to his decision. I'd taken his car without consent. The accident was 100 percent my fault, and he deemed my negligence would result in the loss of forty hours' pay. Damn! But he was absolutely right. Oh yes, I needed to be brought down a peg or two. Several weeks later, I was ceremoniously presented with a plaque bearing several pieces of the Dodge 500 recovered by members of my unit. That plaque served as a sober reminder that no matter how full of myself I felt, there is a cautionary tale waiting around every corner. Stay alert and stay humble. That plaque is among my most prized memorabilia: it has followed me throughout my career and has been mounted on one wall or another as I've moved offices.

∞

Tuesday, May 4, 2010, was another tough day. A two-year-old boy was killed in the driveway of his Markham home when a family member backed a car into him. This incident happened around 5:50 p.m. on Bushberry Court, near 16th Avenue and Kennedy Road. Paramedics arrived shortly after the boy was hit but were unable to revive him. He was pronounced dead at the scene. On my arrival, the little boy's body had not been taken to hospital and instead had been laid in his home. I was the duty inspector responsible for overall operational function of the service at that time. It was my responsibility to provide information to the throngs of media present. It took everything I had to keep it together, parsing every word so as not to break down. Here are the details as I knew them then. The mother of the child had gone out to the store to pick up a few items, while her young son was in the company of adults, playing with some of the other children on the street. The young boy saw his mother pull into their driveway when she returned and ran over to greet her. His mother, having remembered that she had forgotten something at the store, immediately reversed the car and struck him. The young couple, believed to be in their thirties, also had a six-month-old girl. They had moved into the neighbourhood about two years prior. It was one of the saddest situations I experienced in my career.

∞

Routine patrol, working out of 4 District (Vaughan) in the early '90s, was a blast. Every day was different, with expected and unexpected calls. On this particular day, I was detailed to a sick-and-injured-person call. The information received prior to arrival was that an elderly person was in bed and non-responsive. Now, in almost every case for this kind of call, either the fire department or the ambulance would be on scene prior to the police arriving. They were that good in their response times. As luck would have it, I was only a minute or two away and so was another officer, Constable John Lucas. Both of us arrived almost at the same time. We entered the house and were greeted by a number of people who were in distress, some in panic mode. They were crying, shaking, and moaning. "Thank God, thank God, officers, she's upstairs. She went to bed last night and we tried to wake her this morning and we couldn't."

Both John and I bounced up the stairs and were directed to one of the bedrooms. As we entered the room, there was an older lady lying flat on her back on the bed, dressed in her nightgown. We both had seen enough bodies to recognize immediately that she had been dead for a while. There were a couple of other people in the room at that time. They were begging us to do something. "Help her, please!" We both moved in close to the body and operated as if we knew what we were doing. John was attempting to take a pulse, and I acted as if I was gauging her temperature by placing my hand on her forehead. John whispered to me, "Let's do CPR." I said to him at an almost imperceptible volume, "John, she's dead!" His immediate response was, "Get the fucking mask from the car!" As he was the senior officer on scene, that's what I did.

I hopped down the stairs past wailing voices and grabbed the mask from the trunk. Not missing a step, I ran up the stairs back into the room. John was still working on taking her pulse. He got into position to start the compressions, and I put the mask over her nose and mouth. We were both thinking, *Where the hell is the friggin' fire department or ambulance?!*

Not knowing what I was doing, without thought, I put my mouth over the mouthpiece of the mask and proceeded to blow in two quick breaths. I inhaled at the same time as John pushed down on the lady's chest. I had no idea that the one-way valve in the mask was faulty. All that dead air from her lungs came up into the mask and into my mouth, which I inhaled and ingested fully and completely, causing an immediate gag reflex. A nauseating vomit mixed with saliva came out of my mouth onto the patient. Oh shit! I just vomited on Grandma! Now, it wasn't a lot, but it was enough to be seen by the bystanders.

I then went into a coughing fit. I couldn't get that dead air out of me. Death carries a certain smell that is distinctive. It was in my nose and lungs and stayed there. One of the bystanders ran to my aid, providing me with a towel. I used the towel to wipe the mess off the patient and dabbed the corners of my mouth. John didn't miss a beat. All the while, he continued the chest compressions — a thousand and one, a thousand and two, and so on. Totally embarrassed and endlessly apologetic, I could do nothing else other than wait for John's counting to stop, then blow into the mask providing two quick breaths as required by the St. John Ambulance CPR training at that time. I'm aware that the CPR procedures have since changed.

We spent only a few more minutes in what we both knew was a futile attempt to resuscitate until the fire department finally arrived with their equipment and expertise. They transported the patient to the hospital via ambulance. I was required to take a preliminary report from witnesses. I remember trying to hide myself in my notebook, not wanting to face them as I asked for information. The reality was that their concern was for the patient, not me. With more maturity on the job, I would have known this. At the time, I felt I had lost my professionalism in front of these folks, who were looking to me for help. This was no ordinary day, and certainly one that I have not forgotten. Would you believe that death scent stayed with me every waking hour for over a week? However, if I were able to blush, you would still be able to see the embarrassment on my face even now as I relate this story.

∞

The morning of August 2, 2007, is indelibly seared in my mind. I was enjoying some well-deserved time off between shifts. That morning, I woke up, fiddled around, then decided it was time for some brunch . . . yes, the start of a real lazy day. For ambient noise, I turned on the television, which was tuned to one of the local news channels. What I saw took the wind out of me. The headline was that a York Regional Police officer had been killed in the line of duty. When? Who? Details were just emerging and sketchy. I called the station and was told that it was Constable Robert Plunkett. I was in total disbelief; Rob had sat with me in my office just a week earlier, and we'd had the best conversation. This man was truly one of the best people I have ever met during my policing career. I don't know how to state it any better than that. He was that man who had that imposing physique, handsome as they come, extremely athletic, gentle, caring, great sense of humour, and smart, with a heart of gold. Rob would come looking for me and I would look for him whenever we were in each other's vicinity, not wanting to miss an opportunity to chat for however long. His favourite greeting was, "Hey, chum," a term of endearment that most of us received from him upon meeting.

That fateful morning, Rob had been working as a part of a special services surveillance unit tasked with investigating suspects connected to the theft of airbags from vehicles. This was a big thing back in the day. There had been a rash of airbag thefts to the tune of forty-three since January of that year. Stolen airbags were netting between $1,500 and $2,000 apiece. The surveillance team spotted two vehicles leaving an address in Toronto and believed that one of them was indeed stolen. The vehicles were followed to an address in Markham where the bandits began removing the airbag. By this time, it was just after 5 a.m. The team moved in to arrest the two culprits, with Rob approaching the open car door. In an attempt to evade police, the suspect put the vehicle in reverse, pinning Rob between the door and a tree, ultimately causing his death.

My friend was married with three children. He'd joined the service in 1985, just a year before me. He was the chair of the Ontario Special Olympics in 2000 and was recognized for bravery for saving the life of a senior citizen who'd ended up in the freezing waters of a lake in Markham. His police funeral was as magnificent as they come. A true testament to a fallen hero. Rest in peace, Rob.

∞

In 1993, I attended the Ontario Police College for certification as a Use of Force instructor, which required me to take up residency there for a few weeks. On this particular Friday, I had decided that I would stay the weekend at the college, avoiding the long three-hour drive home only to return in a couple days to continue the course. It was not uncommon for the rookies to venture outside of the college grounds into the so-called "town" to blow off steam at the receiving end of a pint or two or three. For me, having the benefit of half a dozen years under my belt, attending a course that was familiar and not so taxing, my decision for the evening was to simply go to bed.

In the early hours of the morning, I woke up feeling the urge to surrender to the call of nature. I left my room and walked across the common area of the pod to the bathroom. That part of the exercise went well, but what did not go so well was my return to my room. As I opened the room door, I came face to face with a young lady asleep in my bed. She was out cold, half dressed — exposed from the bottom down — clearly breathing, and not in any visible distress. However, she did reek of alcohol. I had no clue who she was or where she'd come from. Knowing instinctively how bad this would appear, I immediately grabbed my pants from the edge of the bed, left the room, and ran down the hall to find the overnight security officer, who was in the main rotunda. I was now having a full-blown panic attack. It was difficult for me to construct a sentence to explain what had just happened. The optics were so bad. She was clearly a student, based on my assessment of her age. I was a mature officer on course. I had no idea how she would explain being in my room that morning.

He accompanied me back to the pod and I stayed back a distance as he woke her up and walked her from my room. As it turned out, this young lady was a new officer working out of one of our nuclear facilities, attending the college as part of her progressive training. She had gone out on the town with several of her classmates. She'd clearly had way too much to drink, had stumbled into the pod believing that she was in the female unit, saw my door open, and, I'm assuming, felt that this was either her room or as good a spot as any to get some sleep.

The fallout was epic and, of course, the talk of the college. I was interviewed by several senior administrators and required to submit a detailed incident report. It's my understanding that the young lady was eventually released from her position as a security officer. The ramification of her poor decision was, in my view, severe and unfortunate.

∞

Who remembers the year 2000, most notably known as Y2K? Let me give you a short account of the infamous panic preceding it. It was all based on computer systems used at that time. Because of the inherent cost of memory space storage, programmers used two digits as opposed to four to indicate the date. An example would be 99 representing the year 1999. Therein lies the problem. As the year approached 2000, it would be as if the clocks went backwards to the year 1900. The fear was that as the clocks struck midnight on January 1, 2000, the systems would now be using the wrong date, making computers unable to operate properly. You were now looking at both software and hardware failures, with worldwide implications. This became a huge problem, affecting almost everything imaginable. Mainframe systems operating in huge companies and organizations, such as banking, military, insurance, the auto industry, real estate, high tech, manufacturing, etc., would fail, including store cash registers, ATM machines, and home desktop computers. The effects of these issues were predicted to be catastrophic.

In the policing world, this was a daunting problem because most of our operating systems were based on hardware and software functionality, from our call-taking operations to our computer-aided dispatch, record-keeping and retention systems, ongoing investigative tools, and future operations. With this looming crisis, our security apparatus would be severely compromised and susceptible to all manner of attacks. We were in big trouble. I would say six months prior to this anticipated catastrophe, the service started preparing. New equipment was purchased to reinforce or supplement existing gear. This included a fleet of brand-new, right-off-the-line 2000 Ford Crown Victorias, complete with the special police package. The cost for one of these bad boys at the time was around $40,000.

I was working out of 5 District headquarters as a detective constable (DC), assigned to the Criminal Investigative Branch. We were awash with Y2K preparations and literally within weeks of doomsday. There were folks who'd sold their homes and moved to the mountains or made and/or purchased a bunker to save themselves and family. People bought generators and hoarded food and water. Planes were predicted to fall from the skies. It was the craziest of times. The world was coming to an end! People were freaking out. The world was tossed into this collective groupthink that the last days were upon us. Preachers preached Armageddon. Cult leaders exalted the Most High Creator, who, in their mind, had predicted these last days. Naturalists pointed to the peculiar behaviour of animals, which signalled end times. Tea readers and tarot card interpreters made claims to know the future, which would not exist for us as of January 1. This shit was crazy!

Well, DC Rod Ramage was having none of this. Rod was a competent, seasoned investigator who was subject to deep mood swings. Rod made it known vocally and with reckless abandonment that this Y2K was bullshit and was pissing him off more and more every day. It irritated Rod that he had to participate in nonsense that took him away from real police work. With a limited sense of humour and an aversion to large-scale rapid change, Rod grew angrier every day that this had been thrust upon him.

And then . . . Y2K came and went with a whimper.

With billions of dollars spent and millions of hours invested, nothing significant happened. Literally nothing.

The *Oxford Dictionary* defines the word *apoplectic* as "overcome with anger; extremely indignant." That was DC Rod Ramage. Eleven days after the clocks reached midnight to bring in the New Year, Rod was still raging. The morning of January 11, I had been assigned to accompany Rod to locate and arrest a wanted person. This particular day, he was at his worst. He assigned himself SP50, one of the brand-new unmarked Crown Victorias in the station lot. This particular vehicle had seen very little usage, having only forty or so kilometres on the odometer. Rod jumped behind the driver seat as I sat in the passenger side.

It was downhill from there.

Rod, with determined clarity, had decided that he would break in the new vehicle, ensuring the department got their money's worth. We left the lot with unmentionable haste. No gradual speed or slow descent. It was all hard starts and screeching stops. In those moments, more than once I might add, I saw a white light and family members who had long since passed away. I saw my Sunday school teacher reciting her version of the song "Yes, Jesus Loves Me." I felt the call of nature — what will be will be. In essence, I had resigned myself to the fact that I had had a good life, nothing to complain about, and if I got through this, I would spend the rest of my life in a remote monastery in Tanzania, feeding the hungry.

Somehow, we made it to the residence of the wanted party. Within a few minutes, we had assessed he was not there.

Our next assignment was to attend police headquarters, pick up another vehicle, and return it to our home location, 5 District. I took charge of that second vehicle and Rod followed me in the SP50. The drive back was cathartic. I felt joy and relief that I would be able to live a long and hopefully rewarding life, reneging on my previous vow of feeding the hungry but committed to self-improvement. I pulled into the parking lot at 5 District and parked the van. As I exited the vehicle, I saw Rod make the turn into the lot. Gear in hand, I walked towards the side door, with the building's wall to my right, obstructing my view of the west side of the parking lot. That's when it happened. I heard a loud screeching of tires immediately followed by an enormous explosion. Oh shit! A terrorist attack! A bomb had gone off! I dropped to the ground, drew my firearm, and pressed up against the wall. Completely paralyzed with fear and exposed to a possible second attack, I willed myself to crawl along the side of the building to where I would be able to see the point of attack. That old fight-or-flight instinct had kicked into gear. I remember taking a deep breath and renewing my promise of servitude; well, partially. I took a quick peek around the corner of the building and saw the wreckage.

SP50 was completely demolished. The back end of the vehicle was wrapped around a concrete lightpost that used to illuminate the lot. The back window was blown out, back doors crumpled, and the back seat now formed part of the front seat structure. Still not sure what had happened, I stayed low, pointing my firearm from left to right and back again while making my way to the vehicle. My concern now was Rod. By this time, a number of officers were exiting the building upon hearing the explosion. As I approached the car, I saw movement on the driver's side. He was alive.

As I opened the door, there was Rod, rocking back and forth, completely in shock. DC Ramage had not been injured, and with the assistance of other officers, he was helped out of the car. It hadn't been a terrorist attack at all, just what was known in police circles as a single MVC (motor vehicle collision). While reversing into one of the parking spaces, Rod had unintentionally used the accelerator as the brake. There is no one on this planet who can tell me that this accident was not in part due to his state of mind. I'm convinced it was. One thing was made abundantly clear on that day: Y2K had come with unintended consequences. There was damage in the wake of that event, and DC Ramage was the irrefutable evidence of that.

WORDS OF WISDOM

I have put together some thoughts that have not steered me wrong, principles I have followed throughout my career. I hope in some measurable way that, in part or in whole, what I present will work for someone reading this book. I will call them "Principles of Success."

Start with a vision. See the future and where you fit in. What would you really like to do? What are you good at? What would you like to be good at? What are your strengths? Focus on those things that really matter to you . . . on your terms.

Have a plan. Remember the old saying, "If you fail to plan then plan to fail." It's as simple as that. Planning must be continuous. The plan must live with you and be subject to change. The core of the plan must be solid and manageable. Seek advice. Use the experience and wisdom of those around you. Be prepared. Folks, preparation is a central principle for success. You need to be ready for when opportunity presents itself whether created by you, for you, or whether it materializes organically. In whatever way it occurs, you need to be ready. In his book *Outliers: The Story of Success*, Malcolm Gladwell speaks to the difference between good and great. He talks about how the great got great. There are two central principles of how this is accomplished: One is preparation — a minimum of ten thousand hours in their respective fields — and the second is being prepared and ready when the opportunity is presented. In terms of work and career, what should we be looking at? Well, Malcolm Gladwell speaks to three things that most people agree are the qualities that work has to have if it is to be satisfying: autonomy, complexity, and the connection between effort and reward. I direct this next comment to the young people reading this book. "It is not how much money we make that ultimately makes us happy." To cement his point, Gladwell cites the example of offering a choice between working as an architect for $75,000 a year and working in a tollbooth every day for the rest of your life for $100,000 a year. Chances are, due to the complexity, autonomy, and the relationship between effort and reward in doing creative work, one would probably choose to be an architect. So look for work that has those qualities built in.

Execute the plan. No more excuses. Nobody is going to put a silver spoon in your mouth. You have to be courageous, strong, determined, willing to stand back up when knocked down. The pain of failure is not as hard as the pain of regret. It will take hard work, but you can change your future. Build in contingency plans and find alternatives. Many people have a vision and can see the light at the end of the tunnel, but what they are really seeing is the light of the train coming towards them. So here is the solution: recognize that the light could be the end of the tunnel or it could be the train. If it is the train, what do I do? How do I get out of the way and still make it to the end?

Network. Specifically in the Black communities, we have the knowledge, skills, and abilities to be successful. What has been achieved to date is a testament to that. The world is full of successful people. What we are not successful at is working together. We are still a very fragmented people who severely underutilize our collective potential. We need to do a better job of networking, mentorship, and knowledge exchange. When there are networking events offered, particularly in the Black community, we should be attending. Then open up to meeting others. Leave your comfort zone. Learn the art of mingling, introduce yourself, engage in conversation, have your contact information available. Utilize the opportunity of meeting others with whom you may have meaningful exchanges, relationship-building, and the like.

Give back. For those who have achieved a modicum of success, I hesitate to consider you successful if you have not contributed in some meaningful way to the success of others. For real, true success is achieving in the collective, not the singular. The commitment to service needs to be added to your portfolio. On your way to being successful, consider these things: Be kind. Treat people with respect. Who among us wants to be disrespected? How would *you* react? What results do you expect from people whom you disrespect?

Operate with humility and grace. Give people the room to make good judgements. Allow them a degree of autonomy. Allow them to grow. (It works!) Learn the art of making people do what they don't necessarily want to do, but because of your influence they buy into it and take ownership of it. That's called leadership. I truly believe that if the noted principles are applied with the required dose of hard work, persistence, and due diligence, success however you measure it will be yours. I have followed these principles as I moved through the ranks within my organization. I found them to be sound, directional, and with the right amount of clarity that supported my career.

· PART FIVE ·

STILL MOVING
FORWARD

BLACK IN BLUE

A mechanic was removing a cylinder head from the motor of a Harley motorcycle when he spotted a well-known heart surgeon in his shop. The surgeon was there, waiting for the service manager to come and look at his bike. The mechanic shouted across the garage, "Hey, Doc, can I ask you a question?" The surgeon, a bit surprised, walked over to the mechanic working on the motorcycle.

The mechanic straightened up, wiped his hands on a rag, and asked, "So, Doc, look at this engine. I open its heart, take the valves out, fix 'em, put 'em back in, and when I finish, it works just like new. So how come I get such a small salary and you get the really big bucks, when you and I are doing basically the same work?" The surgeon paused, smiled, leaned over, and whispered to the mechanic, "Try doing it with the engine running."

That joke kind of sums up my policing career in a peculiar way. To some degree, I felt as though I was operating with the engine running. It has to do with all the other things that most other officers didn't have to deal with. Policing is a real-world deal that at times is unforgiving. The additional burden of having black skin in a blue uniform formulated a uniquely harsh, discordant mixture of experiences that the majority did not have to face. The cacophony of ambient noise surrounding these two combinations was consistent both within the service and as a lived experience while I performed my duties.

There were two occasions where a request for police service was ultimately declined because the victim did not have the stomach to deal directly with the attending Black officer: me. In one case, the older woman was the victim of a domestic dispute and had called the police. I was the first officer on scene, and I approached the front door. The lady viewed me through the glass window but refused to open the door. She instead placed another call to the dispatcher to send a white officer. I have been asked, on a number of occasions, to use the servant's entrance while my companions were allowed to enter through the front door. There have been occasions where I was the lead investigator conducting the interviews and the subject would only respond to the questions posed by the white officer.

Fighting the system was exhausting. The internal strife continued from the day I was hired to the final months of employment. Although I left the organization on my own terms with no bitterness in my heart, I did carry away with me a profound disappointment that the fairness component I desired all those many years was too elusive, no matter the immense effort applied.

This disappointment invaded my soul in June 2016. At this point in my career, I had thirty years of exemplary service and had obtained the rank of inspector. In fact, I'd had eight years at this rank, serving in the capacity of duty inspector, officer-in-charge of investigative services responsible for the Integrated Crime Analysis Unit, Special Services Surveillance Unit, Interception of Private Communications, Technical Support Unit, and Covert Operation Unit. I was the officer-in-charge of the Organized Crime Bureau, responsible for the Guns and Gangs Unit, Drugs and Vice Unit, and Major Fraud Unit, and the officer-in-charge of the Professional Development Bureau, responsible for the Staff Development and Uniform Recruiting Unit. By this time, I had competently managed what would be considered in any policing organization to be premier portfolios.

In April 2016, a posting for a promotional opportunity to the rank of superintendent was issued service-wide. It turned out that there were two positions available as part of the competition. I saw this as my opportunity to advance to the next level based on my pedigree and service performance. Interestingly enough, I had competed twice before for promotion to this level and had not been successful. My not being promoted at those times was absolutely the right course of action. I had not been ready at the time, nor had I been the best candidate. There were a number of successful officers who were deserving, having put in the time and effort, gained the right amount of experience, and demonstrated the ability to do the job. No complaints from me.

This time was very different. Eight officers applied for the two positions, and none of them had the overall time on the force and range of experience that I brought to the table. I had just made the Uniform Recruiting Unit the envy of other services with the percentage of visible minority candidates that we were able to garner in a short amount of time. This was a badge of honour for our executive command as they were now able to boast to their counterparts about the diversity of this division. My career to this point was stellar, including outstanding community engagement. In my mind, the impending position of superintendent was mine to lose. No way was I going to screw this up.

By all accounts, I was the lead candidate, which inflicted undue pressure that was self-imposed. There were a number of steps I needed to complete in order to be considered. Candidates needed to submit a cover letter with a résumé that outlined their qualifications for promotion. They were also required to submit a two-thousand-word written essay relating to cost-effective solutions to alternative service delivery now and into the future. Finally, candidates were provided a scenario illustrating a superintendent's competencies, requiring a written response followed by an interview with the Executive Command Team. It was no easy feat, but definitely not insurmountable. I applied myself to the task of preparation, leaving no room for mediocrity, understanding that I needed to once again operate at that next level; there could be no shortcuts or excuses.

Having run the gauntlet set out by the service, I felt very satisfied by my performance in every area of the competition. The whole process had been a strong demonstration of my ability to take on more responsibilities at the next level, and I sensed that had come through in the interview process involving three members of the executive branch (the chief at the time and two deputies). On June 22, 2016, there was word that there would be an announcement that day on the results of the competition. That evening, I sat in my office with two members of my staff — Sergeant Greg Connolly and Staff Sergeant Peter Casey. We were in a jovial mood in anticipation of my pending promotion. At 5:09 p.m., an email was released service-wide:

> The Executive Command Team is very pleased to announce the promotion of two Inspectors to the rank of Superintendent.
>
> The members being promoted have a wide range of experience throughout their careers, including District, Investigative, Support, and Administrative duties.
>
> The members are:
>
> Inspector [Not My Name #1]
>
> Inspector [Not My Name #2]
>
> Congratulations to our newest superintendents — both of whom have and will continue to make a difference in our community by ensuring our citizens feel safe and secure through excellence in policing.

My name was not on that list. The three of us sat in that room stunned. Both of these newly promoted inspectors had only two years in the rank, and one of them had never held a command position in the organization. The other had one command during the two years he served in that role. Before I go any further, I will state emphatically that I both liked and respected the two successful candidates and hold absolutely no animus or malice towards them. My argument going forward was how was it possible that both of them had beat me out for one of the positions? That decision lies squarely at the feet of the Executive Command.

Saying I was disappointed is the ultimate understatement. I felt betrayed. I had invested thirty years in that organization with not a single blemish on my record. I had consistently proven my knowledge, skills, and ability to competently do the job with exemplary dedication. The Executive Command knew me. We had worked together over many years, always with the professional decorum that was expected. I knew I'd done exceedingly well in the various phases of the competition, so how did this happen?

No, the right question was why? *Why* did this happen?

News of what had happened travelled exceedingly fast. The phone calls were immediate from colleagues, friends, acquaintances, family, community organizations, and even several news media outlets asking my opinion as a Black senior officer being surpassed by two white junior officers and how I planned to deal with it.

I had been wounded once again by an organization that had demanded and received much of who I was and what I had become. What now? Well, in my mind I had two options that manifested this way: one was to acquiesce; the other was to resist with every fibre in my being. I'm sure the prevailing thought from the Executive Command was that I would do the former, and just accept the situation for what it was. Naw! They truly underestimated the fight left in me. With the need to understand exactly why this decision was made, the following day I contacted one of the deputies who had formed part of the interview process and requested a meeting, which was granted.

There is no need to bore you with exact details, but I will summarize the meeting this way. I asked, "What happened in the process that resulted in me not being selected?" He started by saying that I'd had an excellent interview and was his choice for promotion into one of the superintendent's positions. He'd advocated for me, but the situation was they had to make a decision that was best for the organization as it pertained to how long the superintendents would be in the positions. It was felt that the two promoted individuals would be around for a longer time. I reminded him that I had been a part of this organization for the past thirty years, and when he was speaking about the organization, he needed to remember that the organization was people like me, who have invested sweat equity so people like him could rise to command positions. Suffice it to say, he was genuine with me but surely didn't offer up the whole story.

Not satisfied with that meeting and still very much in resistive mode, I requested a meeting with the Executive Command Team. This was a swing for the fences meeting where once again, I felt that my job was on the line and I was prepared to lose it if that's what it took to regain my dignity. Armed with a list of questions and an invited witness (Staff Sergeant Ezra Browne), I began the meeting hot and stayed that way until the end. Here is a list of eight questions that were tabled in the meeting that to this day the Executive Command was unable to answer:

- Where in the promotional process did I fall short in relation to the two successful candidates?
- What were the determining attributes of the two successful candidates compared to mine?
- The Executive Command set the essential qualifications and the points to be considered for promotion — where did it say that overwhelming consideration would be given to the length of time that the candidate would commit to his/her tenure in the rank?
- What service time in the rank commitments did you get from the successful candidates?
- Why would you take their word for it and not mine?
- Where did I place in the competition?
- One of you stated that they had favoured me for the promotion. Why did the other two not agree with his assessment?
- How and when are you going to correct this injustice?

The same nonsense was offered to me about the longevity in the position being the reason that the other two members had been selected. What garbage. I countered with the fact that in the previous promotional process a year earlier, there'd been two inspectors who'd been promoted to superintendent who'd had more years on the job than I did. One had thirty-two years of service and the other *thirty-eight*, so how is it possible that you would try to use longevity in the position as a disqualifier? Besides, during the interview, I'd been asked about my commitment if I were to be promoted, and I'd stated a minimum of five years. It had been a reasonable response, I thought, given that most high-level contracts, the chief's included, were on average three to five years.

This was one of the most intense and contentious meetings that I have ever endured. The range of emotions that ran through my body, the hurt, utter disappointment, and rage I felt were palpable. This was not okay. Not this time. Not again. This was my moment once again to resist the nonsense and confront the system head-on. The meeting devolved into the likes of an epic street fight. There was no give in me whatsoever. None! They were challenged on every word and action that they took. They had no satisfactory comeback to the questions posed, nor were they prepared to defend their position.

Without being disrespectful but definitely with an air of defiance, forty-five minutes later, I stood up, picked up my notes, turned to the team, and said, "We are done here, you leave me no choice but to challenge this decision," and left the room. I was livid! I was so angry that I'd been passed over for promotion for two white junior officers with the reason offered being longevity — not qualifications, not experience, not performance, talent, competency, or any of the other attributes that one would use as a differentiator. The rationale was bad but the optics were worse. It was so blatantly obvious that the pigment ceiling was in play, even if it had not been intended in that manner. It looked that way and felt that way.

Fifteen minutes after leaving the meeting, I received a phone call from one of the deputies advising that the chief would like to see me in his office in the morning. This meeting was quite different, as the chief and I were the only ones in the room. He did most of the talking, using a mostly apologetic tone. He basically admitted that they'd got it wrong and had reconsidered. He said it was his decision that I be promoted to the rank of superintendent.

Showing very little in the way of emotion, I thanked him for his demonstrated courage and the willingness to make things right. Deep down in my core, I was hurt — hurt because it had to come down to this for me to be recognized in an organization to which I had contributed all those many years, given what I had definitely earned. It saddens me that the right thing was not done in the first place due to some unknown agenda in which I was collateral damage. The joy of being invited to the command table had been stripped from me and replaced with the bitter sweetness of having fought and won only to suffer devastating wounds that will never heal properly.

In September 2016, I was officially promoted to the rank of superintendent. The irony in all of this was I was given not one but two commands within the organization to manage at the same time. I was the only superintendent in the service, at that time, to have two portfolios. I was now the bureau commander of Information Management and Court Services. Both were very large commands with over three hundred members combined under my authority. That alone is a testament to the belief of the Executive Command Team that I was indeed capable of operating at that level and that they had the confidence in me to be able to manage the enormous load. However, the damage had been done. At that point in my career, I had yearned for this acknowledgement and support from my organization, which in the end eluded me. The feeling of abandonment, in that time of need, turned a stellar employee into a disappointed soul. My win was a loss. Less than a year later, I was retired. The joy of the promotion and the drive to operate at a sustained optimal level had been sapped from me.

MY FINAL THOUGHTS

In May 2021, after what could be called a mild winter, the air was abuzz with folks escaping lockdown fever from many months of off-and-on restrictions, courtesy of the COVID-19 pandemic ordeal. My neighbourhood was flush with people outside, tending to their lawns: aerating, raking, fertilizing, watering, and finally cutting the grass. Not wanting to be outdone, I quickly got in gear, donning my workboots and gardening gloves and adopting a mindset that I would not be outdone by any of my neighbours this year. I made several trips to a number of local nurseries. It worked; my lawn sprang to life with the agility and conditioning of a world-class athlete. I purposely waited until the grass was many inches tall before the first cutting, to ensure the best growth. The cutting time was now at hand.

I rolled out my gas-powered lawnmower, filled it with gas, and topped up the oil. One pull, two pulls, a dozen pulls on the crank starting cord, and nothing. It appeared that the engine had seized over the winter. I took off the plastic casing covering the top portion of the engine and attempted to examine the issue. On removal of that cover, there it was, as bold as any highway billboard. Etched into the dirt and grime on top of the engine was a swastika and two lightning bolts. How the hell did that get there? I made the connection instantly.

Several years earlier, I'd brought my mower into a local small engine store for servicing. I had purchased it several years prior, brand-new, out of the box, and the mower had been with me ever since. I had not lent it out to anyone, and had only ever stored it in my garage. The only time that that lawnmower had ever been out of my possession was that one particular service call — the only person who had ever been under the hood had worked there.

I documented the offensive graffiti by way of pictures on my phone, loaded the lawnmower into my van, and headed to the same service shop that had done the work. I met with the manager, who was beside himself at the prospect that someone in his employment could have possibly committed such a vile act. He checked the store records and located my service record. On discovery of the technician who had actually worked on the mower, he gave me an implicit denial, stating that this particular employee had been working there for many years and was a good man who would never do such a thing. As we spoke further, the manager realized that this denial was not the right approach; a resolution was. He offered to take the matter to corporate (the store's overseeing body) with his assurance that he personally would ensure that all employees would be cautioned and would receive training on race relations and sensibilities. He further offered — no, *pleaded* — to make this right, starting with fixing my mower at no cost.

The next day, I did receive a phone call from corporate expressing shock and horror that this could have happened. They apologized profusely with an assurance that they would look into the matter and deal with it appropriately. This was a small local store, and I had no intentions of causing harm or destroying the reputation of the business, so I opted to meet them where they were and agreed to their commitments.

∞

The Black experience in North America, by any reckoning, has been particularly deprived since the beginning. When will we find the peace we seek, the equality we demand, the justice that should be afforded to each person on this continent? When will we earn the respect, the rights and privileges given to some by virtue of pigmentation, while we are relegated to second-class-citizen status, shackled by conditions and systems designed to bind and restrict? When will enough allies engage at a level to tip the scales towards deconstruction, culminating in monumental efforts to rebuild proper working and living conditions conducive to regenerative status for all? How much more of this can we bear? The truth is, we are tired. We are burdened and fatigued, yet we will never stop resisting.

What we want is quite simple: Stop killing us! Stop profiling us! Allow our existence as equal members of society. No more discriminatory practices. No more mass incarcerations. No more imbalance of justice at the hands of systems designed for that very reason. Allow equal competition where warranted, staying true to the essences and spirit of righteousness, the law, and fairness, knowing that the current practice of the law is often neither equal nor fair. Right the wrongs that have unfairly disadvantaged minorities for generations, putting the burden on them to convince those in authority that they are worth taking a chance on. Stop resisting us, for the uncompromising truth is, until equity in all its iterations is achieved, we will never stop resisting.

None of us can stop the future from happening. The inevitable is playing out right in front of us with a clarity and predictability that, if you're paying attention, will make your pronouncements almost prophetic. The world's a-changing. Oh yes, there has never been a time in world history when people have had this degree of connectivity, whether through communication devices or access to rapid transportation to whisk us away to any place on earth. I am exposed to it by virtue of my existence in the world as I engage in the wonderful pastime of global traveller. I have two beautiful grandchildren who are the result of an interracial marriage: Nova, who is three years old, and Dash, who is near his first birthday. One day, racial differentials will no longer be a thing, making discrimination on those grounds obsolete. It may not happen in my lifetime, and perhaps not in the span of my offspring's, but make no mistake — it will happen. And oh, what a glorious time that will be, provided that we, the people, don't create something just as insidious or worse to replace it. In the meantime, why are we not working towards tranquility, wrapped up in the love for one another based on our humanity? According to the U.S. Declaration of Independence, "We hold these truths to be self-evident, that all men are created equal, that they are endowed by their Creator with certain unalienable Rights, that among these are Life, Liberty and the pursuit of Happiness." That sounds good to me.

Retirement has afforded me the luxury of hours of introspection, with a maturity gained over the years. It has cemented my resolve that I must tell my story, hoping that whatever impact it may have will land positively in the hearts and minds of a reader or two, empowering them to act. The word *ally* has found its way into today's lexicon. Someone who is committed to helping, working in unity with the oppressed group in the fight for equality and justice, all the while staying true to the cause, even though it may compromise their privilege. The cornerstone of this book is to garner allies in order to advance the struggle that has devoured countless Black and Indigenous people of colour and ravished many who just want to operate in a world on an equal footing.

One of the hardest tasks I had to perform in my capacity as a police officer was my final sign off, 10-7. Yes, it's the end of a chapter, but not the book. My policing career has come to an end. Folks, it's as real as it gets. At the end of this chapter, I fell back into the role of a civilian member of society and started what is affectionately known as part two. As the lights dim on part one, part two illuminates an equally glorious future. The cord that attaches me to my past life is that gold retiree's badge that always and forever resides in one pants pocket or the other. I have served, and now it's time for some rest and relaxation. It's time to get up when I feel like it, wash the car when I feel the need to do something productive, play golf on my timeline (well, with the wife's approval, of course), and the best part about all of this is that the government will top up my bank account every month, come rain or shine.

As some of us move into our retirement age, there is a certain irony that life brings. We get to a stage where we can finally afford steaks and lobster, and we're told it's no longer healthy for us. Retirement age is when you're faced with two temptations and you choose the one that will get you home by 9 p.m. Retirement age is when you're told to slow down by your doctor and not by the police. Retirement age is when you can live without sex, but not your glasses. You know you are at retirement age when you have to write a note to yourself reminding you not to take a sleeping pill and a laxative on the same night.

Although aspects of my career in law enforcement were bittersweet, now that I am enjoying a life in retirement, looking back, I have no regrets. There is plenty I would have changed, but even during the years when fairness and equity eluded me, I spent my career committed to excellence, fairness, and common sense. That makes me content. Policing is indeed a noble profession. Community service is a must. The commitment to family, friends, and duty are what shaped my life and why, looking back, I can hardly find regrets. Disappointments, in my view, were lessened by the very fact that my commitment brought me utter joy. My sense of duty and character bears no repentance.

There is a deep, profound respect and sadness I have for the fallen officers who, in the line of duty, have paid the ultimate price. Their loss is a sacrifice that must never be taken for granted or disrespected. As I write this book, within a span of seven months we have witnessed the tragic death of nine Canadian police officers, eight of whom were killed in the line of duty. I had the honour of attending the funeral services of Constable Devon Northrup and Constable Morgan Russell, both South Simcoe police officers, who were responding to a call for service and were gunned down. It was a sobering reminder to all of us that all life is precious and that this particular profession, in real ways, exposes our service providers to the inherent dangers of doing this job. Trois-Rivières Quebec Sergeant Maureen Breau was fatally stabbed while in the process of arresting a suspect. Edmonton Police Service officers Constable Travis

Jordan and Constable Brett Ryan were shot to death while responding to a 911 call about an out-of-control teenager. Constable Grzegorz Pierzchala of the Ontario Provincial Police was ambushed and shot to death while answering a call for service. RCMP officer Shaelyn Yang was stabbed and killed serving her community of Burnaby, B.C. Constable Andrew Hong of the Toronto Police Service was shot and killed while on a training assignment in Peel Region. A member of my former service, York Regional Police Constable Travis Gillespie, was killed while en route to work. They will forever be in our thoughts. To the family and friends of those who have been killed or seriously injured, it is my honour to grieve with you. To lament with you. To commiserate with you and to never let their sacrifice be forgotten.

It is worth stating that the majority of officers that I have worked with or encountered along the way were fabulous individuals who joined policing to serve with honour the people of their community. They took an oath to be the guardians of societal values based on the enforcement of the criminal code that is deemed to be the arbiter of the boundaries we wish to exist within. They believed in the noble profession that entrusted them with the power and authority to keep the peace, maintain order, and put themselves in harm's way if necessary for you and me. They were honest brokers bound to do the right things to the best of their ability. The policing profession consists of wives, husbands, cousins, sisters, brothers, aunts, uncles, friends, and acquaintances . . . they are us. They are to be valued and appreciated. I have witnessed officers going above and beyond in their duty to serve. I have seen officers compromise their own safety to save the lives of strangers. I have been involved with officers who thought outside the box to make the situation manageable for victims and families. I have seen the best of policing and the officers who truly love and cherish the job that is required. The majority are very special people. To all the service providers who have and continue to uphold and respect their office, I and many others are truly grateful.

∞

After thirty-one years of service, I left my organization. I have been a proud member of York Regional Police and can truly say it has been an honour to put on the uniform day after day to serve our great community with humility and grace. Looking back, I cannot envision myself doing anything else. I achieved a position of superintendent, one that very few members in my or any other organization will ever attain. It is also true that even fewer members of colour will wear a crown denoting this rank on their shoulders. We still have a way to go, but I'm comforted by the vigilance, the watchful eye, and the unity of our communities to ensure that organizations (not just YRP) continue to move in the right direction to advance we who have suffered so greatly. We as a people know who we are, we know what we are about, we know our worth, we know what we have earned. We know our determination and don't ever underestimate our resolve.

A word to the establishment: until equity and justice for all are applied in the manner consistent with the meaning allocated to those words, we the aggrieved, in and out of uniform, beaten and bruised but not defeated, will never stop fighting for change.

As I speak about my journey, I am reminded that the collective racist, bigoted, discriminatory interactions that followed me, shackled to me like a phantom ball and chain, are always with me. In this book, I have mentioned just a few incidents in an attempt to take the reader into the world of a successful Black man in this country. The price of my achievements was steep, with deep scars to attach to my credentials. Writing this book has been cathartic — as I reflect on my life with the clarity of maturity, I am able to provide wisdom that is worth sharing. I do, however, feel that I have been deeply scarred by the avoidable hurtful events I encountered during the course of my life. In the same breath, I will say all that I have endured has shaped me into a person with whom I would want to be friends. There is a sense of sympathy and empathy that permeates my veins for my fellow people. There is a certain joy in providing truth, in offering learning opportunities to those I meet, whether it be for the first time or during subsequent times. I grow weary of that ugliness of hate, constant conflicts, and the ramifications of malicious actions that lead to the pain and ultimate suffering of minority groups.

The great Dr. Martin Luther King Jr. once stated, "If you can't fly then run, if you can't run then walk, if you can't walk then crawl, but whatever you do you have to keep moving forward." I've done the running, walking, and crawling. I can truly say that what's left for me is to just keep moving forward.

THE INFLUENCERS

I would be remiss if I didn't take the time to mention major influencers in my life and in my law enforcement career. It is difficult to measure the degree of influence each had on me, but I'm comfortable to state that it was significant.

Armand La Barge

For the greater part of my career, there were no Black senior officers who could mentor me. However, there was one white officer I studied from a distance, reducing that gap year after year. He ultimately became chief of police.

Armand P. La Barge was appointed chief of the York Regional Police (YRP) in 2002. He served in this capacity for the next eight years, retiring in 2010. At the time of his retirement, Armand was fifty-six years of age and had given thirty-seven years of service. This man was truly someone special.

I first met Armand as part of the background investigation that applicants to the service received prior to being hired or rejected. Armand came to our house unannounced, but was immediately warm and friendly. The interview was conducted around the kitchen table. Armand took his time and asked a series of questions relating to my application to the service. When he was satisfied with the information that he had come for, we chatted jovially. At one point it dawned on me that there was a police officer sitting in my kitchen. Given all my negative interactions with the authorities in the past, I was a bit stunned. I had very much formulated the stereotypical view of police officers as arrogant, controlling, belligerent bigots. This man did not fit the mould. He was gentle, captivating, caring, and appeared sincere.

Poor Cheryl, on the other hand, was a hot mess that day. Despite being a professional herself, and accustomed to dealing with heads of corporations, my wife was completely beside herself that there was a police officer in her house. Not just any police — this one happened to be in a position to possibly move her husband forward in the process of being hired. Although she kept a good home, the perfectionist in her caused her to inevitably find items out of place that needed to be straightened up right away. With all the exuberance and hospitality that she could muster, she found ways to end up in the kitchen. Armand was astute enough to bring her into the conversation and charmed her to the point of bringing out that shy schoolgirl smile that had eluded me for many years. She also became an Armand admirer.

What I was most impressed with about Chief La Barge's legacy was the cultural change that he imparted on the organization. He was a leader who was determined to deconstruct the old ways of limited inclusion. He set up a Diversity and Public Resources Bureau, understanding that officers needed to hear directly from members of the cultural community. He also brought in special speakers to address his members. He believed that diversity training was for everyone in the organization regardless of station or position. Like me, Chief La Barge believed that sensitivity training, as well as advanced and continuing education efforts and programs, significantly enhance an officer's effectiveness in the field. He recognized that his organization was lacking the diversity and inclusion that he truly believed in. He set about identifying potential officers within the organization with diverse backgrounds, moving them into specialized units providing opportunities for growth, and promoting them within the ranks at a rate that was never seen before within YRP. A number of Black officers eventually ascended to senior management as a direct result of his actions. I was one of those officers. He was not afraid of the whispering or condemnation of some who complained about many of the promotions. Armand knew in his heart that it was the right thing to do, and he did it. That was an exercise in courage.

Armand was in demand from our diverse communities, and he attended countless events at the invitation of hundreds of organizations. At these events, I would soak in the chief's words, mannerisms, posture, and genius as he stood front and centre, most of the time given an opportunity to address the attendees. He would start off with a greeting in any of several languages, including Hindi, Hebrew, Urdu, Chinese, Italian, and French, and I swear I heard some Jamaican patois as well. I witnessed first-hand the connection he engendered and the tangible benefits gained as a result. Armand truly led by example and empowered me to do the same, while embracing who I was and the positions I held. I watched, listened, absorbed, emulated, and ultimately rose through the organization based on the template put forth by this incredible man.

Jay Hope

Those of us who worked with or broke bread with Jay understand how special he was, how stealthily he occupied his various positional authorities, creating immeasurable shifts in equal rights and employment equity. I would describe Jay as ambassadorial in his demeanour, professional in his engagements, fearless in his determination to be who he is: a Black man doing a job at the required level and competence of anyone who should occupy that position. He can be considered one of the early pioneers of Black officers, having joined the Ontario Provincial Police in 1979.

In 2004, Jay was promoted to the rank of deputy commissioner of police of the Ontario Provincial Police, becoming the highest-ranking

Black police officer in Canadian history. He spent the better part of his career with this organization, making a difference while serving as a senior investigator for the Ontario Human Rights Commission, a policy analyst for the Task Force on Race Relations and Policing, and director of human resources, earning him a Human Rights Medal for his work. Jay was on the forefront of recruitment of women, visible minorities, and First Nations peoples in the service.

Merely by his presence, stature, and commitment, Jay inspired me to reach for what was possible without compromising who I was. I took his lead by being bold and unapologetic and showing depth of character both in and out of the workplace. He enhanced the uniform with his infectious confidence, integrity, and wit, traits to which all who know him would attest. Most of all, Jay created lateral and upward movements for minority officers, providing opportunities that have had positive, lasting effects. I believe his total contribution in the areas of equal rights and justice will always be underestimated — but not by me.

Dr. Frank Trovato

It is with a profound sense of joy that I write about one of my unsung heroes, who operates with poise and grace but has no doubt influenced thousands of individuals in critical thinking as it relates to diversity, equity, and inclusion. I first met Dr. Frank Trovato in earnest while working on my bachelor of arts degree at the University of Guelph-Humber. Frank was one of the professors facilitating the program. What I most admire about Dr. Trovato is that he is a genuinely decent, likable man who has been engaged in the struggle for equality and justice at a level that influential allies should be operating. He is unapologetic in his commitment to the cause, which he has consistently demonstrated over a great many years. Frank has been there. He is a retired senior police officer from the Toronto Police Service. Moving into the realm of education, he served as a program coordinator for the Police Foundations Program at Humber

College and program coordinator for the Police Foundations Leadership program, and became the program head for the Justice Studies degree program at the University of Guelph-Humber. He received his Ph.D. in philosophy from the University of Toronto.

During my tenure as president of the Association of Black Law Enforcers (ABLE), Frank was an expert consultant who assisted me as I dealt with numerous inflamed and contentious situations, some requiring surgical precision to obtain the proper outcomes.

I recall a class where Dr. Trovato spoke about ethics as it related to the job we were doing or aspiring to. There wasn't a sound in that room other than the professor's voice. With profound delivery and the cadence of a skilled communicator, he walked us through the meaning of ethical behaviour and the reasons why it matters. We were then assigned to write an essay on that very topic. His lesson evoked deep critical thinking and challenged my definitions of ethical behaviour. My previous beliefs clearly cried out for next level-change if I truly wanted to operate in the ethical stratosphere that Dr. Trovato prescribed.

It will never be widely known how influential Dr. Trovato has been in changing the landscape of this country, moving us towards the equity and justice we seek. But rest assured that, both directly and indirectly, he has profoundly changed the lives of so many of us for the better.

David Mitchell

A true game changer, David Mitchell, retired assistant deputy minister of the provincial Youth Justice Division, has dedicated over thirty years to public service. David was born in England of Jamaican parentage, and he unabashedly credits his mother for setting a tone that has carried him through the barrage of storms life has thrown at him. He has some old Jamaican quotes relating to Caribbean upbringing that makes one laugh at the quirkiness, but the point is always relevant and based on truth. David is the founder and past president of ABLE. In his role as president, David provided leadership in areas of advocacy, community engagement, targeted minority recruitment, government consultation, and fundraising. Under his strong leadership, lasting community linkages and partnerships were created.

David enriched my professional development by virtue of his guidance, mentorship, and coaching, which had a direct impact on my career advancement. He provided continuous sage advice and stern corrective edicts when necessary. I listened, watched, and applied the persuasive techniques that David employed to match the specific engagements in which he participated. What was never lacking was his preparation on the topic at hand and his points of reference to support his views.

To this day, David continues to engage in his vision and mission to be an innovative justice leader, committed to public safety through meaningful partnerships with community organizations. His influence in facilitating policy and operational practices and his support of human rights, fairness, equity, and safe law enforcement are a testament to just how important a figure David Mitchell is in our criminal justice system and our country as a whole.

Peter Sloly

Chief of Police Peter Sloly showed me what a true leader and formidable administrator is made of. Chief Sloly was born in Kingston, Jamaica, and immigrated to Canada at the age of ten. He joined the Toronto Police Service in 1988, transitioning through the organization and earning a meteoric rise to the position of deputy chief of police.

To me, Peter embodied leadership. With his robust intellect and no-nonsense approach, he charted his way to the upper echelons of the Toronto Police Service, bringing the citizens of the city along with him. He is extremely bright and definitely a forward thinker. Peter has that intestinal fortitude and intelligence found in exceptional leaders. I admired the courageous and balanced approach, both to the world of policing and life in general — that is part of Peter's DNA. He has played an integral part in my personal and professional development that cannot be overstated.

I am grateful for the many conversations we have engaged in regarding the community in general and the Black community specifically that have helped chart my path towards a deeper, more quality-based engagement in these areas. Each time, I felt that I walked away with newfound knowledge that I was able to use to advance my influence in the social justice arena.

When I first took on the role of president of ABLE, Peter reached out to me and offered his assistance. At that time, he was the deputy chief of Toronto Police Service. He drove from his office to meet with me at my office in Newmarket to chat one on one. This small gesture told me much about who this man really is. He cared. He was humble. When I entered the promotional competition for the rank of superintendent the second time around, Peter provided a mentorship and coaching role. Now, to be clear and completely transparent, after a gruelling and extensive process, I was not one of the selected candidates — I wasn't ready yet. I must admit that a concern I had was that Peter might see this outcome as a reflection of his coaching abilities and my absorption rate. As a coach, one can only do so much with the product they have to work with!

In 2019, Peter was selected as chief of police in the Ottawa Police Service. Chief Sloly advanced the service with an emphasis on public trust, accountability, and equity within the department. He has been influential in his quest to bridge the gap between the citizenry and police. To this end, he has been included in this book as one of the icons I met along the way.

Herbert H. Carnegie and Bernice Carnegie

The phrase "one of the greatest hockey players never to play in the National Hockey League" is synonymous with the man I refer to as one of the nicest, most positive and respectable persons I have ever met. The legacy of Herbert H. Carnegie is that of a man who, because of his skin colour, was denied a lifelong dream of becoming a member of the NHL. By all accounts, Herb was the best player in the semi-professional league and should have been the number one draft pick, but his skills on the ice were no match for the discrimination surrounding the National Hockey League at the time. I first recall meeting Herb at a community event where he spoke to an audience of over three hundred people, relaying his story about his beloved game and the trials and tribulations embedded in hockey in the 1950s.

This powerful and empowering speech brought us through his life's journey, concluding with an impactful message about unselfish acts, giving of one's time and energy. He emphasized the personal transformation that can be achieved by uplifting those around you.

It was a call to action. At least it was for me. The influence his speech had on me is still felt, and I still credit him for many of the ways in which I too have overcome trials in my own life and career. He did all of this and inspired the rest of us to climb and lift, despite the unjust and inexcusable way he was treated during his hockey career.

I approached him after the speech, and we spoke for several minutes; he was even more impressive one on one. This man's tone, cadence, politeness, and positive message affected me to a degree that is hard to explain other than I wanted to be more like him. From that point on, I followed his appearances and speaking engagements just so I would have an opportunity to engage him in conversation. Herb was always accompanied by his daughter Bernice, whom I came to know very well. There was no Herb without Bernice. By the time we met, Herb was aging and partially blind. She was his sixth sense.

Sadly, on March 9, 2012, at the age of ninety-two, Herbert Carnegie passed away. My heart was heavy with the news but filled with the joy that I was blessed to have met and spent time with him during his stay here on the earth. Bernice has kept the legacy alive and has come into her own as a global ambassador for the nobility of service to others, equal rights, and driving a generational shift in our youth with the spirit of love for one another at the core.

Ina Ermina Merith

Ina Ermina Merith passed away on the September 30, 1995. Her last days on this earth were spent in a coma, languishing in a sterile room at the Etobicoke General Hospital in Rexdale, Ontario. My responsibility was to spend every spare moment of the six-week journey at her bedside, hoping, wishing, and praying that I would not lose her, that she would somehow miraculously recover and make me whole again. It proved to be an exercise in futility. I intuitively knew that she would never leave that hospital alive.

I loved my mother to the depth of my soul. In those six weeks, I could do nothing but exude my love by gently stroking her hands, lightly kissing her cheeks, and softly whispering in her ear how much she meant to me. I cried openly, spoke lovingly, and feared internally. I wanted my mother — no, I *needed* my mother — in my life forever. This, of course, was not to be. People come in and out of one's life for a reason. Ina's purpose was to fill me with a mother's love. A love that dwells inside of me and that I have shared with my two daughters.

Ina was not only my mother; she was my life coach. She watched over me, loved and cared for me, and guided me, ultimately leaving me with the skills necessary to navigate this world until it's time for me to take my leave and join her in rest. It would not be possible to write this book without paying homage to Mom.

My mother was small in stature but a giant of a woman. She was a strict disciplinarian who had a profound view of what should be considered right and wrong. Her view of the world was based on Christian biblical doctrine centred on the King James Bible. The values held by my most prominent mentor were ingrained in my personality, providing a moral road map leading to my ultimate vocation to serve and protect. I must say that exposure to the multitude of different religions and what I have come to know as natural law did dilute significantly my personal take on morality and value-based decisions on how one should live, but she nevertheless set the foundation. Her priorities in life stayed in her children. She raised us to be significant men and women with character as the staple of our existence. I learned about love, trust, and leadership from her. Traits that I brought to my policing career.

As a maturing young man, in our quiet times alone, I would engage with my mother, taking a temperature read on how we were feeling and the state of current affairs. My mother often spoke to me about being Black in this world. She would express how she had been hampered by her golden-brown hue but was so very proud to own it. We often spoke about freedom not being free. Ina would tell me to be careful as I navigated, integrated, and manoeuvred through this white-dominated world; she had the wisdom and experience necessary to insert that knowledge into my core. She was right, of course. All that she said came to be. We often spoke about how hard her life had been, confiding in me some details that made me weep. Ina was not a complicated woman. Not at all. Born in 1920 to parents of humble means, she grew up in the parish of Hanover, Jamaica. As a young woman, she met and married my father, Leonard, and immigrated first to England and then, with kids in tow, to Canada. My mother loved her children, ensured that we were always fed, clothed, and educated. For as long as I can remember, she worked tirelessly on a factory assembly line for a company that made cereal. She spent as much time as she could with her children, imparting as much wisdom as she possessed.

She always remained optimistic and felt her children completed her. I know one of her proudest moments was when she attended my police swearing-in ceremony in 1986. She told me so.

Yea, though I walk through the valley of the shadow of death, I will fear no evil: for thou art with me; thy rod and thy staff — and my mother — they comfort me.

∞

I would like to recognize a number of supporters who believed in the project and were willing to commit, ensuring a final product. It is with gratitude and respect that I recognize the following people:

Mark Altermann

Dr. Michelle Anderson &
    Maurice Smith

Rahel Appiagyei-David &
    Ainsley David

Kenrick Bagnall

Audrey Barclay

Kirk & Manda Barclay

Dahlia Bateman

Ron Begg

Tessa Benn-Ireland

Katherine Beveridge

Ned Blair

Phil & Betty Broome

Shawn Brown

Ezra (Tony) Browne

Kenton & Kimberly Chance

Charlene Charles

Dianne Charles

Hazel Charles

Lizette & Winston Chong

Marie Clark-Walker

Melody Clarke & Dale Williams

Alan Cooke

André & Dr. Janet Crawford

Daniel Dos Santos

Monica Edwards

Gerry & Carmen Gentile

Fabian Graham

Kevin Gutierrez

Hugh & Caroline Graham

Lorna & Owen Green

Diego Herrera

Maureen Johnson

Archbishop William Kimando

Slava Levin

Andrea McCormack

Brianna Merith

Cheryl Merith

Shirley Merith

David (Dave) Mitchell

Claudine & Horace Nairne

Michael Olderr

Hana Pika

Dr. Dionne & Robert Poulton

Elder Lloyd Ricketts

Claudio & Ada Romano

Maria Rosaria Fontana

Joan Russell

Michael & Sharon Ruscigno

Andy & Hema Shah

Brock & Jasmine Sinden

Marlin Taylor

Sonia Thomas

Dr. Frank Trovato

Audrey M. Walters

Don Yirenkyi

KEITH MERITH is a retired police superintendent, serving thirty-one years with the York Regional Police Service. Superintendent Merith held command positions in Information Services, Court Services, Corporate Development, Intelligence, Special Services Bureau and Organized Crime Bureau. He has worked in Criminal Investigations, Training and Education, Drugs and Vice, and Uniform Patrol and is a former Provincial Weapons Enforcement Unit member.

Superintendent Merith served two terms as president of the Association of Black Law Enforcers (ABLE), which focused on advocating for members operating within the Criminal Justice System. He is also the co-founder of the Citizenship Initiative Group (CIG), an organization that assists permanent residents in applying for and receiving Canadian citizenship.